# Encyclopedia of
# French
# Period
# Furniture
# Designs

## José Claret Rubira

Sterling Publishing Co., Inc.   New York

Distributed in the U.K. by Blandford Press

**Library of Congress Cataloging in Publication Data**

Claret Rubira, José.
  Encyclopedia of French period furniture designs.

  Translation of: Muebles de estilo francés.
  Includes index.
  1. Furniture—France.  2. Furniture—Drawings.
I. Title.
NK2547.C5413  1983     749.24     83-18220
ISBN 0-8069-7750-7 (pbk.)


Edited and designed by Barbara Busch

# CONTENTS

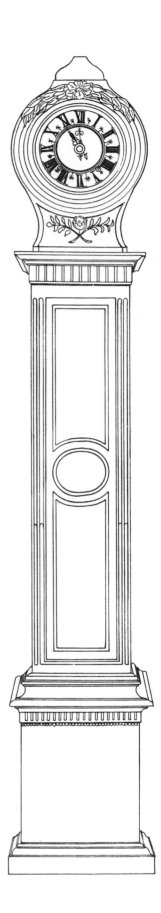

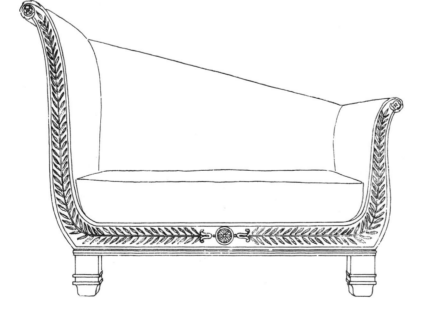

# PUBLISHER'S PREFACE

Cabinetmakers, decorators, historians, collectors, artists, stage designers and restorers—all will appreciate this comprehensive source book on French period furniture designs. The more than 3,000 illustrations on the following pages show French furniture from the mid-seventh century to the late nineteenth. Here are examples of almost every important period piece one might wish to build, collect or refer to, with closeup views of some of the more elaborate details. Scattered among the beds, sofas, chairs, cabinets, desks, and wardrobes are interesting footnotes to history: the desk of Louis XV, Marie-Antoinette's jewelry cabinet, the bed of the Empress Josephine, the cradle of Napoleon's son. All of the drawings are based on actual pieces of furniture in the finest museum and private collections.

Furniture-makers and restorers will find this book a treasure house of ideas either to be looked through casually or in search of a specific item or even a finish detail. The index will direct you to all the friezes and key escutcheons as well as wardrobes and armchairs.

Historians and sociologists will find much of interest in the chronological arrangement of the plates in the sense that furniture reflects the culture and life style of its times. On the facing page is the earliest piece shown—the chair of King Dagobert I, who reigned from 629 to 639. This chair is one of the few pieces from the Romanesque period that could be described as truly French. The furniture of the time was imitative of Roman and consisted mostly of tables, tripods and beds—the sort of thing one finds in Pompeii.

During the Gothic and Renaissance periods the furniture became more massive and ornate, and even more elaborate under Louis XIV, Louis XV, and Louis XVI. All this was a reflection of the grandeur of France. Although still elegant and often ornate, the furniture of the post-Revolutionary periods was scaled down and made more comfortable—intended for smaller private apartments.

Whatever the style or the period, however, there is a uniquely French character to the furniture represented. In studying these 1200 years of design, readers will find vast differences, but the furniture is always well made and elegant. It is easy to understand why French furniture makers developed such widespread influence, an influence that is still strong.

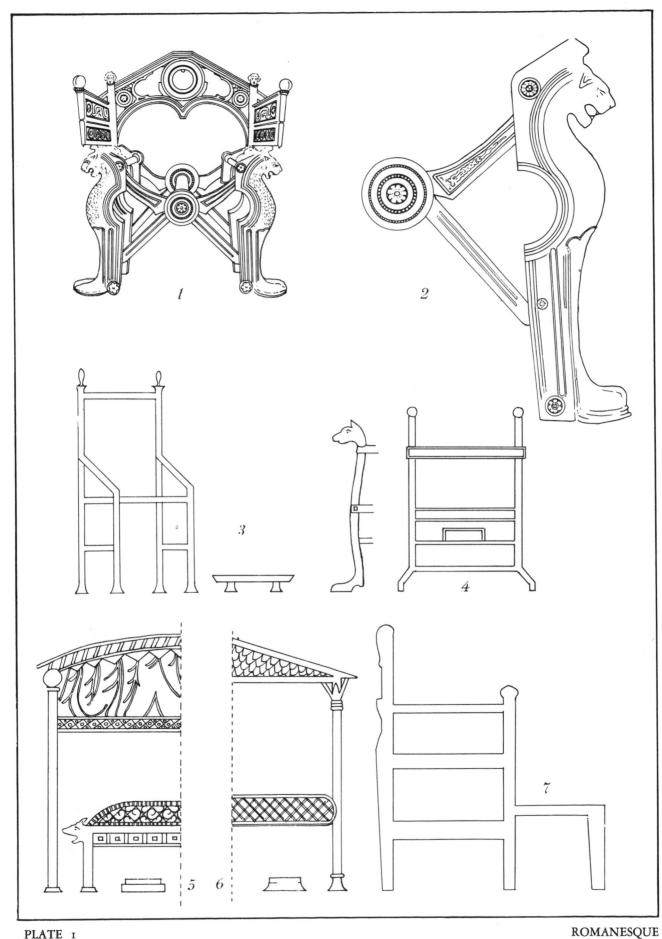

PLATE I          ROMANESQUE

1. Chair of King Dagobert.   2. Detail.   3. Chair and footstool, as shown in a codex.   4, 5 and 6. Chairs and benches taken from codexes.   7. Chair and footstool, as shown in a stone relief.

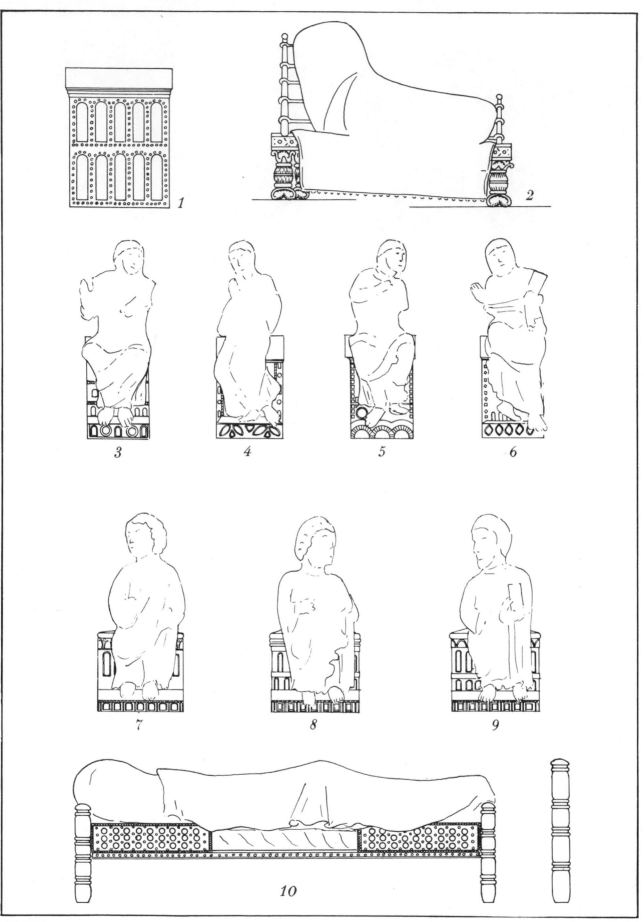

PLATE 2

1. Chair, as shown in a relief.   2. Drawing of a bed, described by Viollet le Duc.   3, 4, 5 and 6. Chairs, as shown in the tympanum of an arch in the church in Carennac.   7, 8 and 9. Chairs, as shown in the sculptures of the porticos of the transept of the cathedral of Bourges.   10. Bed from a stone relief on the lintel of the royal portico at Chartres.

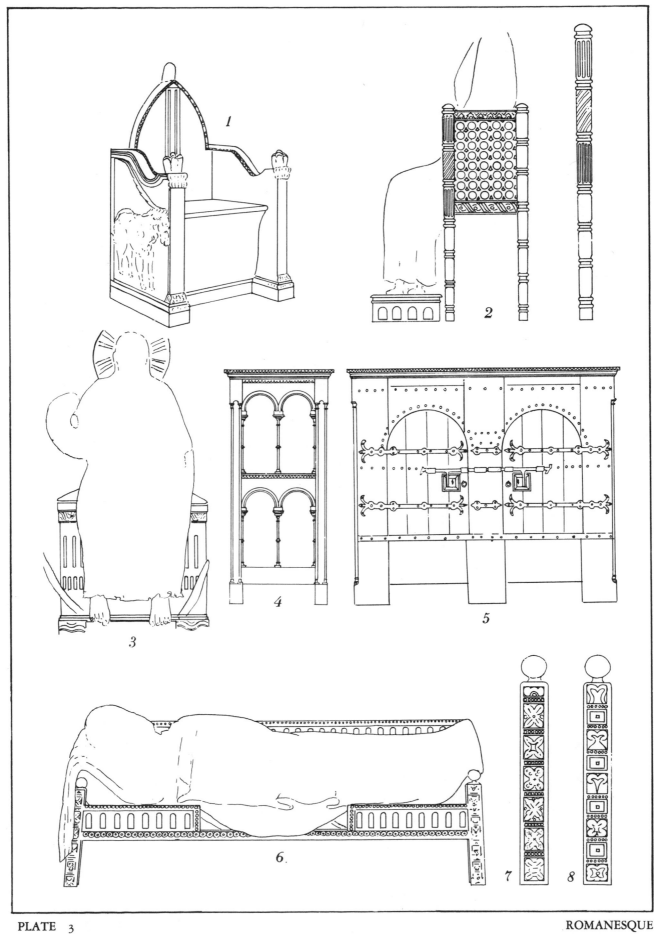

PLATE 3                                                                         ROMANESQUE

1. Stone chair in the cathedral of Avignon.    2. Armchair, as shown in the tympanum of the arch of the door of the church of La Charité-sur-Loire.    3. Chair, after a stone sculpture in a portico of the transept of the cathedral of Bourges.    4 and 5. Wardrobe, described by Viollet le Duc.    6. Bed, as shown in a stone relief on a lintel of La Charité-sur-Loire.    7 and 8. Detail of the posts.          7

PLATE 4                                                    GOTHIC (13th to 15th centuries)
1. Chest from the south of France, 13th century.   2. Oak chest, 14th century.   3, Chest, 15th century.   4, 5 and
6. Details from 1, 2 and 3.

*1*

*2*

*3*

*4*

**PLATE 5**                                                                                           GOTHIC (15th century)

1. Chest.    2. Post.    3 and 4. Details of the carving of the intermediate upright and tracery.

*John Simon collection, Berlin*

**PLATE 6**

1. Chest.   2. Detail of the post.   3. Detail of the carving.

GOTHIC (15th century)

*George Hoentschel collection, New York*

**PLATE 7**                                                                                    GOTHIC (15th century)
1. Chest.   2. Detail of the corner supports.   3 and 4. Details of the front.

*George Hoentschel collection, New York*

PLATE 8

1. Armchair with high back.    2. Detail of the back.    3. Detail of the back post.    4. Base moulding.

GOTHIC

*Figdor collection, Vienna*

**PLATE 9**                                                              RENAISSANCE

1. Early chair.    2. Later style chair.    3 and 4. Detail of the legs.    5 and 6. Details of the backs.

*Louvre and private collection*

PLATE 10                                                    RENAISSANCE (second half of 16th century)
1. Armchair.    2. Detail of the back.    3. Leg    4. Arm support.

*Private collection*

14

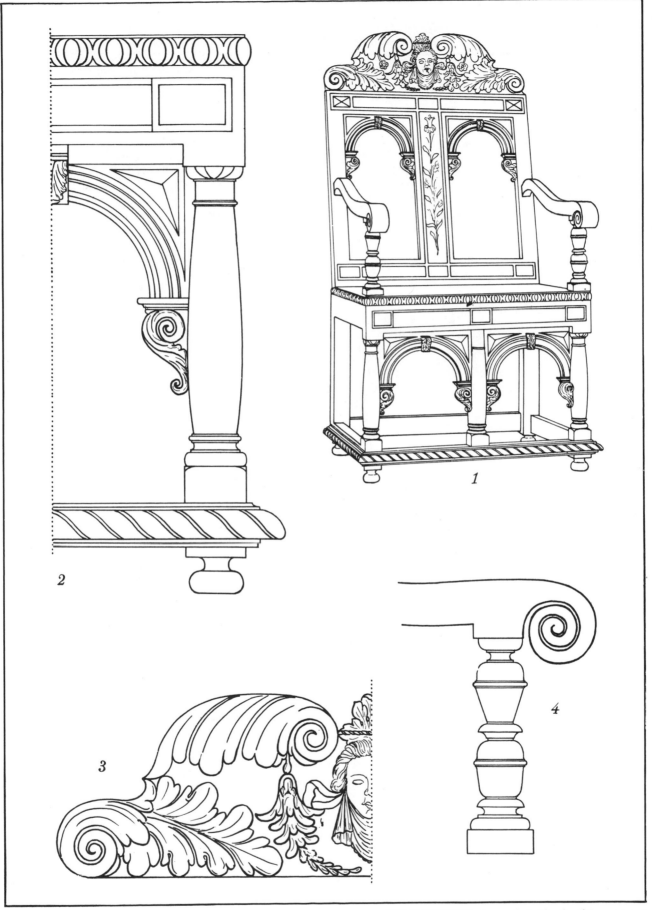

PLATE II                                    RENAISSANCE (second half of 16th century)
1. Armchair.   2. Leg and detail of the front of the seat.   3. Upper crest.   4. Arm and support.

PLATE 12                                    RENAISSANCE (beginning of 16th century)
1. Walnut armchair with high back.    2. Detail of the back.    3. Detail of the arm.    4. Detail of the leg base.    5.
Detail of the front panel.    6. Profile of the panel.

*Museum of Cluny*

16

PLATE 13                  RENAISSANCE (middle of 16th century)

1 and 2. Six-legged walnut chairs, reign of Henry II.    3 and 4. Details of the turned posts.    5. Detail of the seat edge.    6 and 7. Turned posts of the back.    8. Front legs.

*Museum of Cluny*

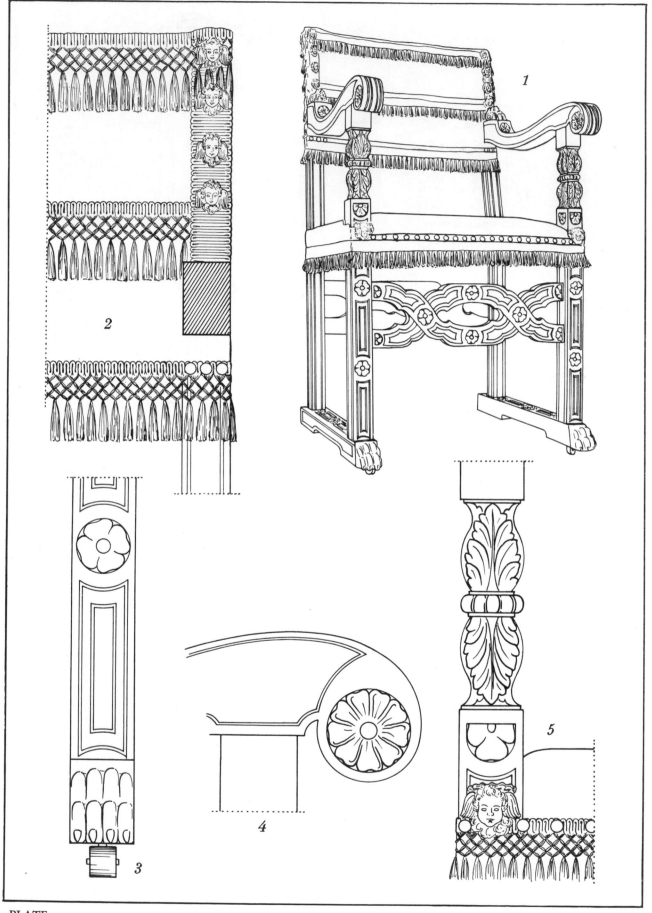

PLATE 14                                        RENAISSANCE (end of 16th century)
1. Armchair.   2. Back.   3. Detail of the leg.   4. Grip of the arm.   5. Arm support.

*Louvre*

**PLATE 15**                                          RENAISSANCE (second half of 16th century)
1. Armchair with high back.   2. Detail of the back.   3, 4 and 5. Profiles of mouldings and decorations.

*Museum of Cluny*

19

PLATE 16                                    RENAISSANCE (second half of 16th century)
1. Armchair with high back.   2. Back.   3. Detail of the lower panel.

*Palace Museum, Berlin*

**PLATE 17**

1. Armchair.  2. Back.  3. Detail of the leg.  4. Turned arm support.

RENAISSANCE (second half of 16th century)

*Private collection*

PLATE 18

1, 2, 3 and 4. Oak panels from the reign of Francis I.

RENAISSANCE (first half of the 16th century)

*Museum of Cluny*

*1*

*2*

*3*

*4*

*5*

PLATE 19                                                  RENAISSANCE (16th century)

1. Front motif of an early chest of the style.   2. Front motif of a chest of the second half of the 16th century.   3. Border.   4. Oak frieze from the reign of Henry III.   5. Border.

*Museum of Cluny*

23

PLATE 20                                    RENAISSANCE (middle of 16th century)

1, 2, 3 and 4. Oak panels, adorned with medallions containing relief figures and arabesques.

*Museum of Cluny*

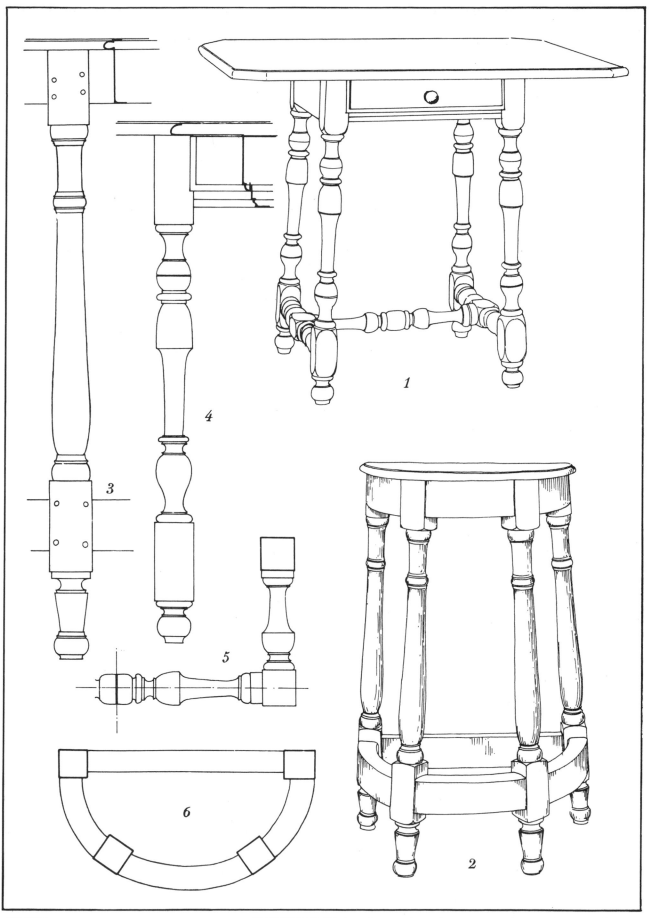

**PLATE 21**                    RENAISSANCE (northern and northeastern provinces, Flemish influence)
1. Small table.    2. Four-legged console table.    3 and 4. Legs.    5. Crosspiece.    6. Base of the console.

*Private collection*

PLATE 22            RENAISSANCE (second half of 16th century)

1. Table.    2. Detail of the legs.    3. Side bracket.    4. Side view and hanging turned ornament.

*Private collection*

PLATE 23          RENAISSANCE (second half of 16th century)

1. Table.    2. Detail of the turned portion of the archwork.    3. Side support.    4. Adornment of the moulding

*Private collection*

PLATE 24             RENAISSANCE (first half of 16th century)

1. Walnut table.    2. Detail of the side face.    3. Detail of a turned piece.

*Museum of Cluny*

**PLATE 25**

1. Table.  2. Detail of the side post.  3. Moulding.  4. Decoration.  5. Turned portion of the archwork.

RENAISSANCE (second half of 16th century)

*Private collection*

PLATE 26                                    RENAISSANCE (second half of 16th century)
1. Table.   2. Column of the archwork.   3. Details of the side support.   4. Moulding.   5. Inside view of foot.

*Private collection*

PLATE 27

RENAISSANCE (last third of 16th century)

1. Walnut table with double-arch support.   2 and 3. Details of the side.   4. Cross section of the support piece between the two arches.

*Museum of Cluny*

PLATE 28

RENAISSANCE (17th century)

1. Carved walnut table.　2. Detail of the legs.　3. Detail of the tabletop.　4. Connection of the arch.　5. Foot.

*Museum of Cluny*

PLATE 29                                                                         RENAISSANCE  (Italian  influence)
1. Door from the reign of Francis I.    2. Detail of the upper panels and pilasters.    3. Detail of the central panel.    4. Drawing of the carving that decorates one of the lower panels.

*Museum of Cluny*

**PLATE** 30

1. Early style credenza sideboard from the reign of Louis XII.   2. Detail of the corner pilaster.   3. Top mouldings.   4. Base mouldings.   5. Detail of the panel sculpture.

RENAISSANCE (transition from the Gothic)

*Museum of Cluny*

PLATE 31                                                   RENAISSANCE (first half of 16th century)
1. Sideboard.   2, 3 and 4. Details of the uprights and crosspieces.   5. Leg.   6. Hanging turned ornament.   7. Escutcheon.

*Palace Museum, Berlin*

PLATE 32                                                                RENAISSANCE (16th century)
1. Walnut credenza sideboard of the Midi.   2. Detail of the post.   3 and 4. Panels.   5. Drawer fronts.

*Museum of Cluny*

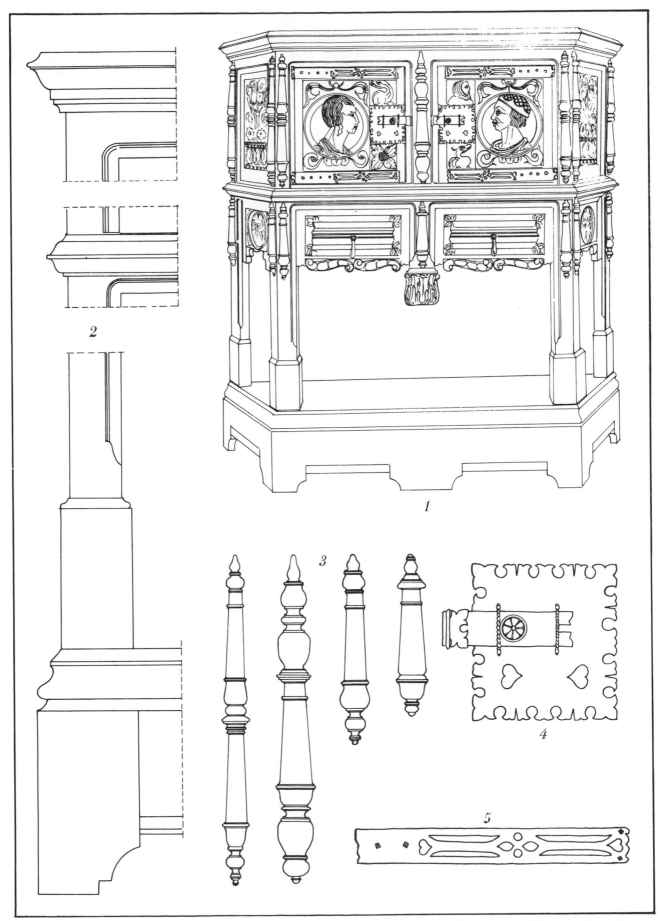

PLATE 33

RENAISSANCE (Spanish influence)

1. Credenza sideboard from the Midi.  2. Detail of the uprights.  3. Profiles of the high-relief turned pilasters.  4 and 5. Details of the latches and hinges.

*Museum of Cluny*

PLATE 34                                       RENAISSANCE (second half of 16th century)
1. Buffet sideboard.    2. Profiles and details of the side pilasters.    3. Detail of the arch.    4. Inside view of the arch.

*Museum of Cluny*

**PLATE 35**

1. Oak credenza sideboard from northern France of the reign of Francis I.
Central panel.

RENAISSANCE (first half of 16th century)   2. Profile and details of the corner pilaster.   3.

*Museum of Cluny*

PLATE 36                           RENAISSANCE (southeastern school—Burgundy, 16th century)
1. Credenza sideboard.   2. Detail of the post.   3. Detail of the panel.   4. Cross section of the panel.

*Museum of Cluny*

PLATE 37
1. Credenza sideboard.　2. Detail of the post.　3. Detail of the panel.　4. Side view of the panel.

*Museum of Cluny*

1

2

3   4

PLATE 38                                                        RENAISSANCE (Burgundian school)
1. Walnut credenza sideboard.    2. Detail of the post.    3. Detail of the panel.    4. Profile of the panel.

*Museum of Cluny*

PLATE 39                                    RENAISSANCE (first half of 16th century)
1. Sideboard.   2. Detail of the post.   3 and 4. Mouldings of the lower part.

*Spitzer collection, Paris*

PLATE 40        RENAISSANCE (first half of 16th century)
1 and 2. Chests (the first from c. 1540).    3. Detail of the central upright.    4. Post.    5. Detail of the mouldings.

*James Simon collection, Berlin and private collection*

**PLATE 41**

RENAISSANCE (school of Tours, 16th century)

1. Walnut wedding chest in the form of a trunk.   2. Profile of the lid.   3 and 4. Detail of the mouldings.   5. Detail of the foot.

*Museum of Cluny*

PLATE 42                                                RENAISSANCE (Flemish origin, 16th century)
1. Coffer.   2. Detail of the post.   3. Detail of the central panel carving.

*Museum of Cluny*

*1*

*2*          *3*          *4*

PLATE 43                                                  RENAISSANCE (16th century)
1. Coffer.   2. Detail and side view.   3. Detail of the mouldings that frame the central panel.   4. Cross section of the central panel

*Museum of Cluny*

PLATE 44                                        RENAISSANCE (Italian influence, second half of 16th century)
1. Walnut coffer from the reign of Henry II.    2. Side view.    3. Detail of the pilaster.    4. Motif of small front panel.

*Museum of Cluny*

PLATE 45                               RENAISSANCE (beginning of 16th century)

1. Chest.    2. Detail of the central panel.    3. Base carving.    4. Upper moulding.

PLATE 46                                            RENAISSANCE (second half of 16th century)

1. Double console.    2. Detail of the post.    3. Detail of the rear pilaster.    4 and 5. Door pulls.

*Private collection*

PLATE 47                RENAISSANCE (influence of the Burgundian school, second half of 16th century)
1. Chest-on-chest wardrobe with four doors.    2 and 3. Details.

*Private collection*

PLATE 48

1. Cabinet wardrobe.  2. Detail of the post.  3. Central panel.  4. Cross section of central panel.

RENAISSANCE (end of 16th century)

*Museum of Cluny*

52

**PLATE 49**

1. Chest-on-chest wardrobe with four doors from the time of Henry IV. lower panel.   4 and 5. Upper and lower parts of the corner column.

RENAISSANCE (end of 16th century)   2. Detail of the front post.   3. Detail of the

*Museum of Cluny*

53

PLATE 50                                        RENAISSANCE (Flemish school, end of 16th century)

1. Wardrobe.    2, 3 and 4. Side view, details of mouldings.

*Museum of Cluny*

PLATE 51                                          RENAISSANCE (end of 16th century)

1. Chest-on-chest wardrobe with two doors, broken pediment, with inlaid marble, attributed to the Fontainebleau school.   2.
Side view and detail of the columns.   3. Upper carving between the columns.   4, 5 and 6. Details of the carvings.

*Museum of Cluny*

PLATE 52                                                    RENAISSANCE (end of 16th century)

1. Chest-on-chest wardrobe with two doors, pediment, inlaid marble, attributed to the Fontainebleau school.    2 and 3. Details.

PLATE 53                                    RENAISSANCE (middle of 16th century)
1. Inlaid mother-of-pearl chest-on-chest wardrobe with four doors, from the reign of Henry II.    2 and 3. Details.
*Museum of Cluny*

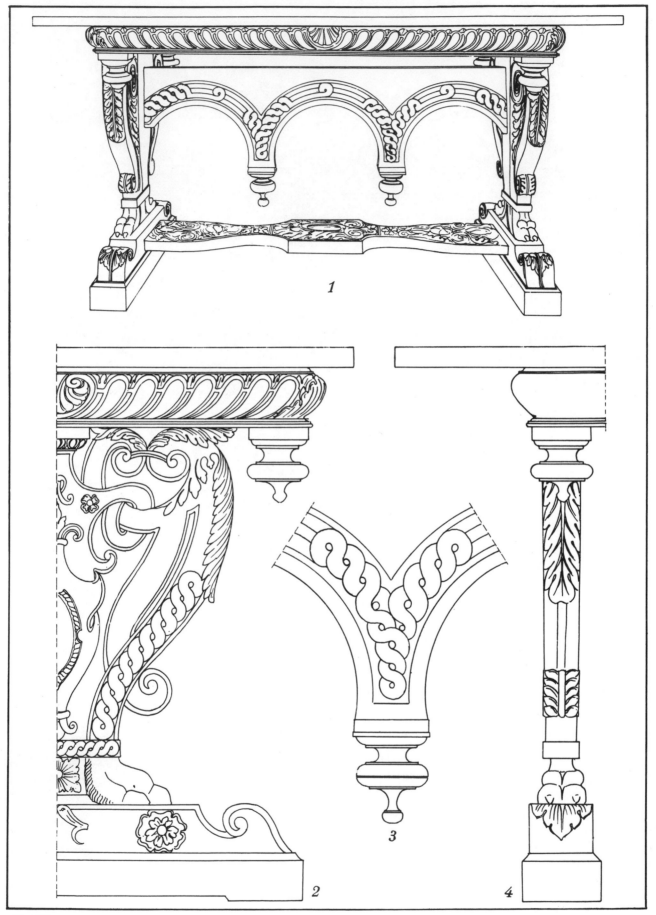

PLATE 54                                                    RENAISSANCE (late style, 17th century)
1. Walnut table from the reign of Louis XIII.   2. Detail of end.   3. Detail of the arch.   4. Front view of leg.

*Museum of Cluny*

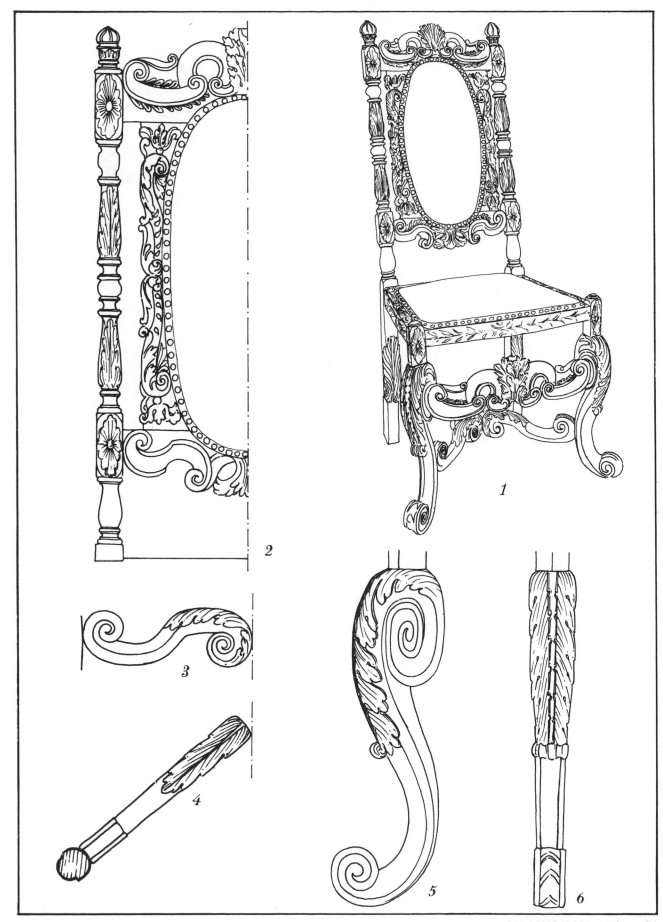

**PLATE 55**

1. Carved chair from the reign of Louis XII.   2. Detail of the back.   3 and 4. Details of the carved crosspiece that unites the legs.   5 and 6. Front legs.

RENAISSANCE (early style)

*Museum of Cluny*

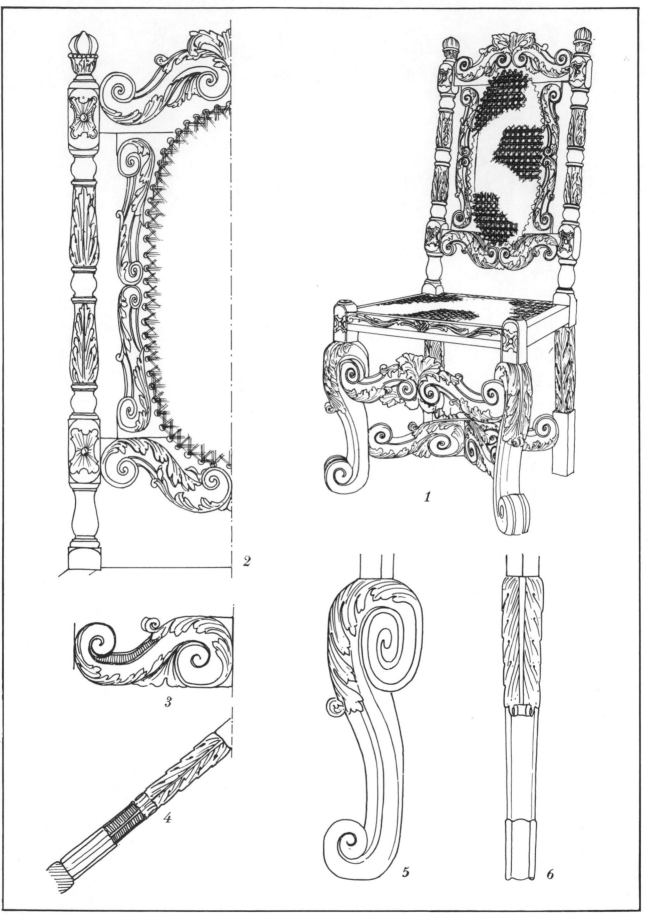

PLATE 56          RENAISSANCE (beginning of 17th century)

1. Carved chair from the reign of Louis XIII.    2. Detail of the back.    3 and 4. Detail of the curved crosspiece that connects the legs.    5 and 6. Front leg.

*Museum of Cluny*

PLATE 57            RENAISSANCE (beginning of 17th century)
1 and 2. Walnut borders from the reign of Louis XIII.    3 and 4. Oak borders from the reign of Louis XIII.

*Museum of Cluny*

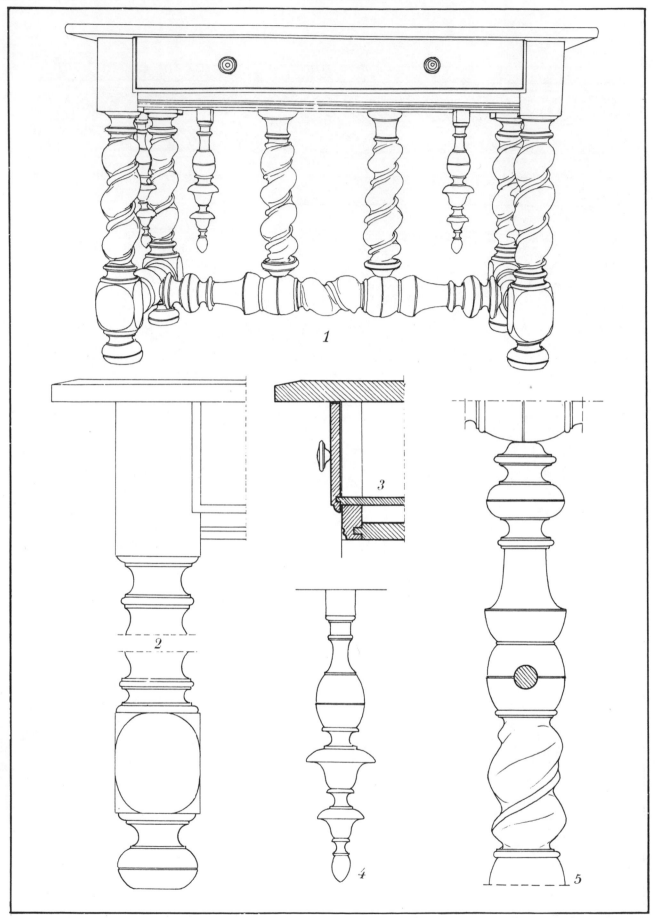

**PLATE 58**　　　　　　　　　　　　　　　　　RENAISSANCE (beginning of 17th century)

1. Walnut table from the reign of Louis XIII.　2. Detail of the legs.　3. Cross section.　4. Detail of the hanging turned ornament.　5. Crosspiece.

*Museum of Cluny*

PLATE 59

1. Table from the reign of Louis XIII.    2. Detail of the legs.    3. Detail of the turned ornament.    4. Detail of the table.

RENAISSANCE (beginning of 17th century)

*Museum of Cluny*

PLATE 60                                    RENAISSANCE (beginning of 17th century)
1. Chest-on-chest wardrobe with four doors and broken pediment from the reign of Louis XIII.    2 and 3. Details of pediment.    4. Details of the upper chest.    5 and 6. Details of the lower chest.

*Museum of Cluny*

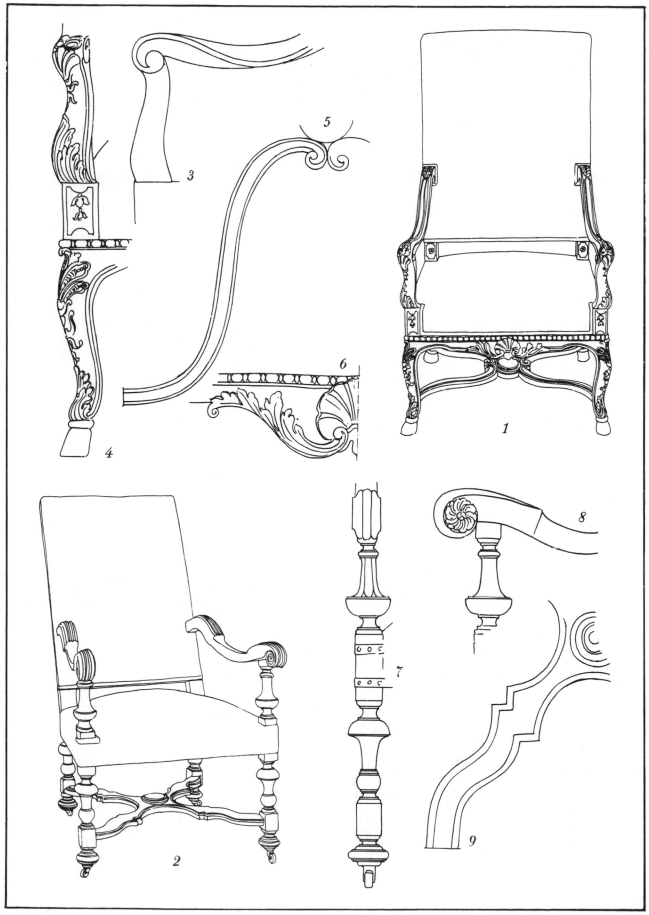

PLATE 61                                                                    LOUIS XIV

1. Upholstered armchair, covered with Gobelin tapestry.    2. Armchair, covered with petit point upholstery.    3, 4, 5
and 6. Details of the arm, leg, trim and central motif of the first chair.    7, 8 and 9. Details of the arm, leg and
trim of the second chair.

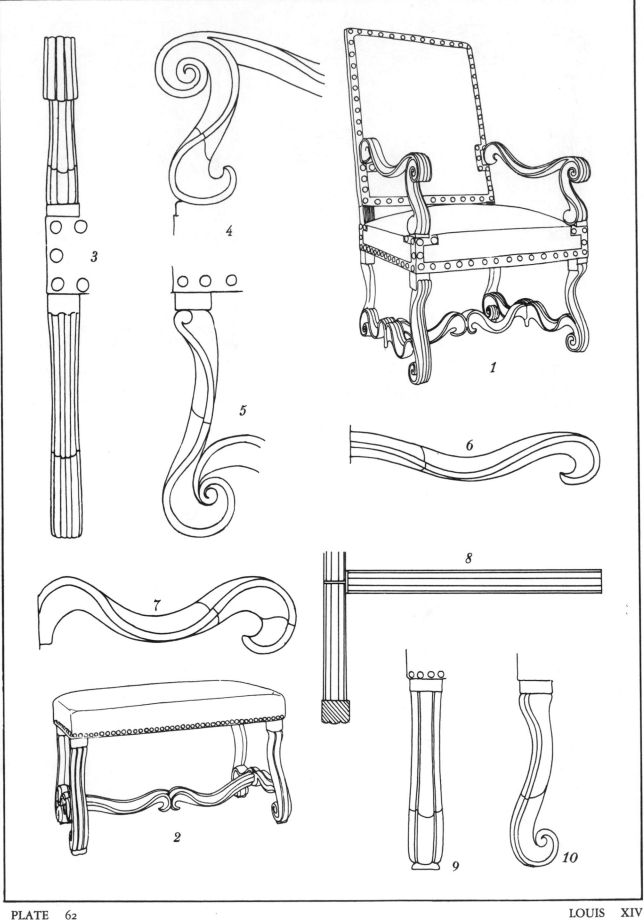

**PLATE  62**                                    LOUIS  XIV

1. Leather-covered armchair of early style.  2. Stool.  3, 4, 5 and 6. Details of the armchair.  7, 8, 9 and 10. Details of the stool.

*Fontainebleau Palace*

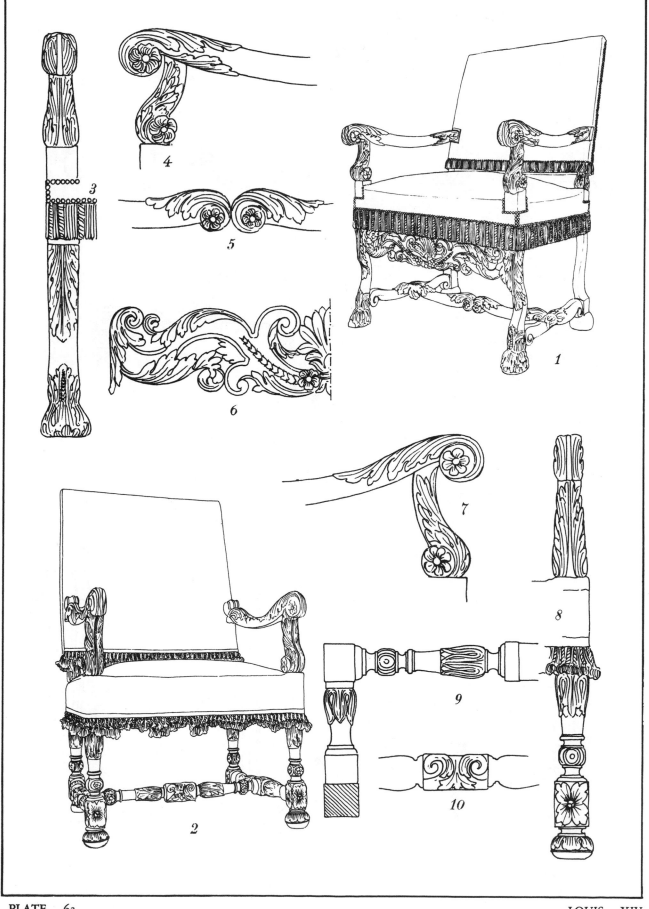

**PLATE 63**

1. Armchair, covered with floral damask upholstery. 2. Walnut armchair, covered with velvet. 3, 4, 5 and 6. Details of the first chair. 7, 8, 9 and 10. Details of the second chair.

*Fontainebleau Palace and Museum of Decorative Arts, Paris*

PLATE 64                                                                    LOUIS XIV

1. Armchair, with petit point upholstery.  2. Sculptured wooden chair.  3, 4, 5 and 6. Details of the armchair.  7, 8 and 9. Details of the chair.

*Fontainebleau Palace and Museum of Decorative Arts, Paris*

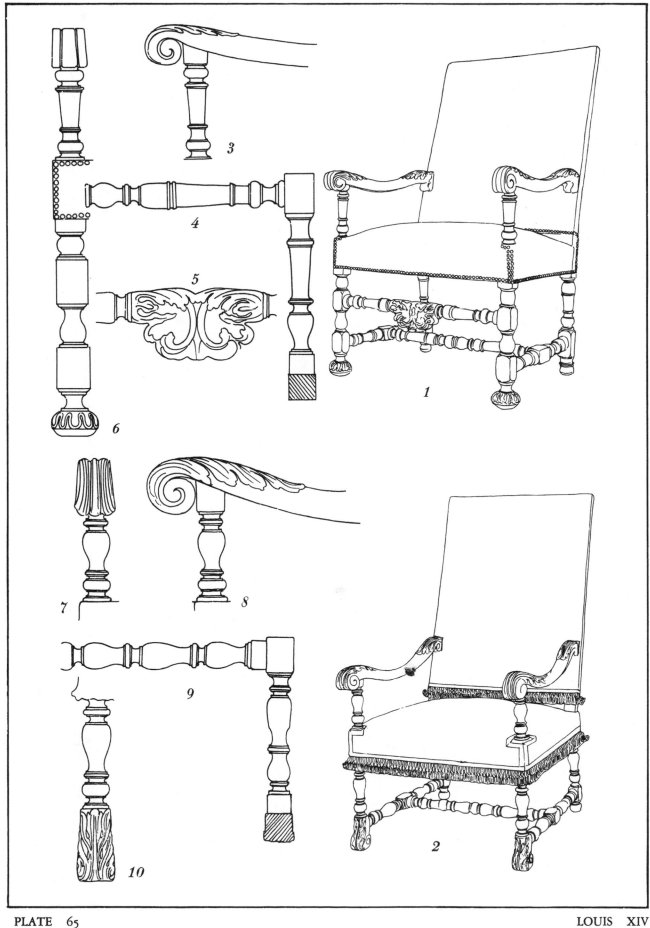

PLATE 65                                                                                    LOUIS XIV

1. Armchair, covered with floral damask upholstery.    2. Armchair, upholstered with petit point.    3, 4, 5 and 6.
Details of the first armchair.    7, 8, 9 and 10. Details of the second armchair.

*Museum of Decorative Arts, Paris and Cinquantenaire, Brussels*

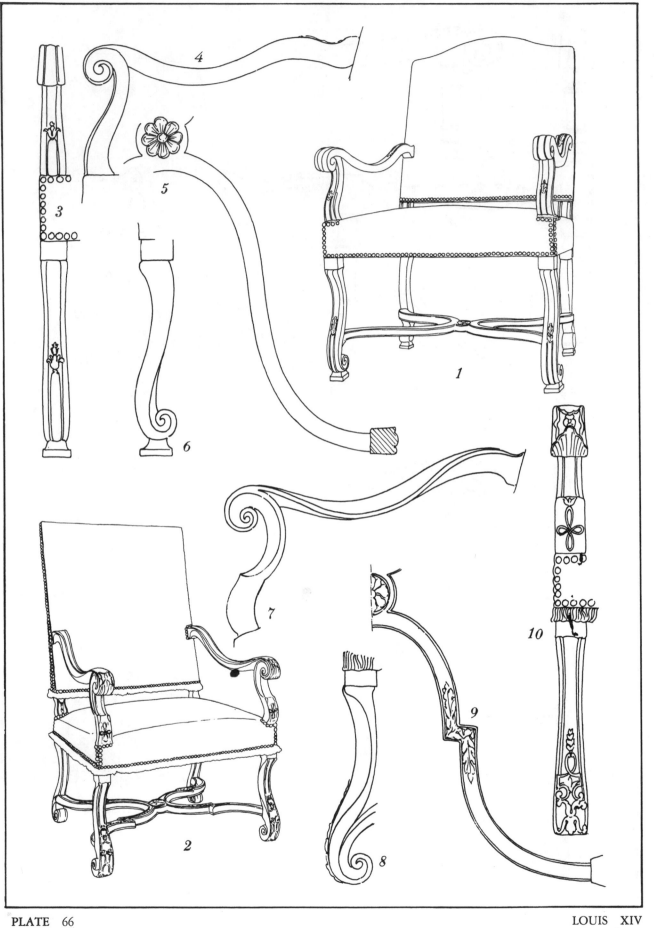

PLATE 66                                                           LOUIS XIV

1 and 2. Armchair, upholstered with tapestry.    3, 4, 5 and 6. Details of the first armchair.    7, 8, 9 and 10.
Details of the second armchair.

*Museum of Decorative Arts, Paris and Metropolitan Museum, New York*

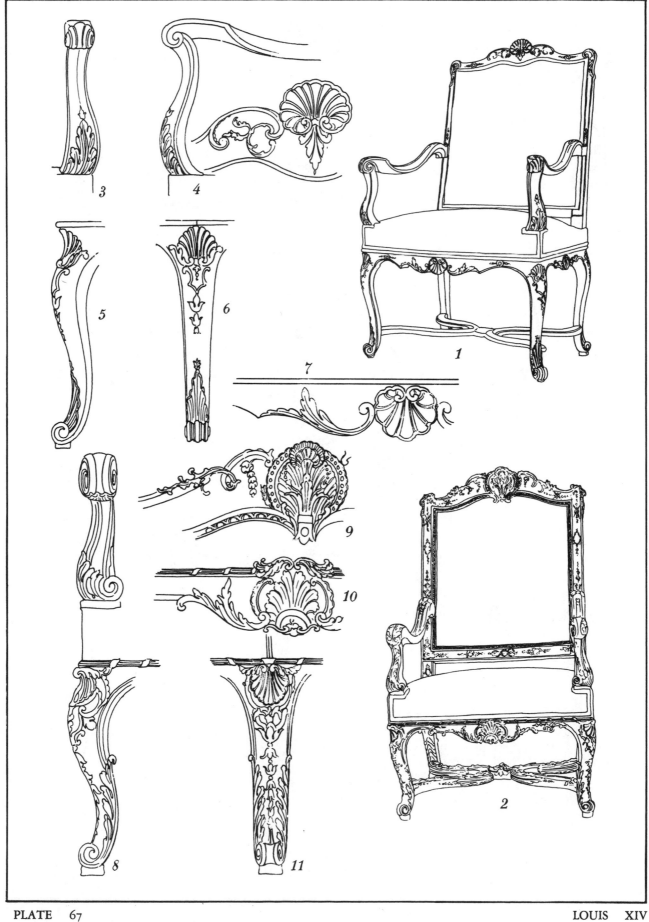

PLATE 67       LOUIS XIV

1. Armchair, upholstered with damask.    2. Armchair, upholstered with velvet.    3, 4, 5, 6 and 7. Details of the first armchair.    8, 9, 10 and 11. Details of the second armchair.

*Museum of Decorative Arts, Paris and the Kann collection*

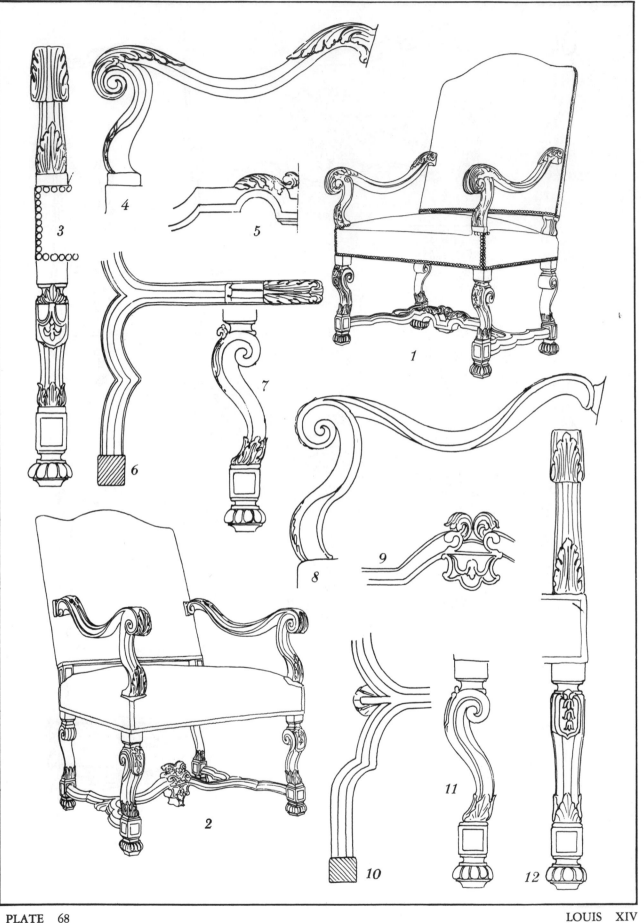

**PLATE 68**                                                                 LOUIS XIV

1. Armchair, upholstered with damask.   2. Armchair, upholstered with velvet.   3, 4, 5, 6 and 7. Details of the first armchair.   8, 9, 10, 11 and 12. Details of the second armchair.

*Museum of Decorative Arts, Paris and a private collection*

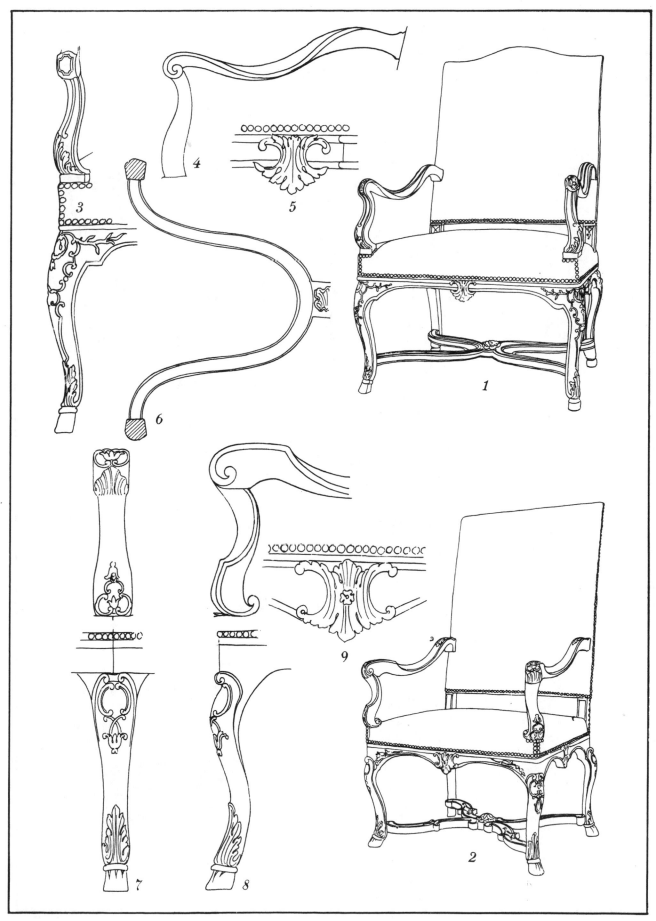

1 and 2. Armchair, upholstered with tapestry.     3, 4, 5 and 6. Details of the first armchair.     7, 8 and 9. Details of the second armchair.

*Museum of Decorative Arts, Paris and Metropolitan Museum, New York*

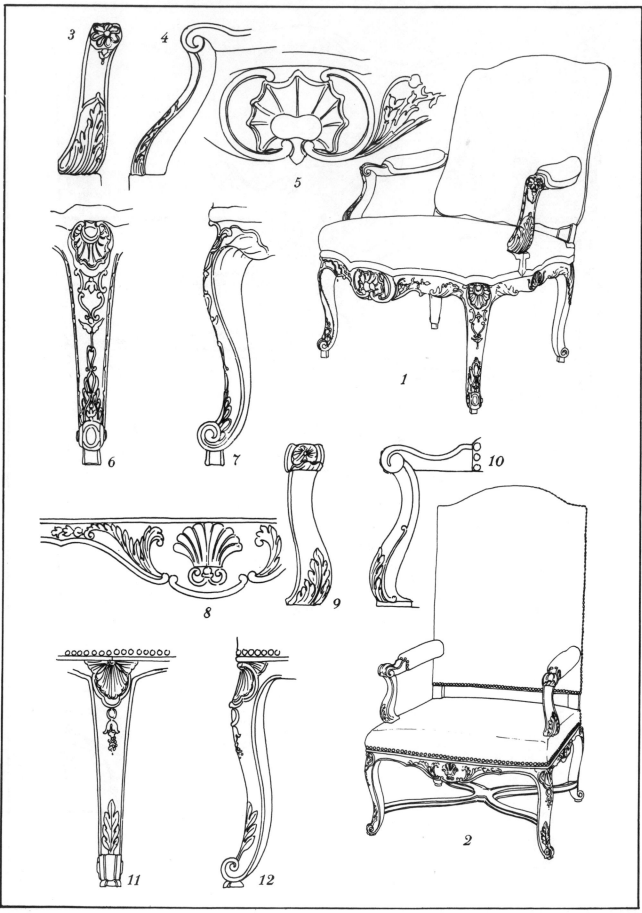

**PLATE** 70

LOUIS XIV

1. Armchair, upholstered with velvet from Genoa.   2. Armchair, covered with petit point upholstery.   3, 4, 5, 6 and 7. Details of the first armchair.   8, 9, 10, 11 and 12. Details of the second armchair.

*Museum of Decorative Arts, Paris and Bernheimer collection, Munich*

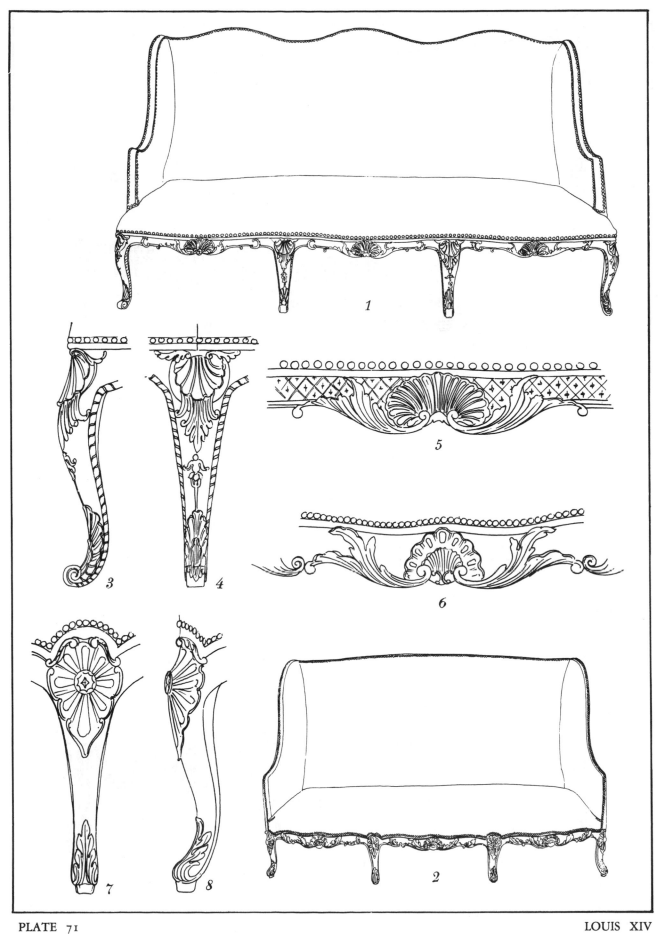

PLATE 71

1 and 2. Wing-back sofas, upholstered with tapestry.  3, 4 and 5. Details of the first sofa.  6, 7 and 8. Details of the second sofa.

*Private collections*

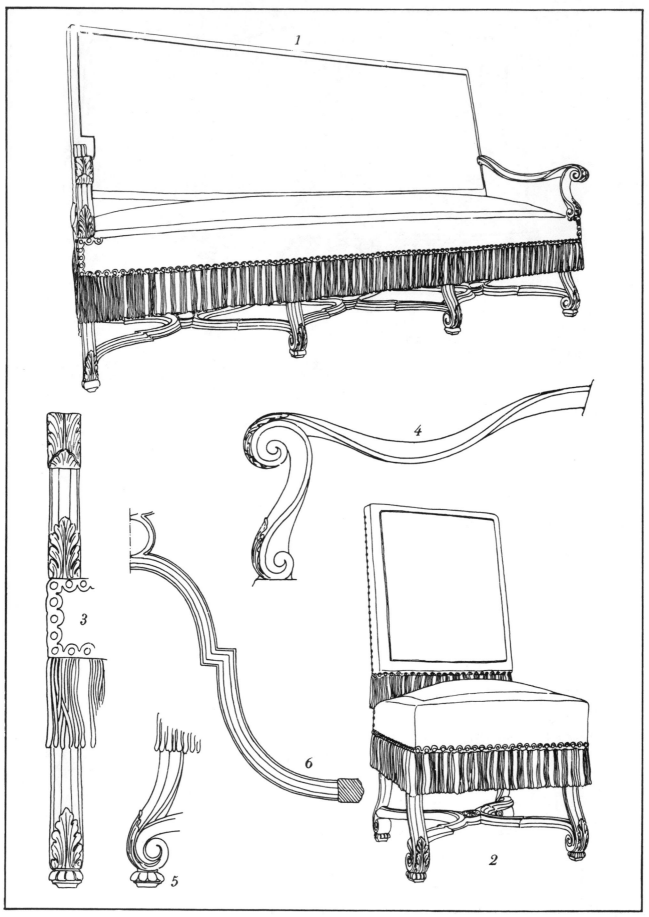

**PLATE 72**

1. Sofa, covered with floral damask upholstery. 2. Carved wooden chair with floral damask upholstery. 3 and 4. Details of the sofa. 5 and 6. Details of the chair.

*Fontainebleau Palace*

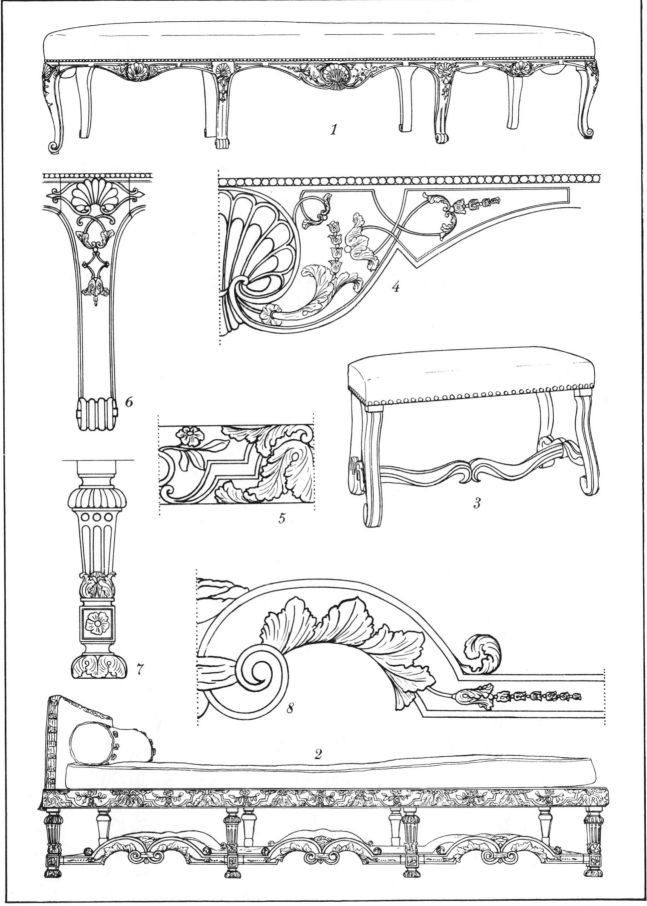

**PLATE 73**

1. Carved walnut bench (banquette).   2. Chaise longue of gilt carved oak.   3. Stool.   4 and 5. Detail of the aprons.   6 and 7. Detail of the legs.   8. Detail of the rails.

*Museum of Decorative Arts, Paris*

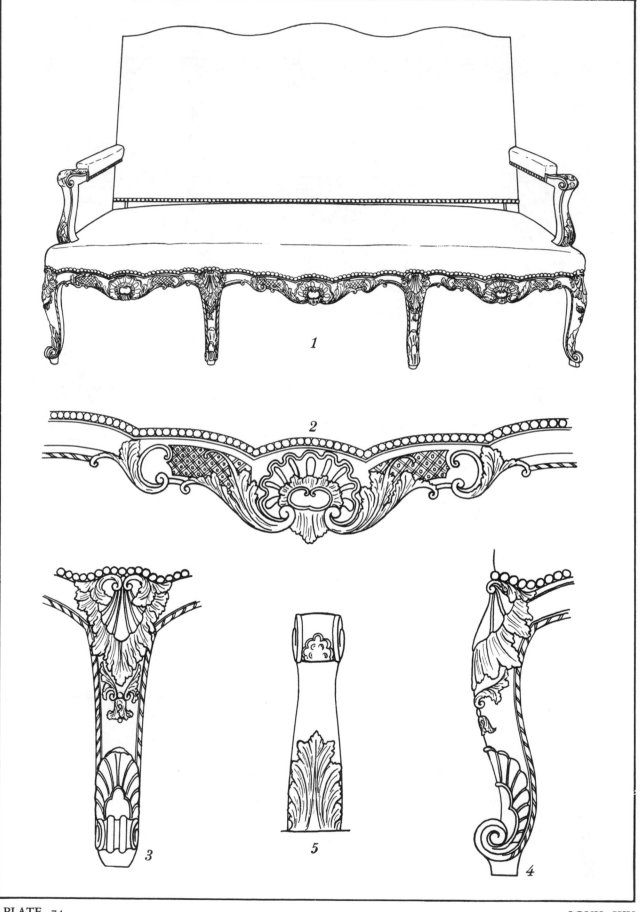

PLATE 74                                                                              LOUIS XIV
1. Sofa, upholstered with Gobelin tapestry.    2. Details of the central motif.    3 and 4. Legs.    5. Arm support.

*Lowengard collection, Paris*

**PLATE 75**

1 and 2. Gilt walnut consoles.   3 and 4. Details of the legs.   5 and 6. Details of the fronts of the consoles.

LOUIS XIV

*Lowengard collection, Paris and Metropolitan Museum, New York*

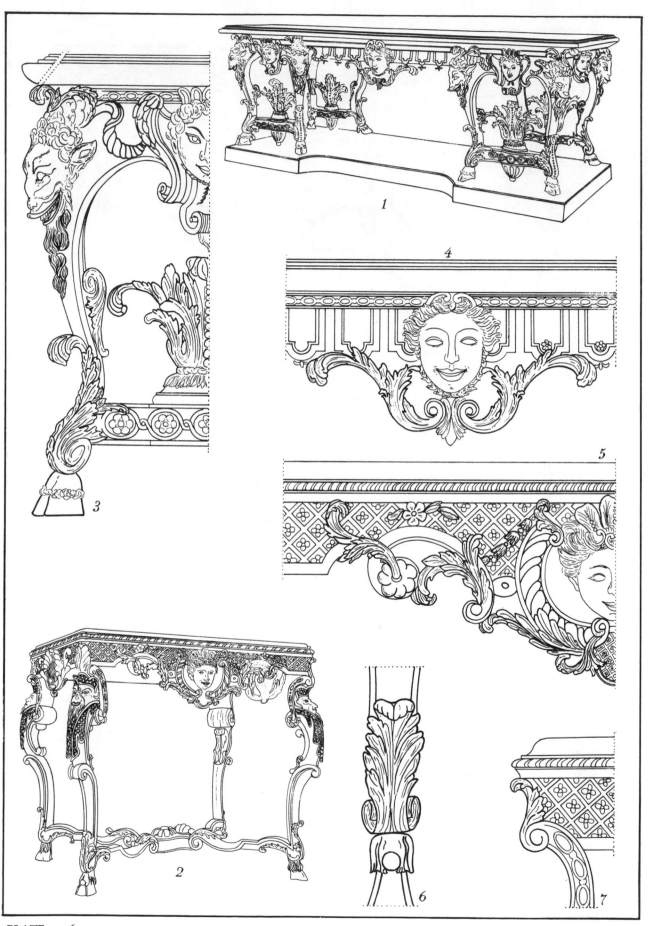

PLATE 76

1. Large natural wood console.   2. Gilt wooden console table.   3. Detail of the legs.   4 and 5. Detail of the central motifs.   6 and 7. Leg and corner of the frieze.

*Bank of France and Museum of Decorative Arts, Paris*

*1*

*2*

*3*

*4*

PLATE 77                                                                    LOUIS XIV
1. Gilt wooden console.    2. Detail of the legs.    3. Middle ornament.    4. Upright crest.

*Bank of France, Paris*

PLATE 78                                                                                          LOUIS XIV

1. Natural wooden console table.    2. Gilt wooden console table.    3. Leg.    4 and 5. Table front.    6. Leg.

*Bank of France and Museum of Decorative Arts, Paris*

PLATE 79

1. Gilt wooden console table.  2. Detail of table front.  3. Top-shaped ornament.  4 and 5. Details of the legs.

*Church of Saint-Jacques, Rheims*

**PLATE** 80

LOUIS XIV

1. Gilt wooden console.   2 and 3. Detail of the leg and table front.   4. Decoration of the crosspieces.

*Museum of Decorative Arts, Paris*

84

**PLATE 81**                                                                      LOUIS XIV
1. **Large** gilt wooden console table.   2. Detail of the leg.   3. Side view of leg decoration.   4. Detail of central motif.

*Louvre*

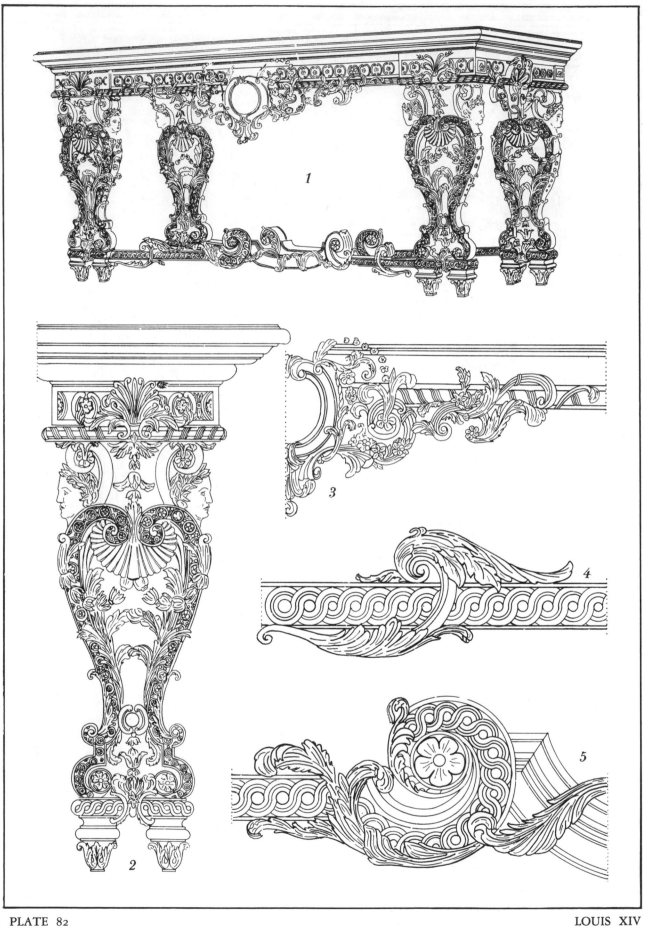

**PLATE 82**  LOUIS XIV

1. Gilt wooden console.  2. Detail of the legs.  3. Detail of the table front.  4 and 5. Details of the decorations of the crosspiece.

*Louvre*

PLATE 83

1. Gilt wooden console.    2. Detail of the legs.    3. Detail of the upper face of the crosspiece.    4. Detail of the table front.

*Achille Seilliere collection, Paris*

**PLATE 84**  COMPARISON OF THE STYLES OF LOUIS XIV AND LOUIS XV

1. Gilt carved wooden console of Louis XIV style.  2. Gilt carved wooden wall console of early Louis XV style.  3, 4 and 5. Details of the decorations of Louis XIV style.  6, 7 and 8. Details of the decorations of Louis XV style.

*Louvre*

**PLATE 85**  COMPARISON OF THE STYLES OF LOUIS XIV AND THE REGENCY
1. Writing table with ebony and copper marquetry, Louis XIV style.  2. Marble-top sculptured wooden pier table, Regency style.  3 and 4. Drawer pulls and escutcheons.  5. Details of the table fronts.  6. Detail of the leg.  7. Moulding.

*Private collection and Castle of Fleury-en-Bière*

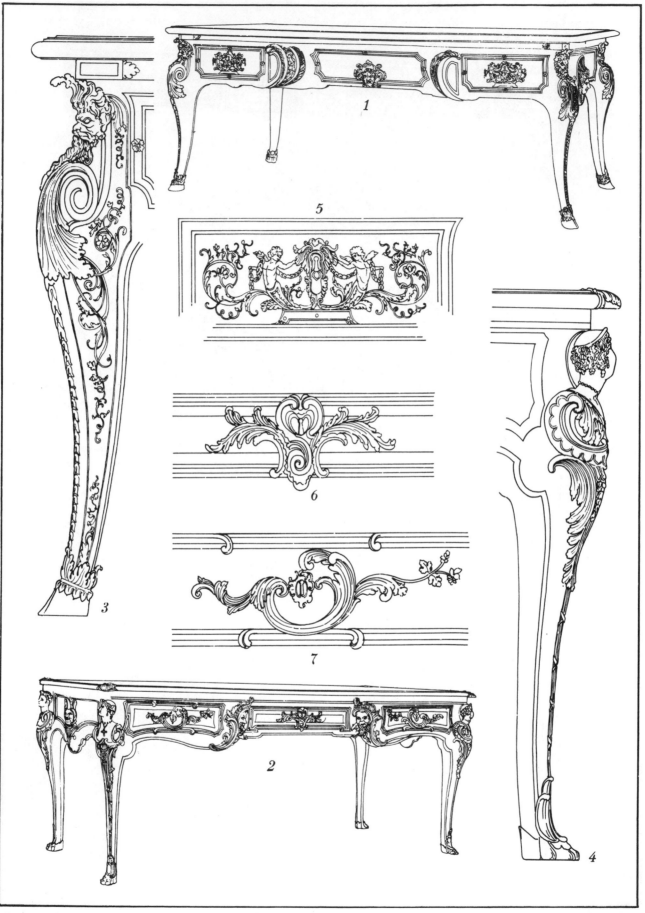

PLATE 86                    COMPARISON OF THE STYLES OF LOUIS XIV AND LOUIS XV

1. Ebony writing table inlaid with gilt bronze decorations, attributed to A. C. Boulle, Louis XIV style (end of the 17th century).    2. Marquetry writing table with gilt bronze decorations by C. Cressent, Louis XV style (early type).    3 and 4. Details of the legs, each drawing indicating the inlays and bronze work.    5, 6 and 7. Details of the table fronts.

**PLATE 87**

1. Marquetry writing desk by A. C. Boulle.    2 and 3. Legs.    4 and 5. Drawer fronts.

*Louvre*

PLATE 88                                                                   LOUIS XIV
1. Marquetry writing table by A. C. Boulle.   2. Detail of the uprights.   3. Escutcheon.   4. Detail of the middle
section.

*Wallace collection, London*

PLATE 89

LOUIS XIV

1. Marquetry writing table by A. C. Boulle.   2. Detail of the upright.   3 and 4. Detail of the leg.   5. Detail of the middle panel.

*Windsor Castle*

PLATE 90                                                                                                                LOUIS XIV

1. Marquetry writing table by A. C. Boulle.   2. Detail of the upright.   3. Detail of the lower section.

*Munich Museum*

PLATE 91                                                              LOUIS   XIV

1. Marquetry writing table by A. C. Boulle.   2. Detail of the upright.   3. Leg.   4. Detail of the middle panels.

*Victoria and Albert Museum, London*

95

PLATE 92 LOUIS XIV

1. Marquetry bureau-type of writing desk by A. C. Boulle. 2. Detail of the post and leg. 3. Detail of the upper face of the crosspiece. 4. Escutcheon. 5. Side view of the leg carving. 6. Detail of middle drawer front.

*Wallace collection, London*

PLATE 93

LOUIS XIV

1. Inlaid ebony commode by A. C. Boulle.   2 and 3. Post and leg.   4 and 5. Outline of the gilt bronze work.

*Louvre*

PLATE 94                                                                                    LOUIS XIV

1. Marquetry commode by A. C. Boulle.    2. Detail of the post.    3. Handle.    4. Upper cross section.    5. Leg.    6.
Detail of lower section.

PLATE 95

LOUIS XIV

1. Marquetry commode by A. C. Boulle. 2. Detail of the post. 3. Handle. 4. Leg. 5. Detail of lower section.

*Louvre*

PLATE 96

1. Low marquetry wardrobe by A. C. Boulle.   2. Detail of the post.   3. Detail of the middle panel.

*Louvre*

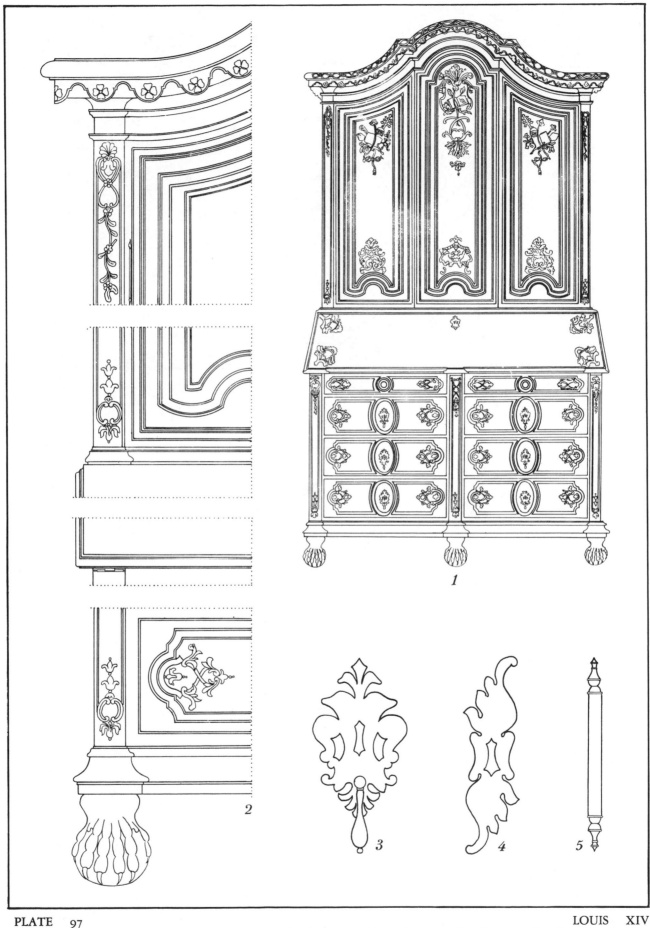

PLATE 97                                                                LOUIS   XIV

1. Sculptured wooden wardrobe-shaped commode with drop-leaf writing table.   2. Details.   3 and 4. Escutcheons.   5. Hinge.

*Cinquantenaire, Brussels*

**PLATE** 98

1. Wardrobe-shaped secretary with colored wooden marquetry.   2, 3 and 4. Details of the uprights.   5. Details of the crest.   6. Pull.   7. Escutcheon.

*Private collection*

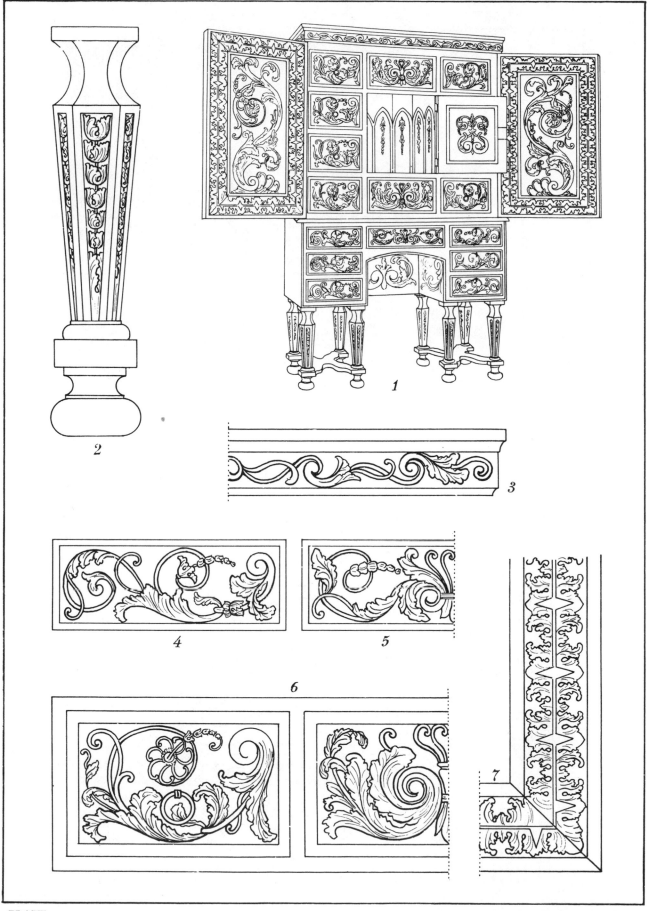

**PLATE** 99                                          LOUIS XIV (early type)

1. Cabinet with copper and shell marquetry.   2. Leg.   3. Drawing of the frieze.   4, 5 and 6. Outlines of the panel designs.   7. Outline of mitred corner.

*Louvre*

**PLATE** 100

LOUIS XIV (early type)

1. Carved ebony cabinet.   2. Leg.   3. Detail of post.   4. Cross section.   5. Detail of lower section.

*Louvre*

PLATE 101                                                                                    LOUIS XIV

1. Chest-on-chest wardrobe of sculpted wood.    2 and 3. Details of the front.    4. Detail of the upper corner of the door.

*Metropolitan Museum, New York*

PLATE 102

LOUIS XIV

1. Wardrobe made of carved wood.    2 and 3. Detail of base and door.    4. Moulding and decorations on panel.

*Metropolitan Museum, New York*

**PLATE** 103

1. Ebony wardrobe with marquetry of copper, shell and blue horn, attributed to A. C. Boulle.   2. Details of the front.   3 and 4. Details of decorations.

*Collection of the Duke of G., Paris*

**PLATE** 104

LOUIS XIV

1. Ebony wardrobe with marquetry of copper and shell, attributed to A. C. Boulle.  2. Details of the front.  3 and 4. Sketches of decorations and the upper central relief.

*Collection of the Duke of G., Paris*

1

2

3

PLATE 105

LOUIS XIV

1. Oversized wardrobe with marquetry by A. C. Boulle.    2. Detail of supports.    3. Bronze design.

*Windsor Castle*

PLATE 106
LOUIS XIV (end of period)

1. Ebony showcase with marquetry of copper over shell. 2 and 3. Details of the bronze decorations. 4 and 5. Profiles of the mouldings.

*Poles collection, Paris*

**PLATE** 107

1. Bed with tapestry canopy.   2. Detail of the legs.   3. Headboard.   4. Detail of footboard.

*Lowengard collection, Paris*

PLATE 108

1. Clock.   2. Detail.   3. Sketch of face.

LOUIS XIV

*Museum of Decorative Arts, Paris*

PLATE 109

1. Clock.    2. Detail.    3. Hands.    4. Detail of lower section.

LOUIS   XIV

*Museum of Aix-en-Provence*

PLATE 110

1. Clock.   2. Detail.   3. Sketch of bronze ornament.   4. Detail of clockface.

LOUIS XIV

*Fontainebleau Palace*

PLATE III

1. Clock on top of a pedestal.    2. Detail of the clock.    3. Detail of upper pedestal.    4. Hands.

*Wallace collection, London*

PLATE 112                                                    LOUIS XIV

1. Clock on top of pedestal.    2. Detail of the clock.    3. Foot of pedestal.    4. Hands.

*Wallace collection, London*

**PLATE** 113
1. Clock.   2. Detail.   3. Hands.

LOUIS XIV

*Museum of Decorative Arts, Paris*

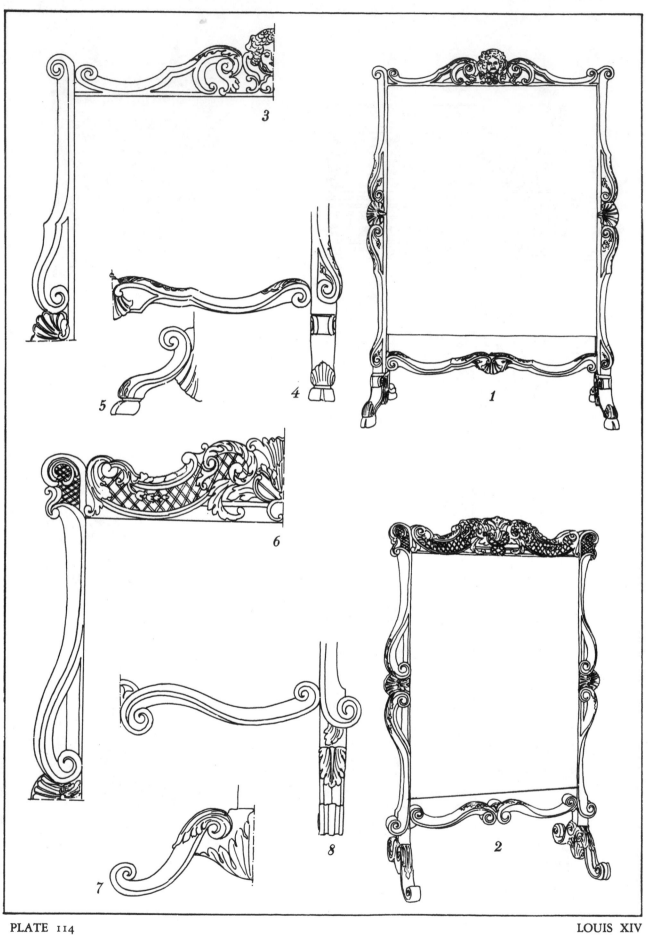

PLATE 114

LOUIS XIV

1 and 2. Fireplace screens with petit point tapestry.  3, 4 and 5. Details of first screen.  6, 7 and 8. Details of second screen.

*Museum of Cluny and Anet Castle*

PLATE 115

1 and 2. Gilt wooden fireplace screens with tapestry.    3 and 4. Details of the first and second screens.

*Private collections*

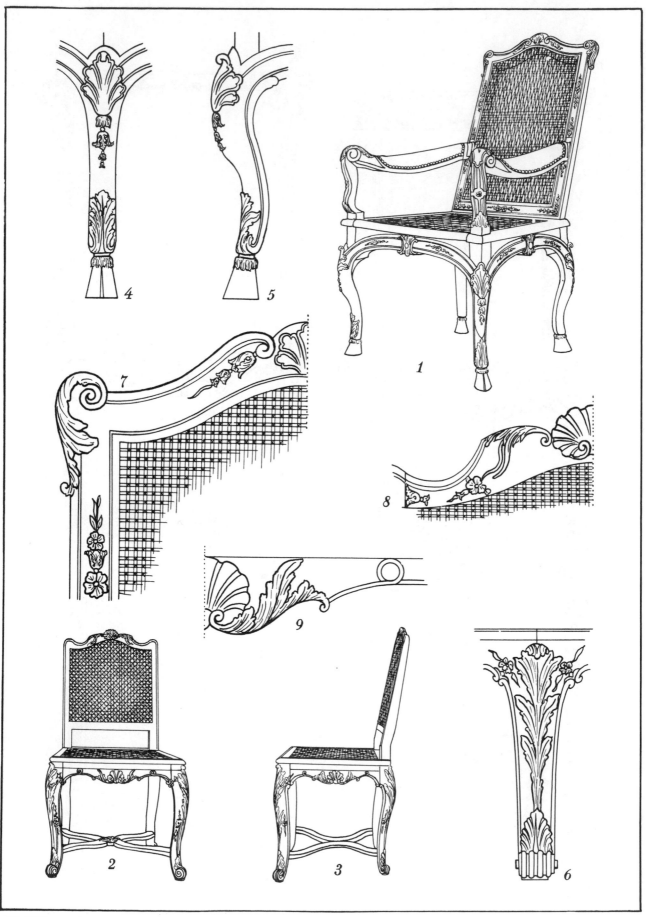

PLATE 116

REGENCY

1. Cane armchair.   2 and 3. Cane side chairs.   4, 5 and 6. Legs.   7 and 8. Details of the backs.   9. Detail of the crosspiece of the seat.

*Metropolitan Museum, New York*

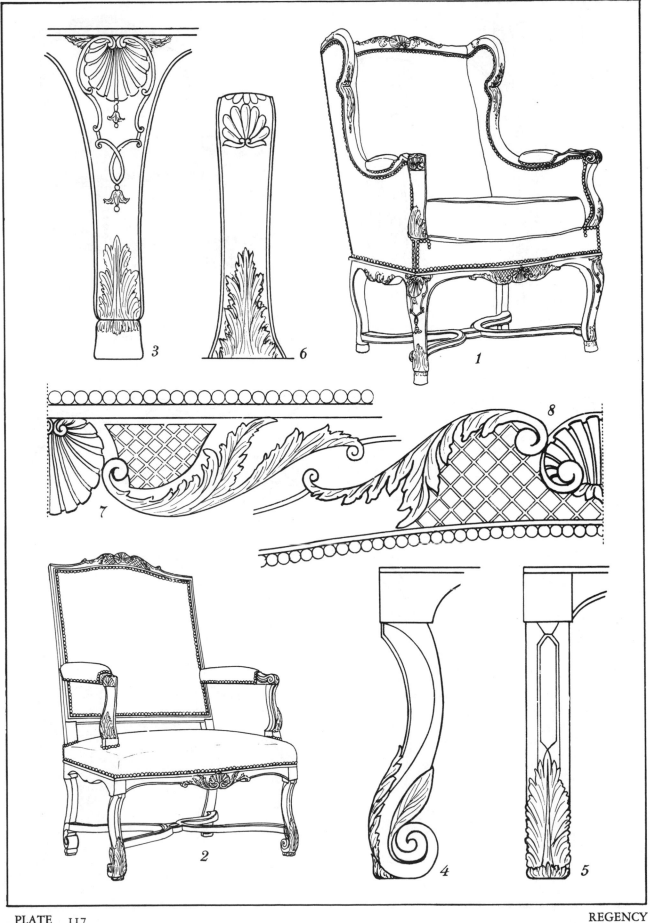

PLATE 117

1. "Country" armchair.   2. Armchair.   3, 4 and 5. Legs.   6. Arm support.   7 and 8. Detail of seat and crest of back.

*Museum of Decorative Arts, Paris*

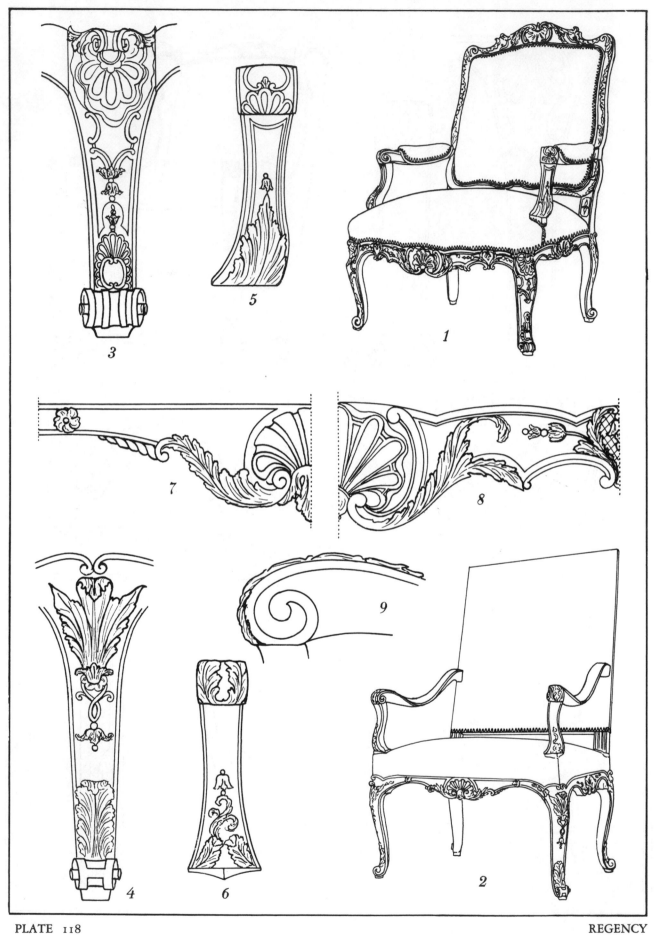

PLATE 118                                                                REGENCY

1 and 2. Armchairs, covered with silk tapestry.    3 and 4. Legs.    5 and 6. Arm supports.    7 and 8. Details of the seat.    9. Front of the arm.

*Museum of Decorative Arts, Paris*

PLATE 119                                                                    REGENCY

1, 2 and 3. Armchairs, covered with tapestry and velvet with different kinds of backs.   4. Side chair.   5, 6, 7 and 8. Legs.   9, 10 and 11. Fronts of the seats.   12. Corner of the back.

*Metropolitan Museum, New York and private collections*

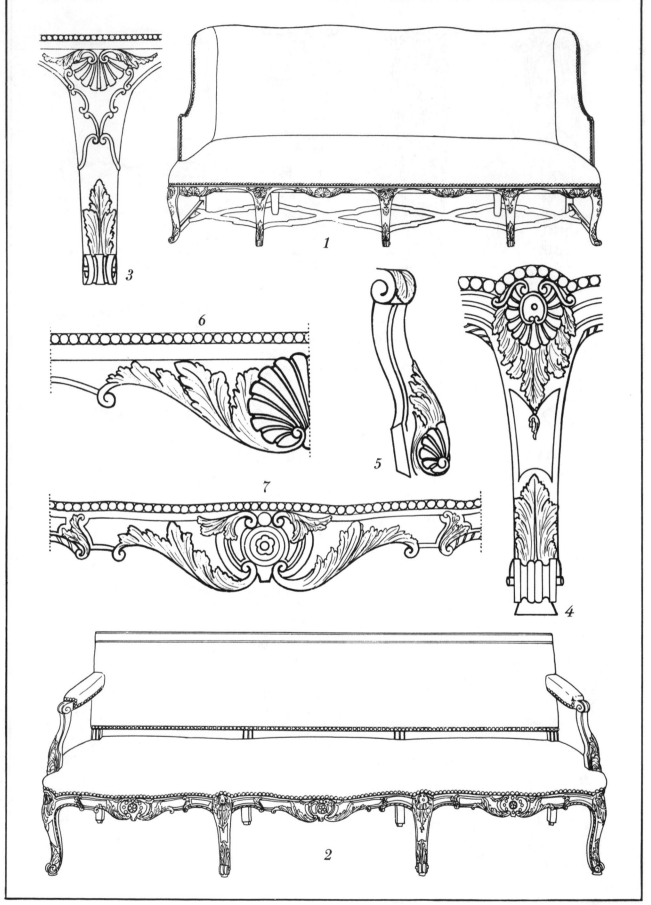

**PLATE** 120  REGENCY

1 and 2. Sofas, covered with petit point tapestry.   3 and 4. Legs.   5. Arm support.   6 and 7. Details of the decorations on the fronts of the seats.

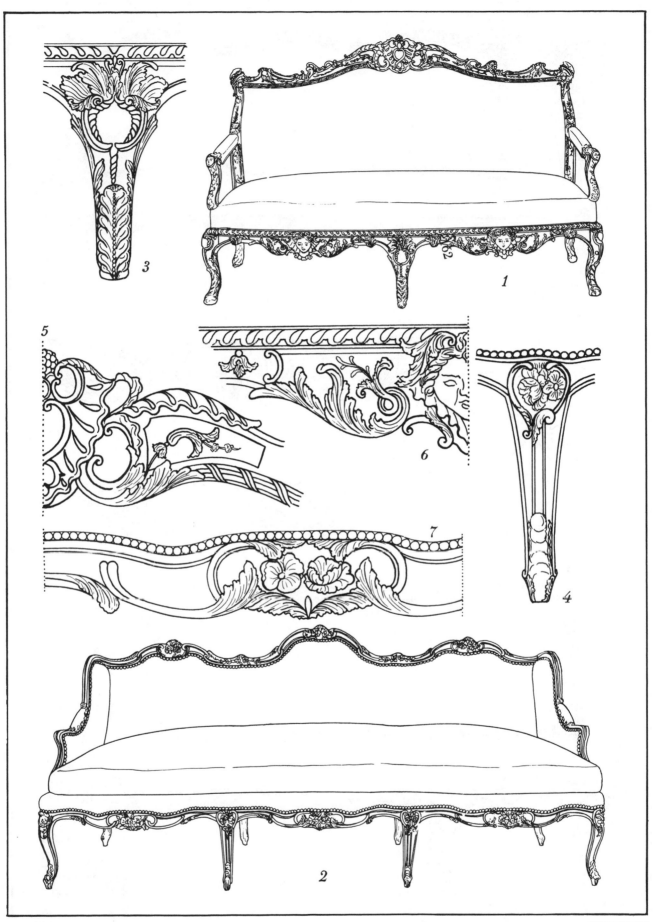

PLATE 121

REGENCY

1 and 2. Sofas, covered with velvet.   3 and 4. Legs.   5. Crest of back.   6 and 7. Detail of the front of the seat.

*Collections of G. Le Breton and Jacques Doucet, Paris*

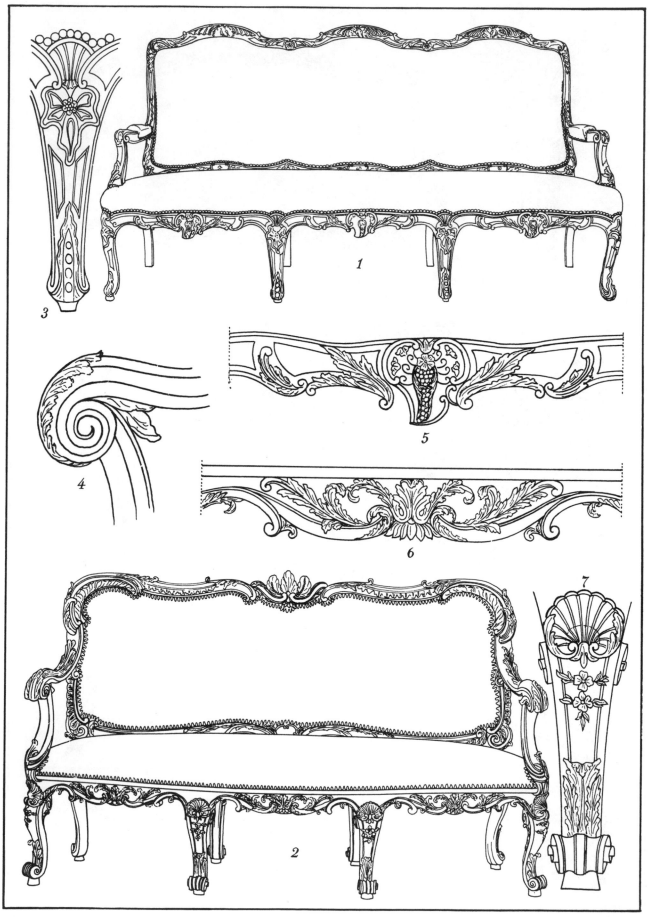

PLATE 122

REGENCY

1 and 2. Sofas, covered with tapestry and damask. 3 and 4. Legs and scrolls at end of arm. 5 and 6. Details of fronts of seats. 7. Leg.

*Collections of Charles and Rodolphe Kann, Paris*

PLATE 123                                                          REGENCY

1. Chaise longue of sculpted wood.  2. Cane chaise longue.  3, 4 and 5. Detail of the decorations.  6 and 7.
Legs.

*Collections of G. Hoentschel and Jacques Doucet, Paris*

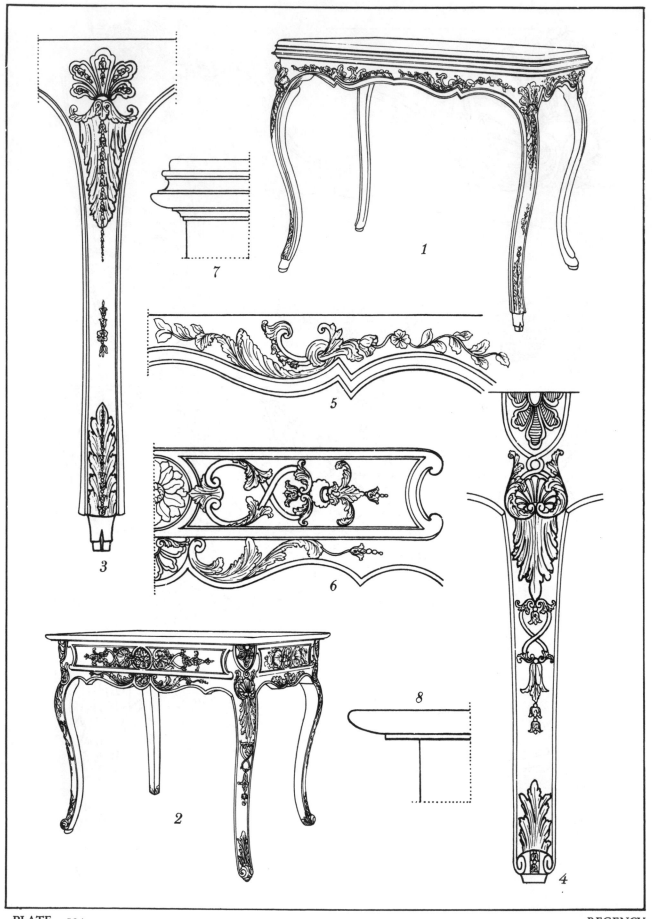

PLATE 124

1 and 2. Tables of carved wood.   3 and 4. Legs.   5 and 6. Details of the front.   7 and 8. Mouldings.

*Museum of Decorative Arts, Paris*

PLATE 125

1. Table of carved wood with mosaic top.    2. Table of carved wood.    3 and 4. Legs.    5 and 6. Mouldings.    7 and 8. Detail of the front.

*Cinquantenaire, Brussels and private collection*

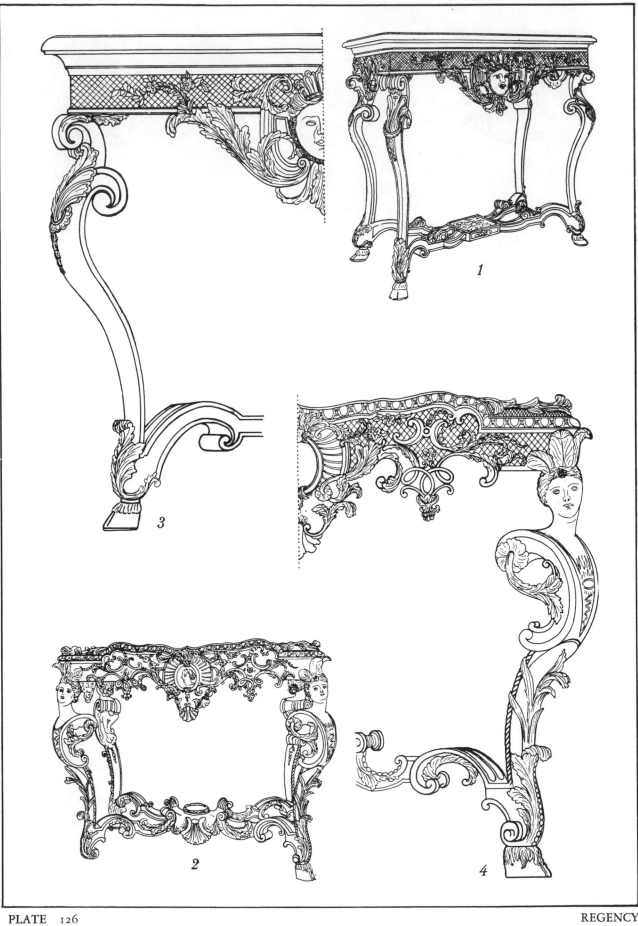

PLATE 126       REGENCY

1. Small gilt wooden table.    2. Gilt wooden console table.    3 and 4. Detail of first and second tables.

*Lowengard collection, Paris*

PLATE 127

REGENCY

1, 2, 3 and 4. Four wooden console tables.   5, 6, 7 and 8. Details of fronts of tables.   9, 10, 11 and 12.
Profiles of the marble mouldings.

*1, 2 and 3 from Aigremont Castle; 4 from Jacques Doucet collection, Paris*

PLATE 128                                                                                                      REGENCY

1 and 2. Large gilt wooden tables.    3 and 4. Legs.    5 and 6. Detail of table front.    7 and 8. Mouldings.

*Lelong and Rodolphe Kann collections, Paris*

PLATE 129

1, 2 and 3. Gilt wooden console tables.   4, 5 and 6. Fronts of tables.   7, 8 and 9. Profiles of marble mouldings.   10. Leg.

*1 and 2, Metropolitan Museum; 3 from Jacques Doucet collection, Paris*

PLATE 130

1. Smooth writing table with metal marquetry.   2. Carved wooden table with bronze decorations.   3. Table with metal marquetry.   4. Commode with four drawers (partial view).   5. Writing table of Prince Max-Emmanuel (partial view).   6 and 7. Legs.   8. Detail of escutcheon plate and drawer pull on Table 5.   *1. Victoria and Albert Museum, London;*

134   *2. Elysée Palace, Paris; 3. Private collection; 4. Wallace collection, London; 5. National Museum, Munich*

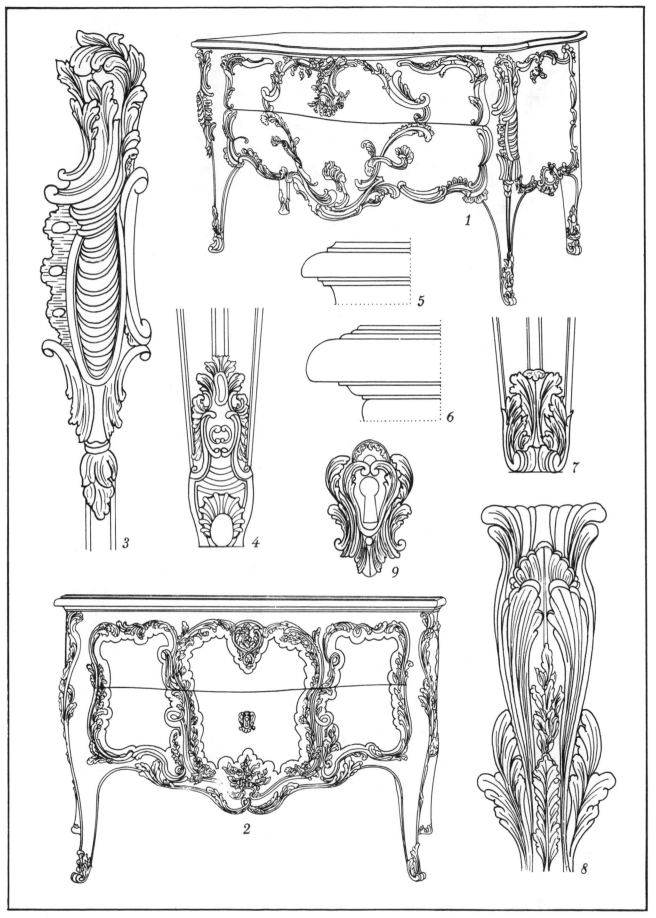

PLATE 131                                                        REGENCY (end of first half of 17th century)

1. Commode with long legs, contoured apron and two drawers, of gilt lacquer on a black background with Chinese motifs, blond lace in form of drawer pull and carved gilt bronzes.   2. Commode with long arched legs, contoured apron and two drawers.   3 and 4. Bronzes on the uprights.   5 and 6. Profile of the marble tops.   7 and 8. Bronzes on the uprights of the second commode.   9. Escutcheon plate.

*Poles and Dutasta collections*

PLATE 132                                                                                                    REGENCY

1. Big-bellied "tomb-shaped" commode made of Brazilian rosewood, with short legs and three drawers. "Pebble" motifs, heads known as "espagnolettes," other carved gilt bronzes and inlaid marble top.    2. Detail of an upright with an "espagnolette."    3. Leg.    4. Drawer pull and escutcheon plate.    5. Escutcheon plate.    6. Bottom decoration.

PLATE 133 REGENCY

1. Short-legged commode, with ten drawers and panels of old Japanese lacquer in the form of mountainous landscapes in gilt relief on a black background, framed with thin copper rods, with bronzes and marble at the top.   2. Profile of the marble top.   3. Leg.   4. Lower middle design.   5. Design at top of upright.   6 and 7. Escutcheon plate and drawer pull.

*Ganay collection, Paris*

**PLATE 134**  REGENCY (end of first half of 17th century)

1. Big-bellied "tomb-shaped" commode with short legs and three drawers, with marquetry of violet, satined Brazilian rosewood. "Pebble" motifs, gilt, carved bronzes and a marble top.  2. Detail of the upright.  3. Lower middle motif.  4. "Pebble" design.  5. Escutcheon plate and drawer pull.

PLATE 135

REGENCY

1. Console table with metal marquetry.    2. Detail of the leg.    3. Decoration and handle.    4. Bronze design.

*Grand Trianon, Versailles*

139

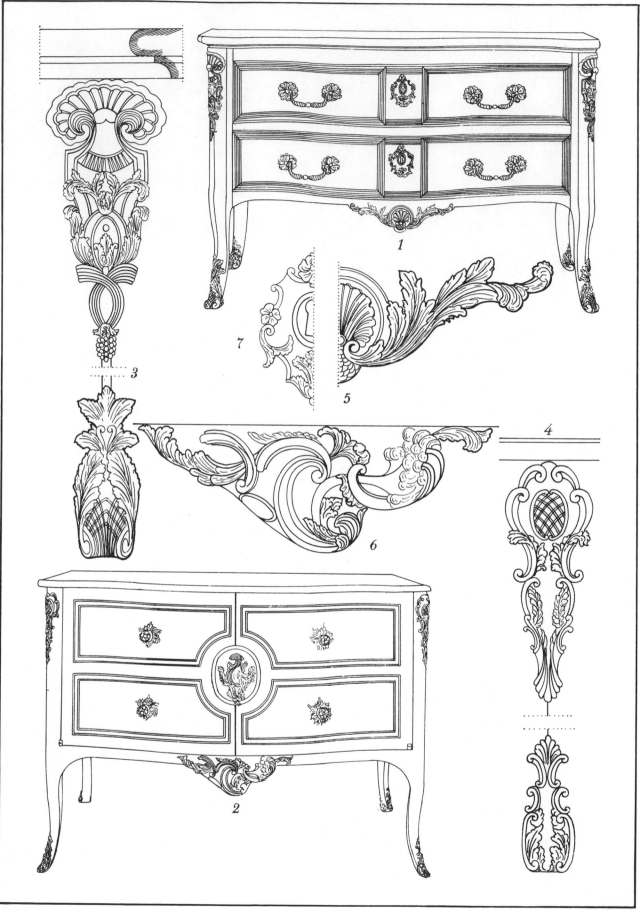

PLATE 136

REGENCY

1. Commode, with two drawers and long curved legs, with marquetry.　2. Commode, with front made of two pieces of wood and long curved legs of wood veneer. Both commodes have carved gilt bronzes and marble tops.　3 and 4. Details of the bronzes on uprights and legs.　5 and 6. Lower middle motifs.　7. Escutcheon plate.

*Darthy collection, Paris*

**PLATE** 137

1. Wood-veneer commode with short legs, three drawers, carved gilt bronzes and marble top.   2 and 3. Detail of the bronzes on uprights and legs.   4 and 5. Bronzes in panel corners and lower middle decoration.   6. Drawer pull and escutcheon pull.

*Parent collection, Paris*

PLATE 138

1. Commode with four drawers.   2. Profile of upper moulding.   3. Corner of drawers.   4 and 5. Escutcheon plate and drawer pull.   6. Leg.   7. Central lower detail.

*Ansbach Castle collection*

**PLATE 139**

REGENCY

1 and 2. Commodes with marquetry.  3 and 4. Detail of uprights and corner decorations.  5. Leg.  6. Drawer pull and escutcheon plate.  7. Drawer pull.

*F. Leuy and Kraemer collections, Paris*

PLATE 140

REGENCY

1. Sideboard with two doors.   2. Detail of upright.   3. Detail of central lower bronze.   4. Escutcheon plate.   5. Sketch of the frieze.   6. Corner of door panel.   7. Middle detail.   8. Marble moulding.

*Versailles Palace*

**PLATE 141**

1 and 2. Carved wooden sideboards.   3 and 4. Detail of fronts.   5 and 6. Details of upper mouldings.

*Cinquantenaire, Brussels and Choquières Museum, Lieja*

REGENCY

1

2

3

4

5

PLATE 142
REGENCY

1. Carved wooden chest-on-chest.   2, 3 and 4. Details of upper chest.   5. Details of lower chest.

*Bernheimer collection, Munich*

PLATE 143

REGENCY (influence of Netherlands, 17th century)

1. Chest-on-chest; upper chest has two doors and lower one has three. Numerous scenes in marquetry of a variety of colored woods; crowned with turned gable.  2 and 3. Details of uprights.  4. Crest of gable.  5. Escutcheon plate.  6. Hinge.

*Private collection*

PLATE 144

1. Carved wooden wardrobe.    2 and 3. Details of door.

REGENCY

*Victoria and Albert Museum, London*

PLATE 145                                                                REGENCY

1. Carved wooden wardrobe.    2. Detail of upper middle section.    3, 4 and 5. Details of the doors and uprights.

*Cinquantenaire, Brussels*

PLATE 146                                                      REGENCY
1. Carved wooden chest-on-chest.    2 and 3. Details of same.

*Museum of Decorative Arts, Paris*

PLATE 147

REGENCY

1. Carved wooden wardrobe.    2. Detail of doors and upright.    3. Detail of gable.

*Victoria and Albert Museum, London*

**PLATE 148**

1. Large wardrobe of satined rosewood, gilt carved bronzes, attributed to Charles Cressent.   2. Profile of the upright.   3. Detail of bronze decoration.

*Poles collection*

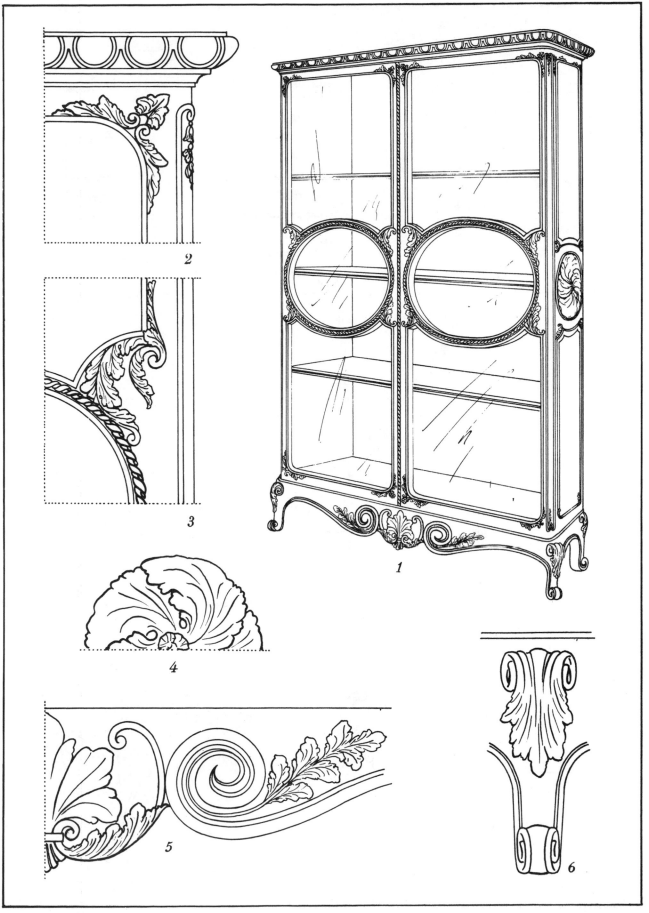

PLATE 149

REGENCY

1. Wooden showcase carved in two pieces.    2 and 3. Details of doors and uprights.    4 and 5. Side and lower crosspiece
motifs.    6. Leg.

*Private collection*

PLATE 150

REGENCY (18th century)

1. Wood-veneer secretary.    2. Details of upright.    3 and 4. Drawer pull and escutcheon plate.

*Private collection*

PLATE 151                                                          REGENCY

1. Carved wooden chest-on-chest.   2 and 3. Escutcheon plates.   4 and 5. Details of upper chest.   6 and 7. Details of lower chest.

*Cinquantenaire, Brussels*

PLATE 152

REGENCY

1. Oak clock.   2. Details of the crest and mouldings.   3. Detail of socle and mouldings.   4. Sketch of hands.

*Cinquantenaire, Brussels*

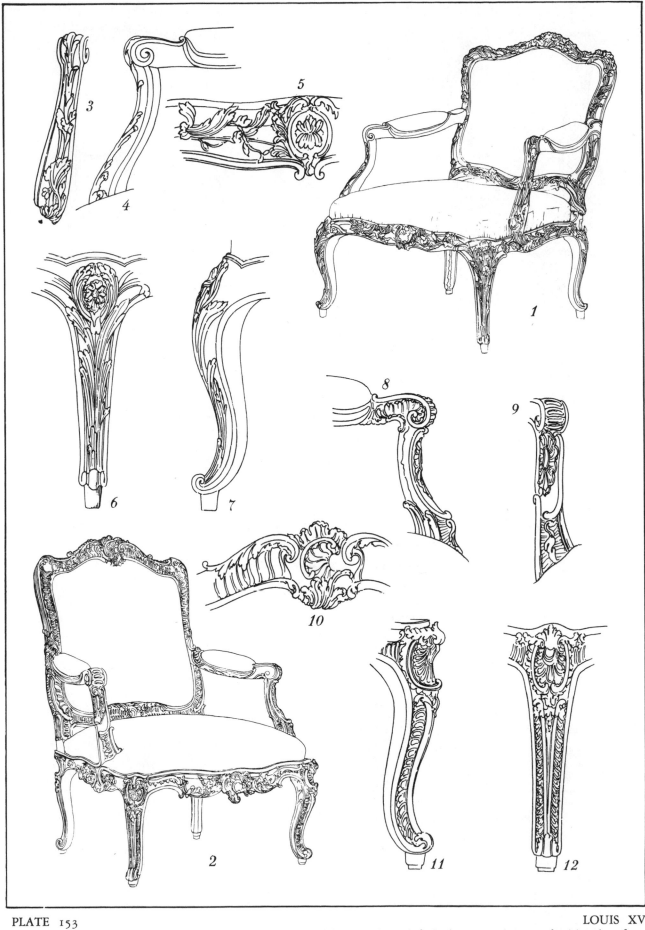

PLATE 153

1 and 2. Carved wooden armchairs. The upper one is painted with colors, and the lower one is covered with velvet from Genoa.   3, 4, 5, 6 and 7. Details of the first chair.   8, 9, 10, 11 and 12. Details of the second chair.

*Louvre*

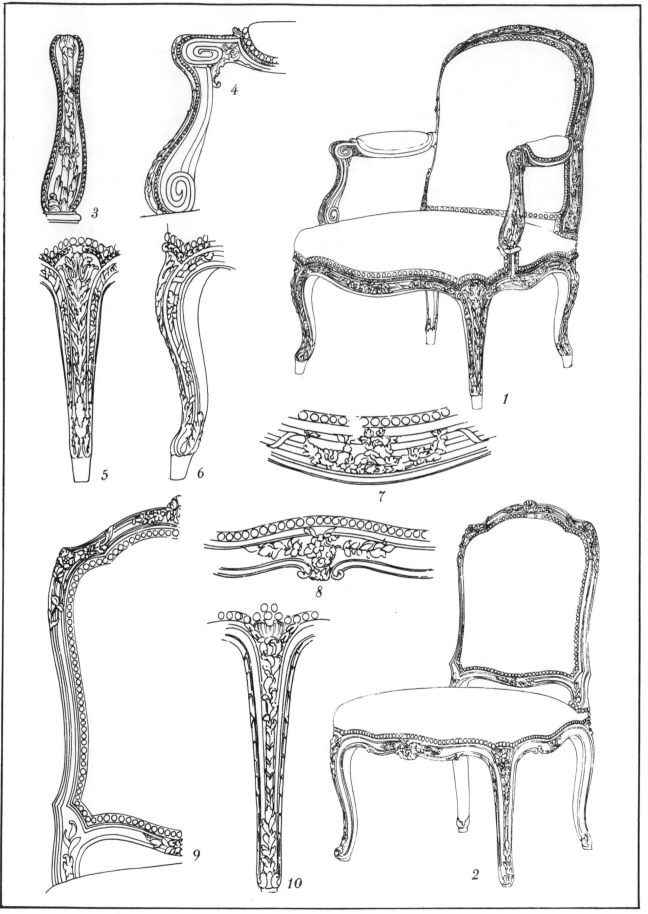

**PLATE 154**                                                                    LOUIS XV

1 and 2. Armchair and chair of gilt carved wood, upholstered with tapestries.   3, 4, 5 and 6. Details of arm supports
and legs.   7 and 8. Details of moulding.   9. Chair back.   10. Leg.

*Louvre*

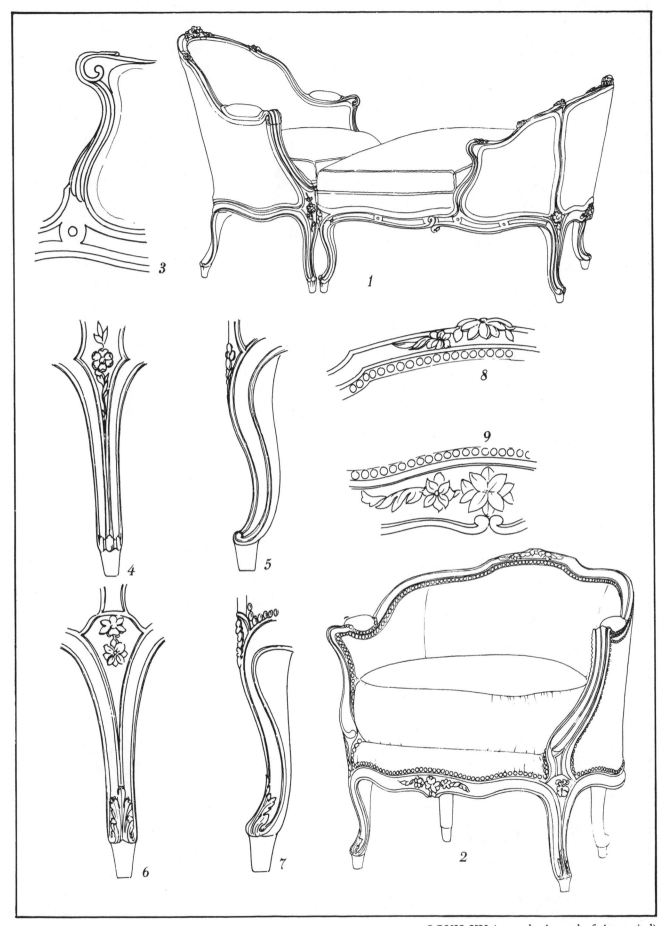

PLATE 155                                    LOUIS XV (towards the end of the period)
1. Gilt carved wooden chaise longue.   2. "Marchioness" armchair of painted and gilt carved wood.   3, 4 and 5. Details
of the arm, back and legs of the chaise longue.   6, 7, 8 and 9. Details of the legs and back of the armchair.

*Louvre*

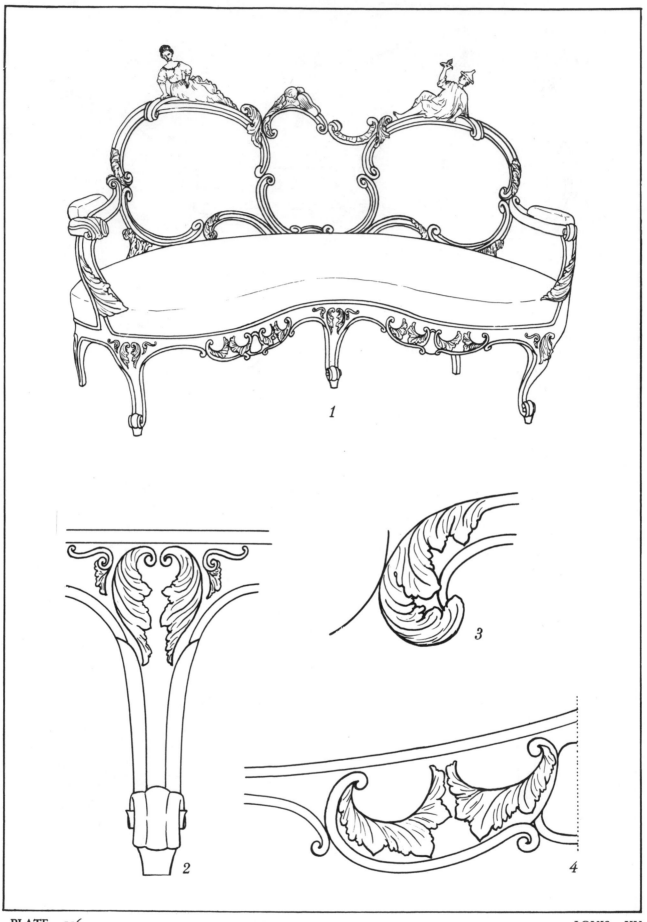

1

2

3

4

**PLATE** 156

LOUIS XV

1. Sofa, showing influence of Far East.    2. Detail of leg.    3 and 4. Decorations.

*Chantilly Castle*

PLATE 157            LOUIS XV (towards end of period)

1. Daybed, also known as a bedroom sofa.    2. Uprights.    3. Leg.    4. Details of middle crest of back.

*Private collection*

PLATE 158                                                           LOUIS XV (end of period)

1 and 2. Small sewing tables. Upper one has removable box.  3 and 4. Uprights.  5 and 6. Escutcheon plates.  7.
Section of upright.  8. Leg.

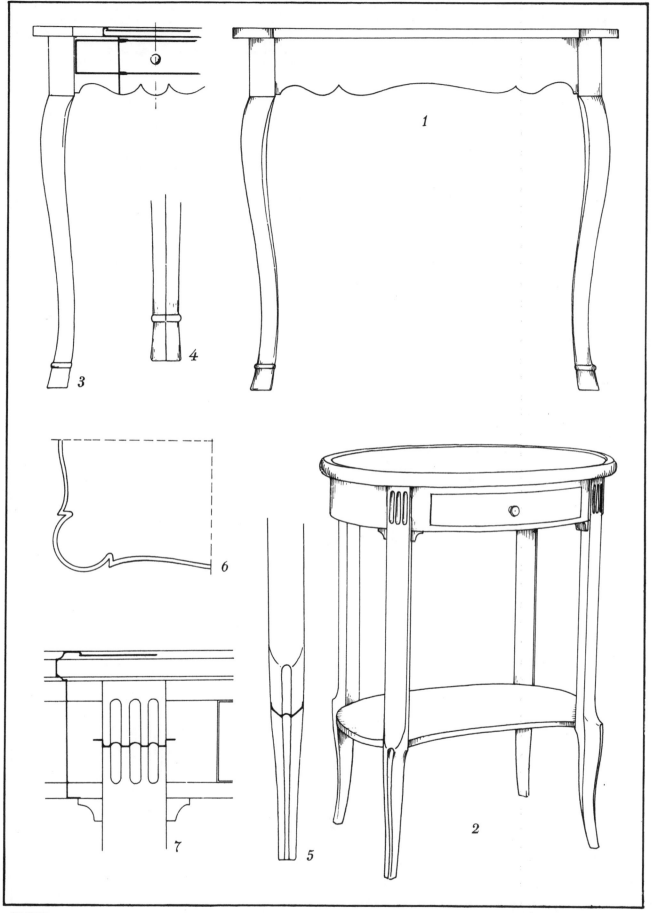

PLATE 159                              LOUIS XV (beginning of Louis XVI. Simple treatment.)
1. Small table.   2. Small oval table.   3, 4 and 5. Details of leg.   6. Silhouette of tabletop.   7. Detail of upright.

*Private collection*

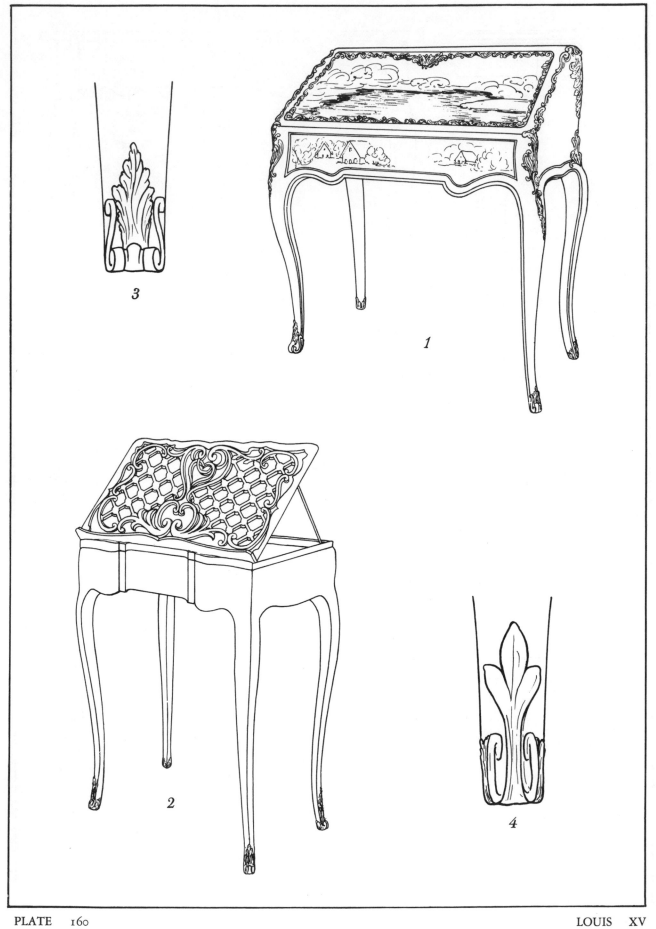

PLATE 160

1 and 2. Ladies' desks.    3 and 4. Legs.

*Private collection*

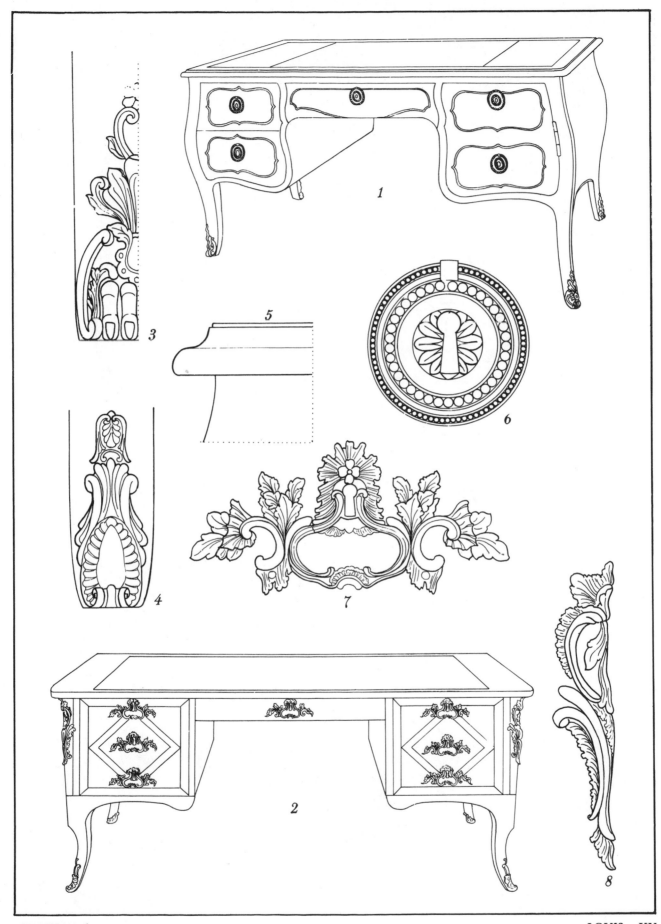

PLATE 161

LOUIS XV

1 and 2. Large writing tables.   3 and 4. Legs.   5. Profile of top.   6. Detail of escutcheon plate.   7. Drawer pull.   8. Corner decoration.

*Mobilier National de France*

PLATE 162

LOUIS XV

1 and 2. Writing tables.    3 and 4. Legs.    5 and 6. Drawer pulls.    7. Moulding.

PLATE 163

LOUIS XV

1 and 2. Writing tables. 3 and 4. Escutcheon plates on first writing table. 5. Details of upright. 6. Leg. 7. Upper moulding. 8. Escutcheon plate.

*Private collection and Dutasta collection, Paris*

PLATE 164          LOUIS XV
1. Writing table with three drawers.    2. Tulipwood writing table.    3. Panel moulding.    4. Escutcheon plate.   5 and 6. Profiles.

*Private collections*

PLATE 165                                                                           LOUIS XV

1 and 2. Desk with paper case and writing table.   3 and 4. Drawer pulls.   5. Detail of desk.   6. Leg of writing table.

*Private collection and Nogent Abbey, Aisne*

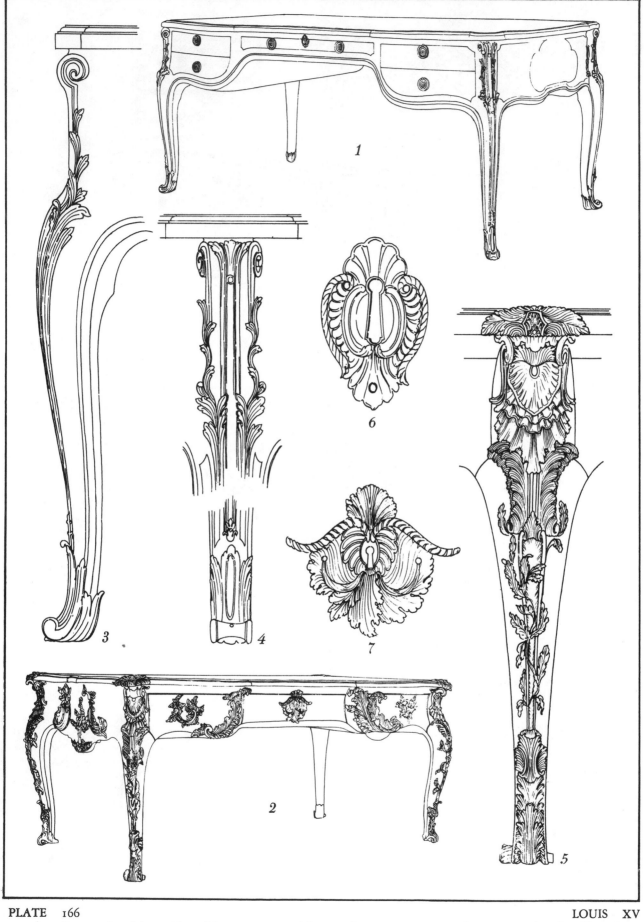

**PLATE** 166

*LOUIS XV*

1 and 2. Rosewood writing tables with marquetry and bronze decorations.  3, 4 and 5. Legs.  6 and 7. Escutcheon plates.

*Louvre*

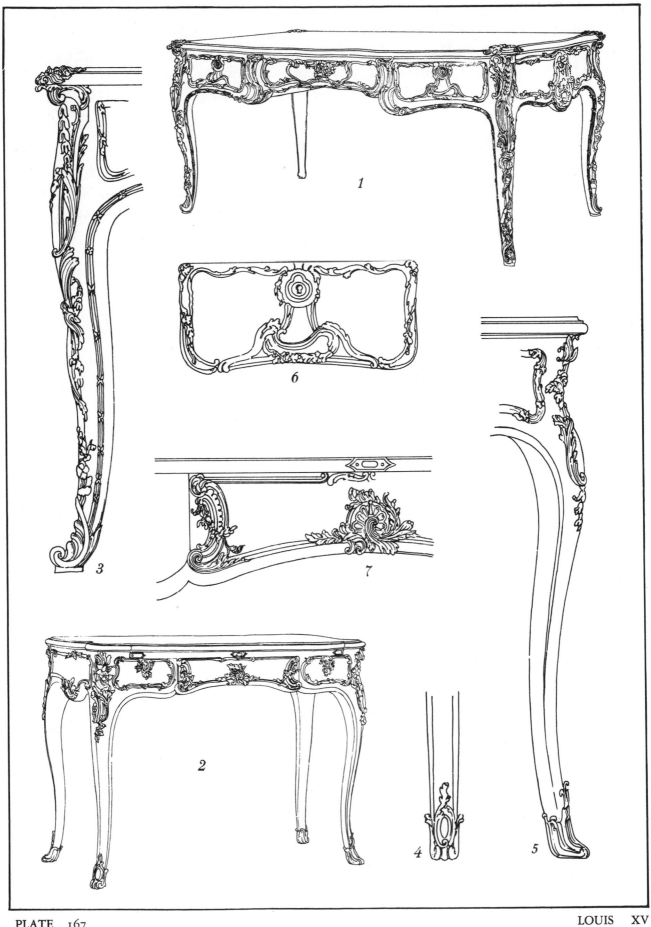

PLATE 167

LOUIS XV

1. Chinese black lacquer desk with gilt bronze. 2. Lady's desk with marquetry and gilt bronze. 3, 4 and 5. Detail of the legs. 6 and 7. Details of drawer fronts.

*Louvre*

171

**PLATE 168**

1 Desk of King Louis XV. Marquetry by J. F. Oeben and J. H. Riesener. Bronzes by Duplessis, Winant and Hervieux (1760–1769).   2, 3, 4 and 5. Details of legs, upright and drawer fronts.

*Louvre*

**PLATE 169**

LOUIS XV

1. Low commode with a "tomb-shaped" desk on top, with marquetry in a "pebble" frame.    2. Low wood-veneer wardrobe with two doors and a drawer on top.    3 and 4. Bronzes on the uprights and legs.    5 and 6. Lower middle appliqué and escutcheon plate.

*Private collection*

PLATE 170

LOUIS XV

1. Louis XV style commode by Ceffieri.  2. Commode in the grand Regency period by Charles Cressent.  3 and 4. Details of the legs.

*South-Kensington Museum, London and Richard Wallace collection, London*

**PLATE 171**

1 and 2. Commodes with marquetry decorated with gilt bronzes. The second commode by Charles Cressent.     3 and 4.
Legs.   5 and 6. Detail of drawer fronts.

*Louvre*

PLATE 172                                                     LOUIS XV

1. Commode with two drawers and marquetry with flower design, forming panels framed by bronzes.   2. Commode
with two drawers with antique lacquers by Coromandel. Both commodes have bronzes.   3 and 4. Details of the legs.   5
and 6. Bronze appliqués on the apron.   7 and 8. Details of drawer pull and escutcheon plate.

*Gentien collection and private collection*

PLATE 173                                                          LOUIS XV

1. Wood-veneer commode with two drawers and bordered by decorative lines.    2. Commode with two drawers and
marquetry in flower designs.    3, 4, 5 and 6. Details of uprights and legs.    7, 8 and 9. Drawer pulls and
escutcheon plate.

*Hodgkins collection and private collection*

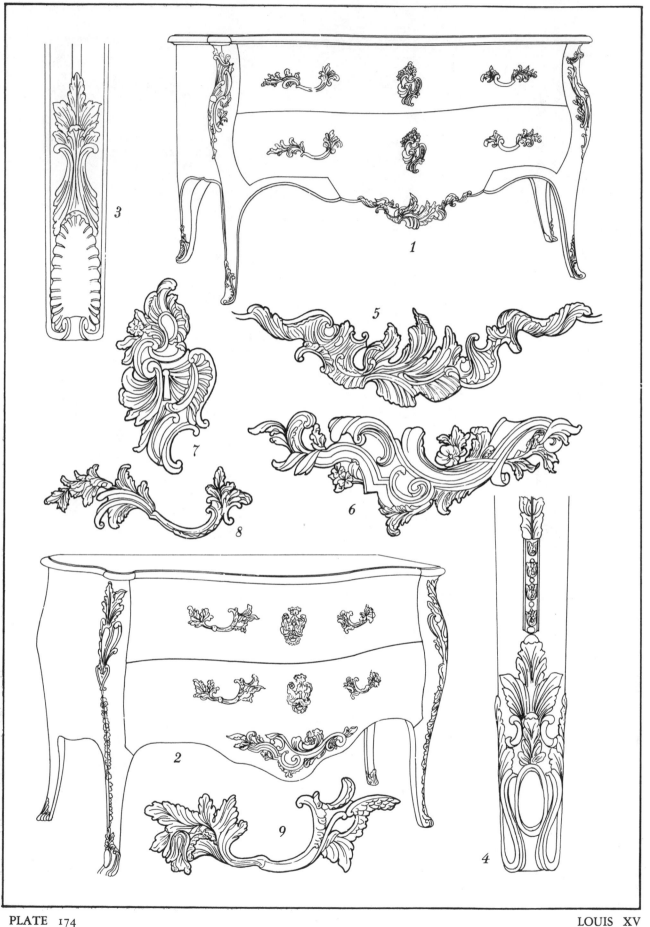

PLATE 174

LOUIS XV

1 and 2. Commodes with two drawers. The lower drawer of the first commode has a middle apron. The marquetry, in floral and leaf design, is in stark contrast. The second commode has gilt carved bronzes.   3 and 4. Details of the legs.   5 and 6. Sketches of the aprons.   7, 8 and 9. Escutcheon plate and drawer pulls.

*Private collections*

PLATE 175                                                                  LOUIS XV

1 and 2. Commodes with curved profiles, with two drawers and marquetry in floral design and gilt carved bronzes.   3.
Bronze on the upright.   4 and 5. Bronze appliqués on the apron.   6 and 7. Escutcheon plate and drawer pull.   8.
Detail of the leg.

*Private collections*

**PLATE** 176

1. "Harant" style commode with curved profile, long legs and marquetry in quadrille shape, surrounding a medallion. 2.
Commode similar in shape to the first one, with marquetry in flower designs. Both commodes have carved gilt bronzes. 3
and 4. Bronze motifs on uprights. 5. Drawer pull.

**PLATE** 177

LOUIS XV

1 and 2. Commodes with curved shape and long legs, with lacquer and carved gilt bronzes.   3, 4, 5 and 6. Details of uprights.   7 and 8. Drawer pull and escutcheon plate.

*Private collections*

PLATE 178

1. Commode with two drawers, marquetry of flowers and leaves. The lower apron is part of the lower drawer.    2. Wood-veneer commode from the mid-18th century, framed with colored decorative lines. Both commodes have carved gilt bronzes.    3. Detail of the upright.    4 and 5. Escutcheon plate.

*Private collection and Dutasta collection*

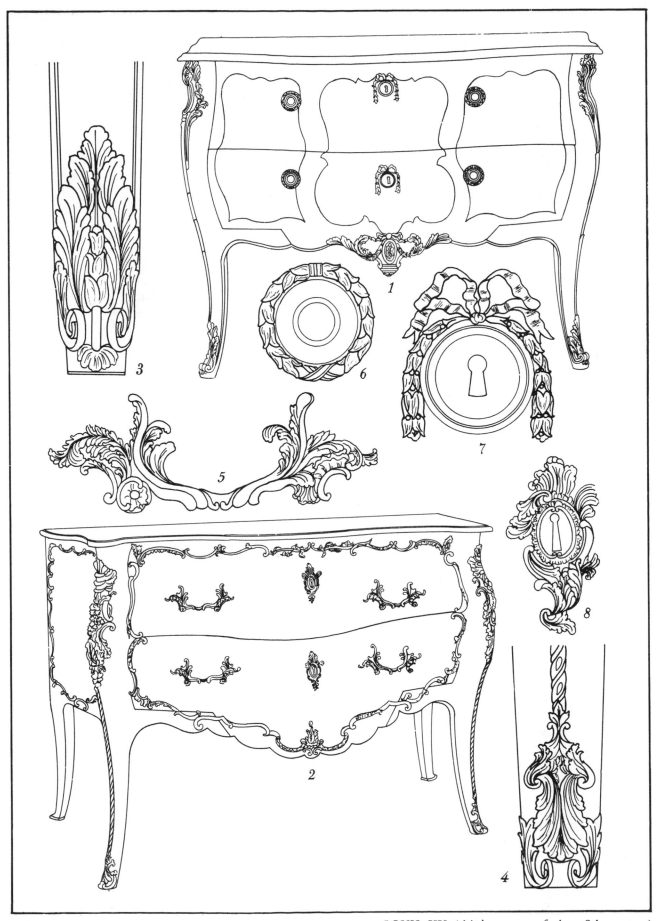

PLATE 179

LOUIS XV (third quarter of the 18th century)

1. Commode from the end of the style, with two drawers, the lower one with an apron. 2. Commode with two drawers, the lower one with an apron. Both commodes have marquetry of flowers and leaves and gilt carved bronzes. 3 and 4. Details of legs. 5, 6, 7 and 8. Escutcheon plates and drawer pull.

*Private collection and Altona-Colonna collection*

**PLATE 180**
LOUIS XV (second half of 18th century)

1. Wood-veneer commode from end of period, with console legs, four doors and three drawers at top.　2. Large commode in shape of low wardrobe, console legs, with two drawers.　3 and 4. Legs.　5 and 6. Detail of the middle bronze appliqués.　7 and 8. Escutcheon plates.

*Collection from Fleury-en-Bière Castle*

**PLATE 181**                                                        LOUIS XV (towards end of period)

1. Small commode with two drawers and marquetry in form of superimposed dados.    2. Small commode with two drawers with marquetry in the corners and frieze of intertwining lines.    3, 4 and 5. Bronzes on uprights and legs.    6 and 7. Details of the lower middle bronze appliqués.    8 and 9. Escutcheon plate and drawer pull.

*Private collections*

PLATE 182                                                 LOUIS XV (late period)

1 and 2. Small commodes with long console legs and two drawers. Upper commode has marquetry and lower one has wood-veneer central panels.   3, 4 and 5. Bronze appliqués on uprights and legs.   6, 7 and 8. Escutcheon plates and drawer pulls.

                                    *Private collection and Darthy collection*

**PLATE 183**                                              LOUIS XV (towards end of period)

1. Commode with three wood-veneer drawers.   2. Commode with two drawers and multi-colored marquetry in diamond shapes.   3 and 4. Details of bronze appliqués.   5. Detail of leg.   6. Detail of top of upright.   7, 8, 9 and 10. Drawer pulls and escutcheon plate.

*Beuret and Ganay collection*

PLATE 184                                                              LOUIS XV (towards end of period)

1. Small commode with two drawers with marquetry.   2. Wood-veneer commode with three drawers.   3, 4 and 5.
Detail of bronzes on uprights and legs.   6. Middle lower bronze.   7. Drawer pull.

**PLATE 185**

LOUIS XV (towards end of period)

1. Wood-veneer commode with three drawers.    2. Commode with two drawers, decorated with squares of marquetry.    3, 4 and 5. Bronzes on legs and upright.    6 and 7. Details of the middle appliqués.    8 and 9. Drawer pull and escutcheon plate.

Private collections

PLATE 186                                    LOUIS XV (towards end of period)

1. Small console table with trapezoidal base, with two drawers in front of two side doors.    2. Small Louis XVI style commode.    3 and 4. Bronze on the upright.    5 and 6. Drawer pull and escutcheon plate.

*Bardac collection and private collection*

PLATE 187

LOUIS XV

1. Sideboard.    2. Wardrobe with two doors and marquetry.    3. Detail of bronze on sideboard.    4 and 5. Door handle and bronze escutcheon plate on wardrobe.    6. Detail of the mouldings and leg.

*Louvre and private collection*

PLATE 188
LOUIS XV

1. Entredeux, a console placed between two windows or openings.　　2 and 3. Details of bronzes on upright and leg.　　4
and 5. Central bronze decoration and escutcheon plate.

*Private collection*

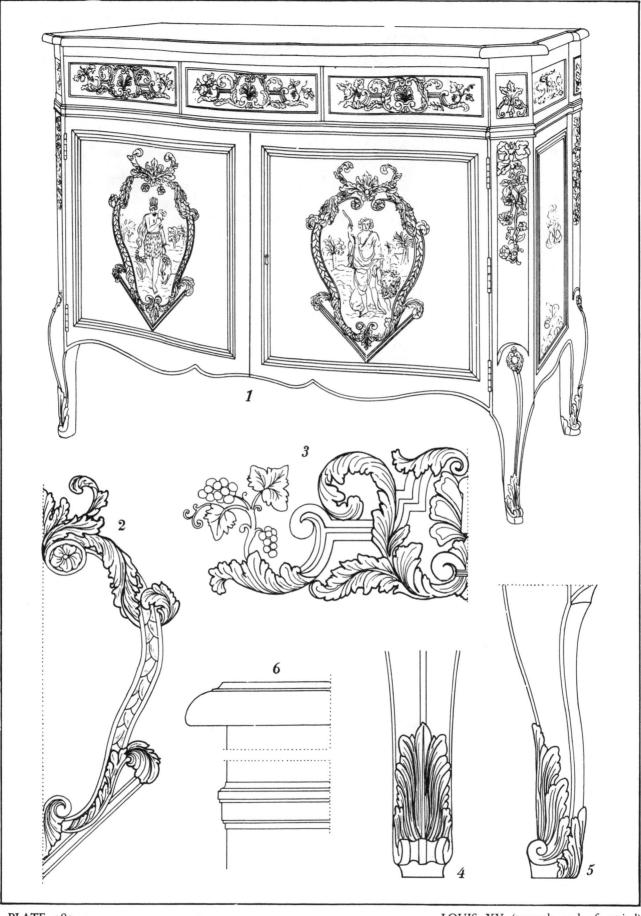

**PLATE** 189                                    LOUIS XV (towards end of period)

1. Wood-veneer entredeux with three drawers and bronze decorations   2. Detail of middle bronze.   3. Sketch of the bronze frieze.   4 and 5. Leg.   6. Mouldings.

*Poles collection*

PLATE 190

LOUIS XV (towards end of period)

1 and 2. Secretary and sideboard ("high support").  3, 4 and 5. Details of the uprights and legs.  6 and 7. Escutcheon plate and door handle.

*Louvre*

PLATE 191                                                                LOUIS XV

1. Wood-veneer wardrobe.   2. Library cabinet.   3, 4 and 5. Details of bronze from wardrobe.   6 and 7. Bronze
door handle and decoration.

*Dutasta and Poles collection, Paris*

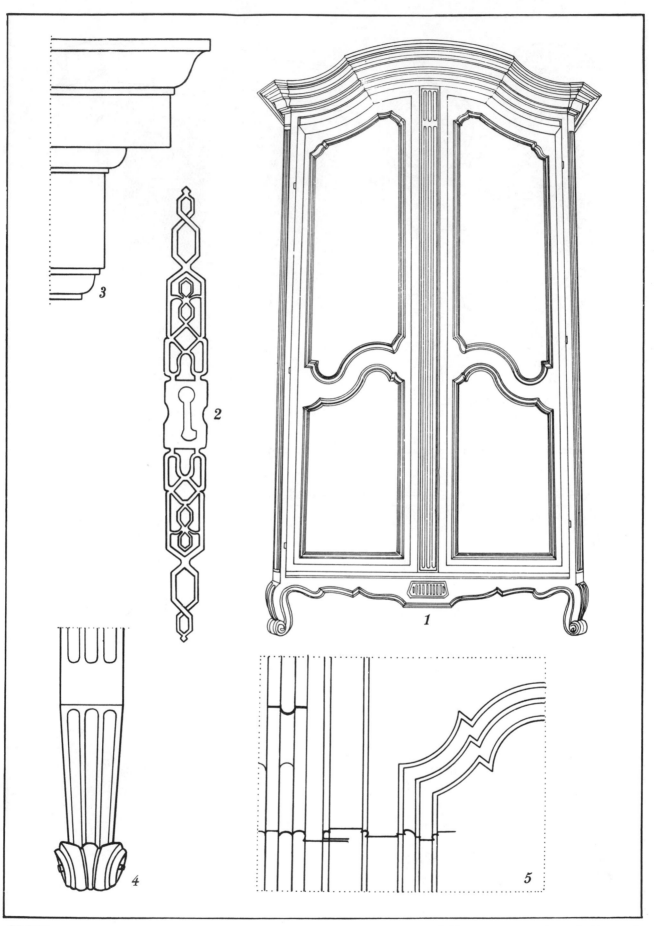

PLATE 192                                              LOUIS XV (towards end of period)

1. Large mahogany wardrobe from the southwest of France. Fluting on uprights, the sloping corners and the sharpness of cornice mouldings and in the style of Louis XVI.    2. Detail of escutcheon plate.    3. Cornice.    4. Leg.    5. Mouldings.

*Private collection*

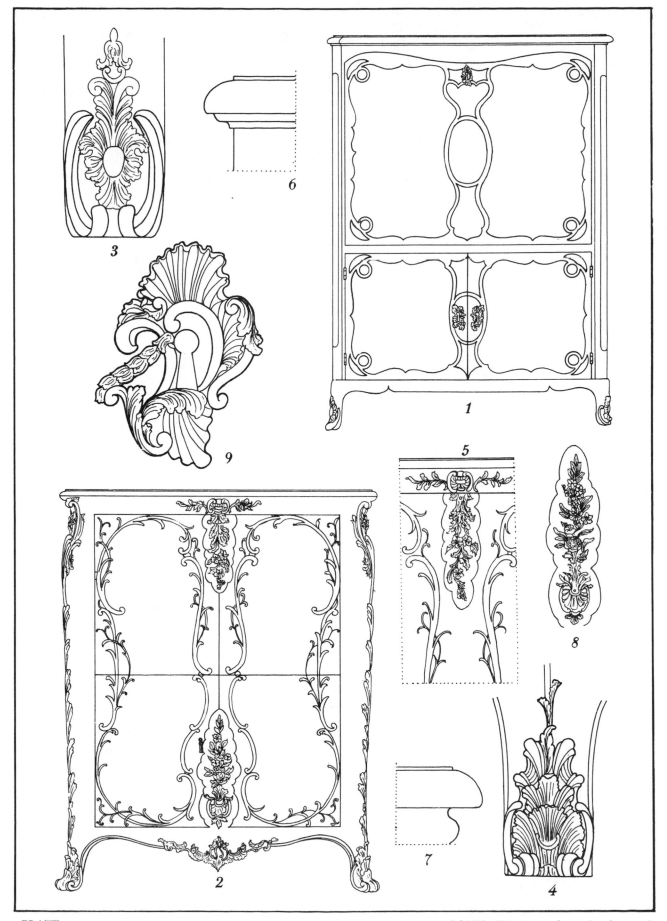

PLATE 193                                        LOUIS XV (towards end of period)

1 and 2. Secretaries: the decorative lines are of marquetry, the rest, covered with bronze.   3, 4 and 5. Details of legs and upright.   6 and 7. Profiles of tops.   8. Bronze design.   9. Escutcheon plate.

*Private collections*

PLATE 194                                    LOUIS XVI (beginning of period)
1. Walnut trough from Arles, the shape is in the style of Louis XV, and the motifs in Louis XVI.   2. Leg.   3. Turned
post.   4 and 5. Details of the work.

*Private collection*

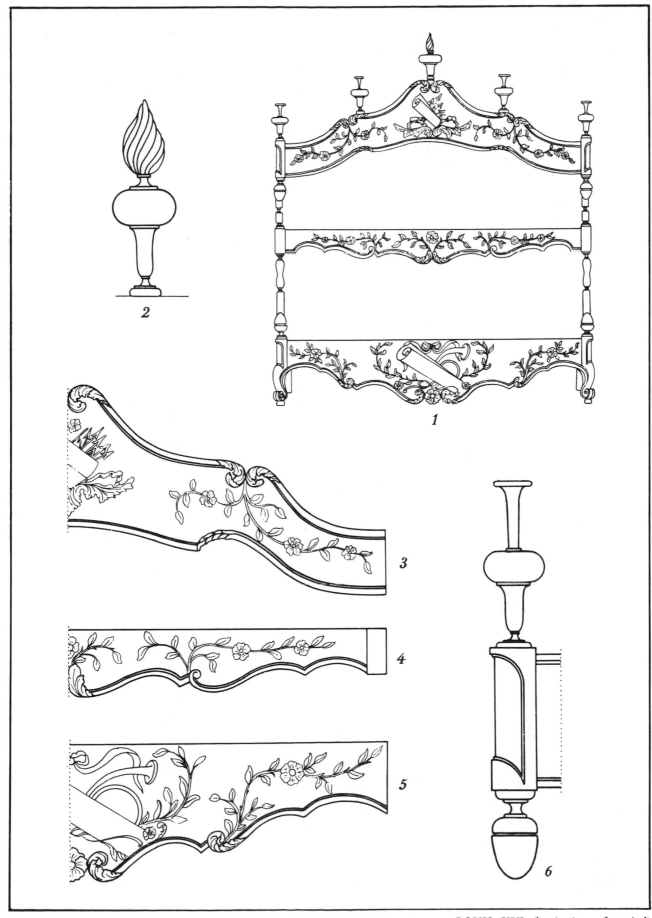

**PLATE 195** LOUIS XVI (beginning of period)

1. Walnut bookcase from Arles. Shape is Louis XV and motifs are Louis XVI. 2. Finial. 3, 4 and 5. Details of the front. 6. Turned post.

*Private collection*

199

PLATE 196

LOUIS XVI (beginning of period)

1. Walnut bookcase from Provence. Shape is Louis XV and motifs are Louis XVI.    2 and 3. Finial and turned posts.    4 and 5. Crest and front.    6. Leg.

PLATE 197

LOUIS XVI (beginning of period)

1. Small rosewood wardrobe, wood grain on bias, contoured with decorative line. Shape is Louis XVI style.   2. Another bias rosewood wardrobe with repetitive panels.   3, 4 and 5. Detail of the bronzes.   6 and 7. Escutcheon plates.

*Private collections*

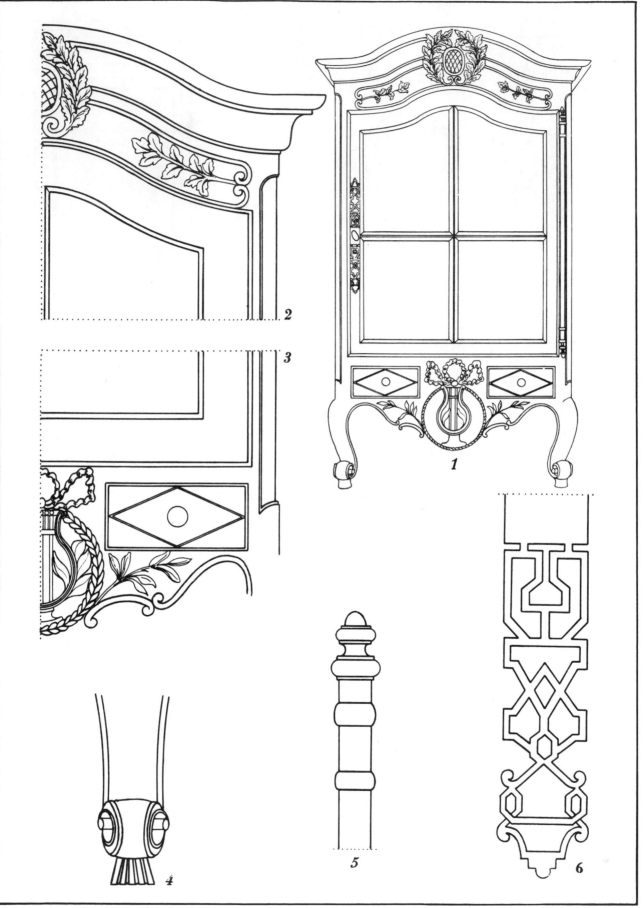

PLATE 198                                             LOUIS XVI (beginning of period)
1. Small walnut showcase from Provence. Shape is Louis XV and motifs are Louis XVI.   2 and 3. Upper and lower
details.   4. Leg.   5. Turned post of upright.   6. Escutcheon plate decoration.

*Private collection*

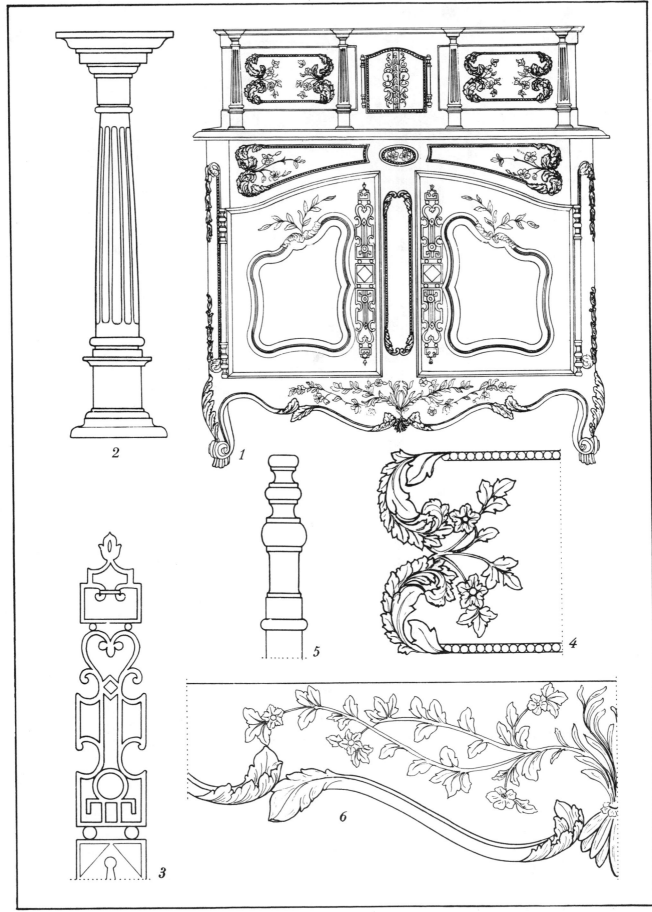

PLATE 199                                                         LOUIS XVI (beginning of period)

1. Walnut sideboard from Arles. Shape is Louis XV and motifs are Louis XVI.   2. Detail of pilaster.   3. Escutcheon plate.   4. Relief at top.   5. Turned post for the position of the hinges.   6. Detail of bottom.

*Private collection*

**PLATE** 200                                                                                        LOUIS XVI (transition from Louis XV)

1. Large semicircular wardrobe from la Gironde. The shape of the panels, the lower crosspiece and the feet are in the style
of Louis XV, the motifs are Louis XVI.    2. Escutcheon plate.    3. Cornice.    4. Detail of bottom.

*Private collection*

204

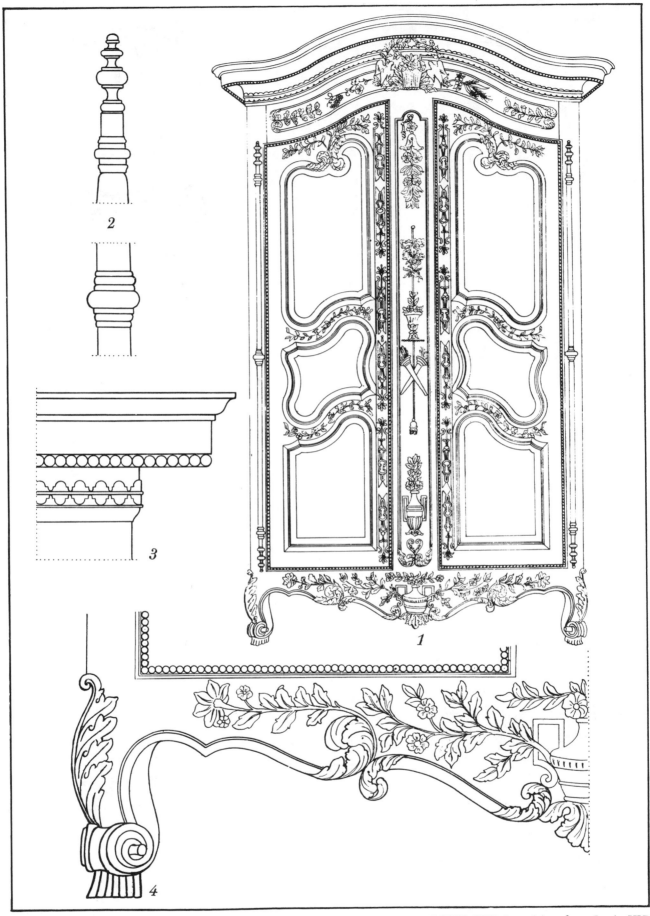

**PLATE** 201

LOUIS XVI (transition from Louis XV)

1. Walnut Provençal wardrobe. The structural lines and the lines of panels are in the style of Louis XV, the decorative motifs in that of Louis XVI. 2. Details of the upright. 3. Cornice. 4. Leg and lower detail.

*Private collection*

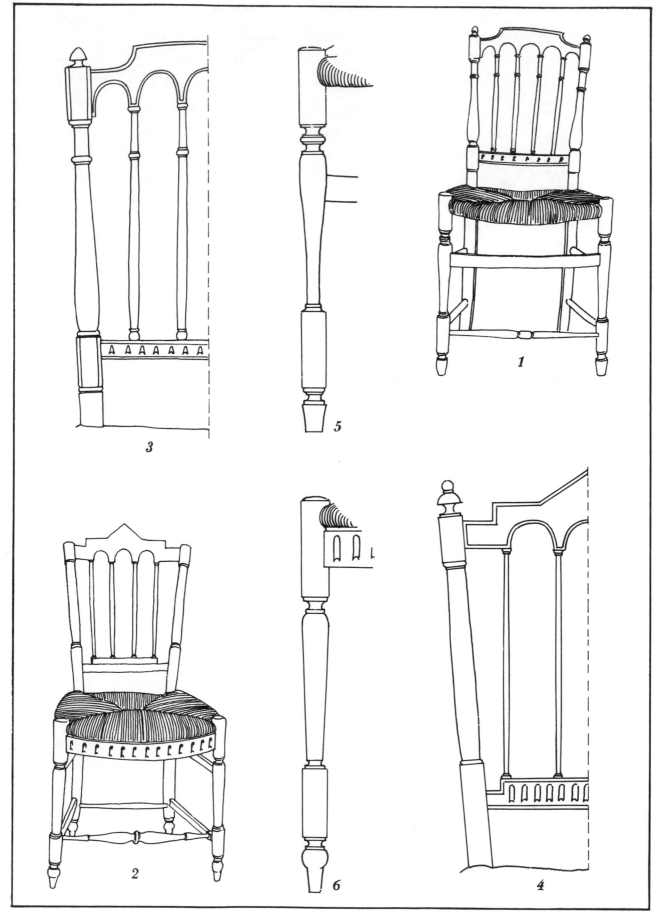

PLATE 202
1 and 2. Chairs with reed seats and backs of thin columns.    3 and 4. Backs.    5 and 6. Legs.

LOUIS XVI

*Private collection*

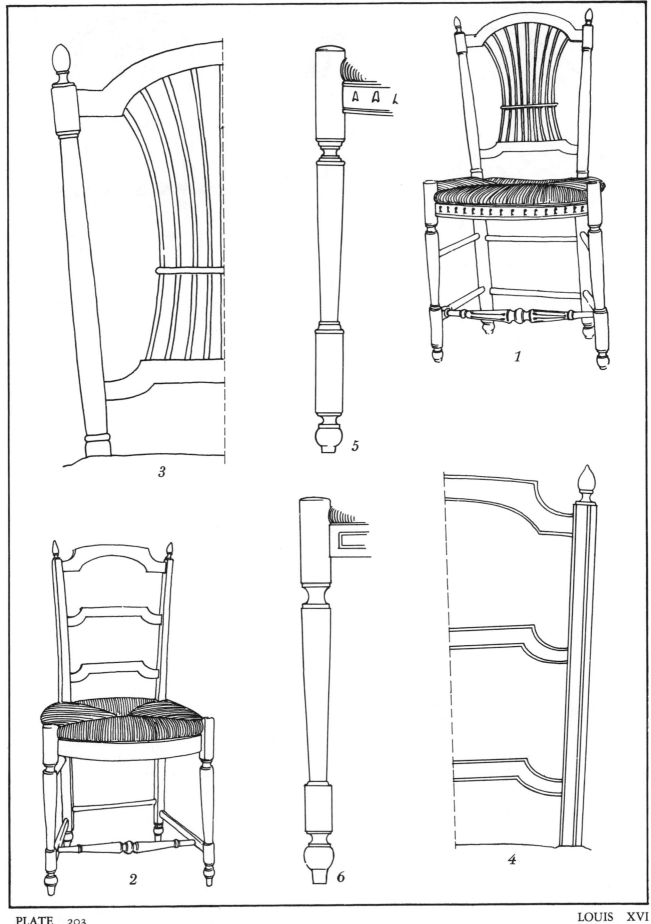

PLATE 203

LOUIS XVI

1 and 2. Chairs with reed seats and fan-shaped backs with horizontal crosspieces curved at the ends.    3 and 4. Backs.    5 and 6. Legs.

*Private collection*

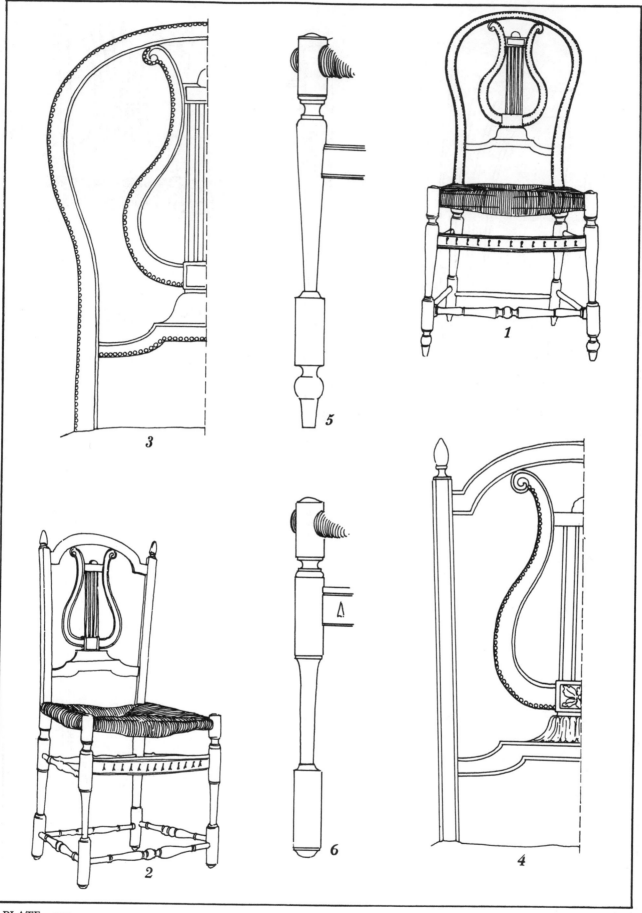

PLATE 204

LOUIS XVI

1 and 2. Chairs with reed seats and lyre motifs. The first chair has a "globe-shaped" back.   3 and 4. Backs.   5 and 6. Legs.

*Private collection*

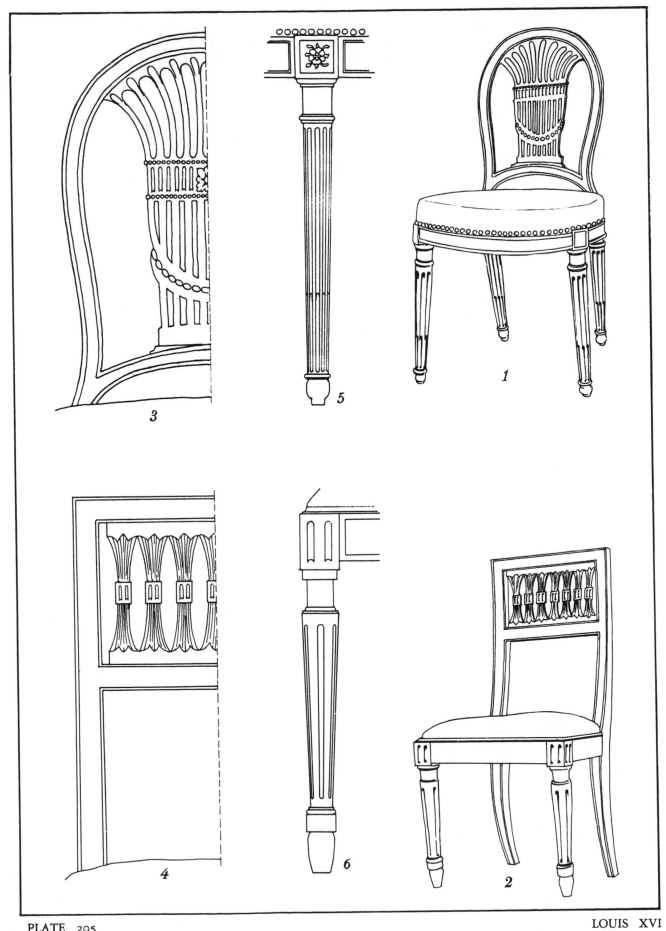

PLATE 205                                                                LOUIS XVI
1 and 2. Dining-room chairs. Back of second chair is in form of basket.   3 and 4. Backs.   5 and 6. Legs.

*Private collection*

209

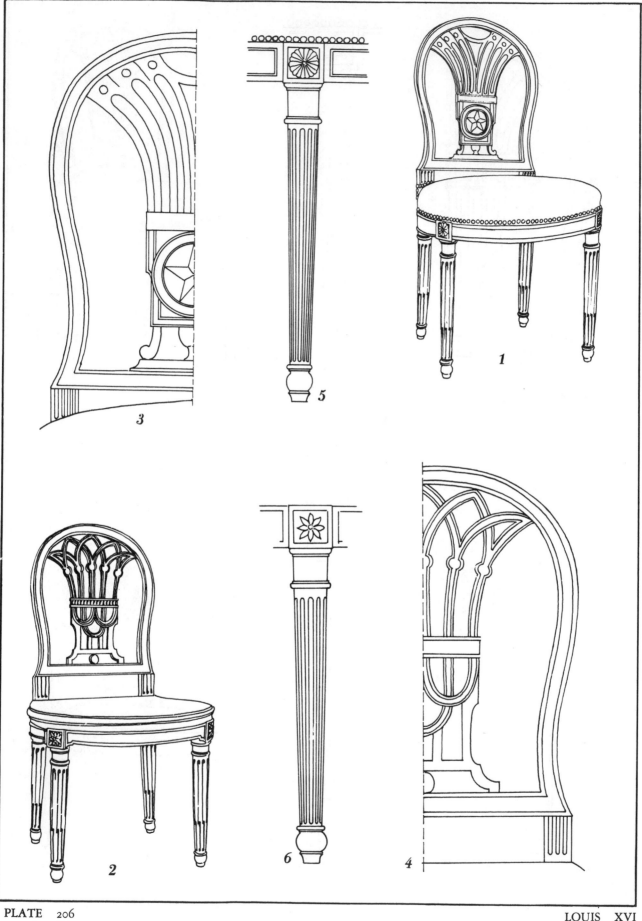

PLATE 206

LOUIS XVI

1 and 2. Dining-room chairs whose backs have central design in shape of fans or baskets.   3 and 4. Backs.   5 and 6. Legs.

*Private collection*

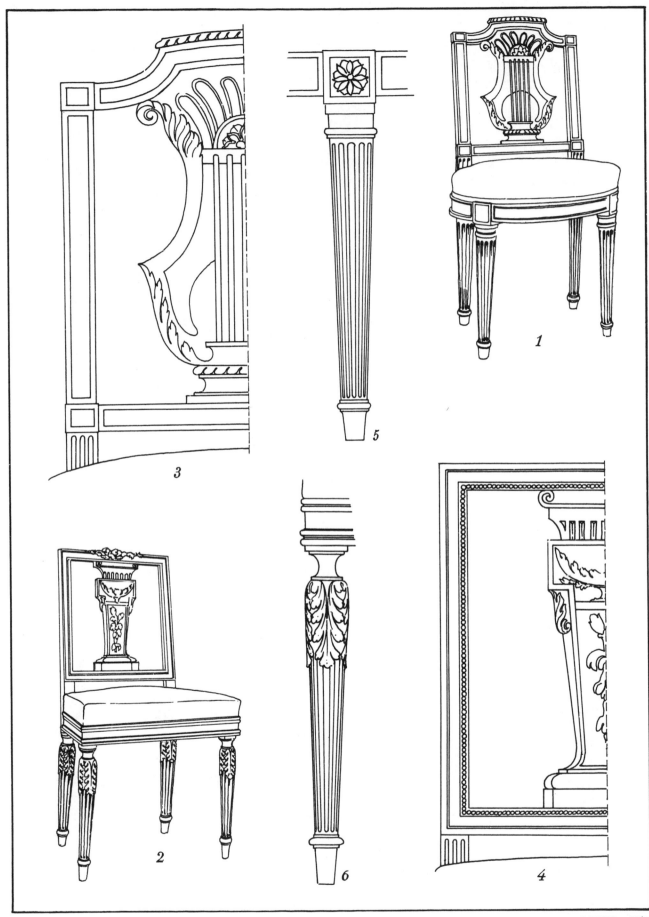

PLATE 207

1 and 2. Gilt wooden chairs with lyre- and baluster-shaped backs.    3 and 4. Detail of the backs.    5 and 6. Legs.

*Private collection*

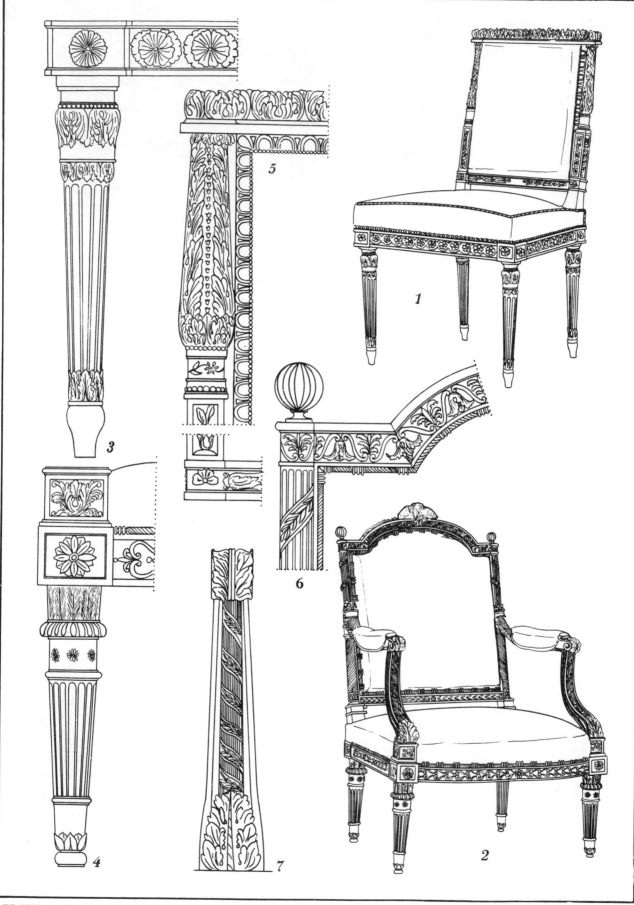

PLATE 208

1 and 2. Gilt carved wooden chair and armchair. Chair is covered with Beauvais tapestry and armchair with silk.   3 and 4. Detail of legs.   5 and 6. Details of uprights of backs.   7. Detail of arm of armchair.

*Louvre*

**PLATE** 209

LOUIS XVI

1 and 2. Carved wooden chair and armchair, both covered with silk. Chair is painted by Dupain and armchair is gilt (Haure, Sene and Vallois).   3 and 4. Detail of legs.   5 and 6. Detail of backs.   7. End of arm.

Louvre

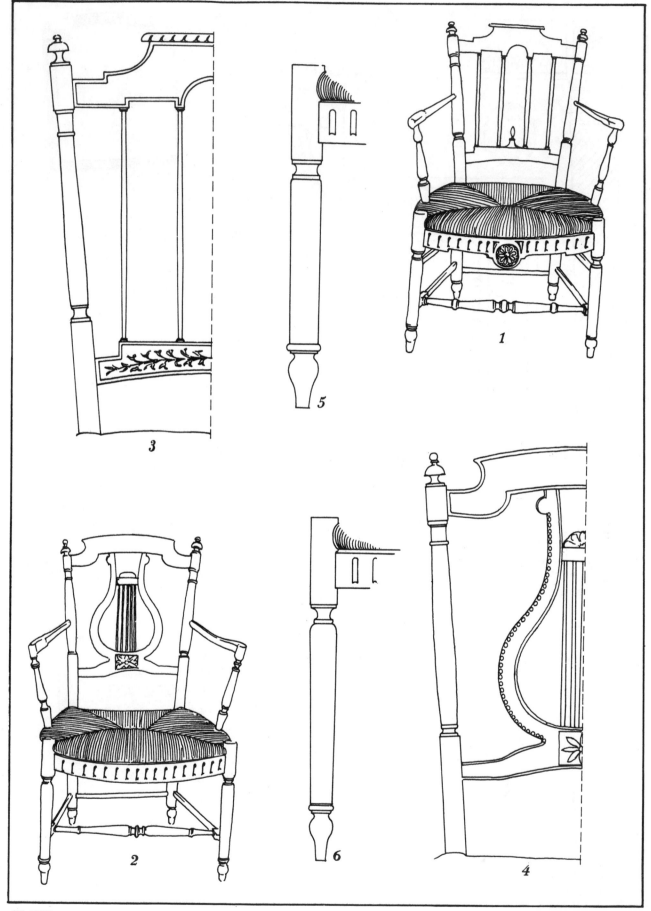

PLATE 210                                                                        LOUIS XVI
1 and 2. Armchairs with reed seats and backs with thin columns and lyre motif.    3 and 4. Backs.    5 and 6. Legs.

*Private collection*

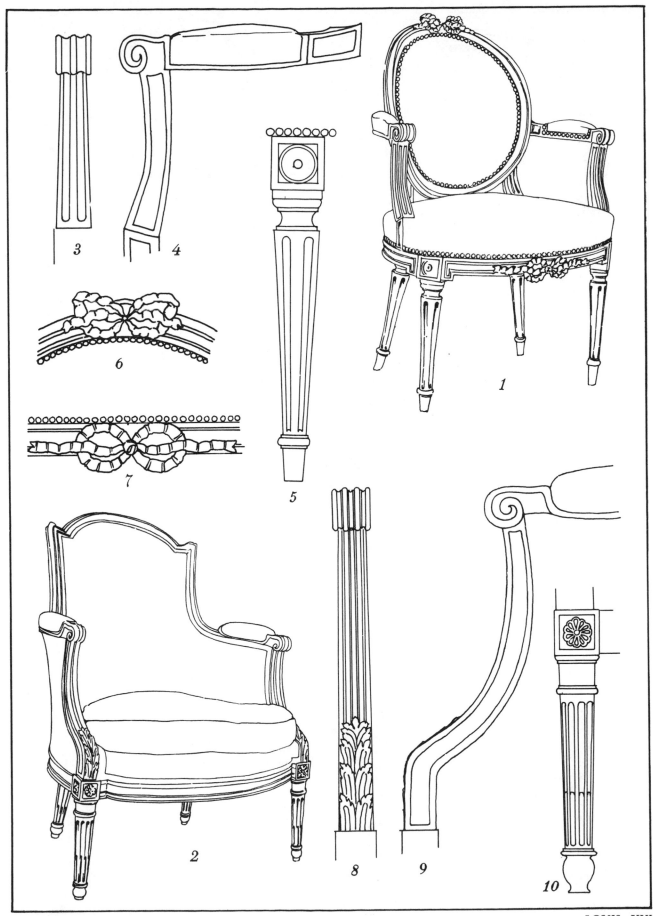

**PLATE 211**

1 and 2. "Carriage" armchair and wingchair.  3, 4 and 5. Details of arm and leg.  6 and 7. Sketches of decorations.  8, 9 and 10. Arm and leg of second chair.

*Private collections*

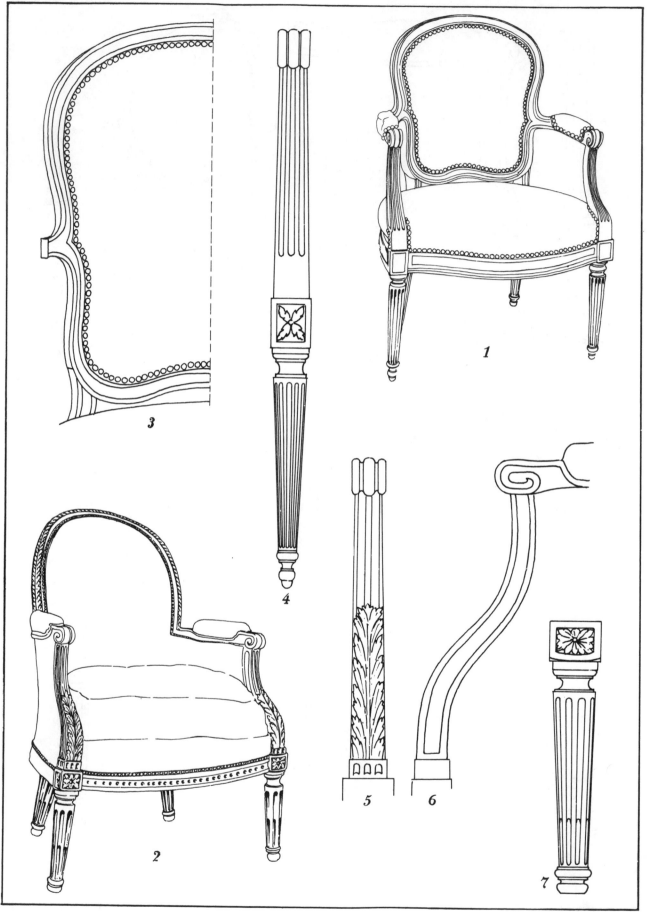

PLATE 212                                                                    LOUIS XVI

1 and 2. "Carriage" armchair and wingchair. The first one has a "violin" back. The second is of painted wood.    3 and
4. Back and front upright of first chair.    5, 6 and 7. Details of arm and leg of second chair.

*Private collection*

216

PLATE 213

1 and 2. Armchairs, the second one of painted wood.    3 and 4. Legs.    5 and 6. Backs.    7. Arm.

LOUIS XVI

*Private collections*

PLATE 214                                                                                    LOUIS XVI

1 and 2. Walnut wing chairs with velvet from Utrecht. The second one, "confessional" style, has raised back and painted wood.    3 and 4. Legs.    5 and 6. Detail of arm.    7. Detail of crest on back.

*Private collections*

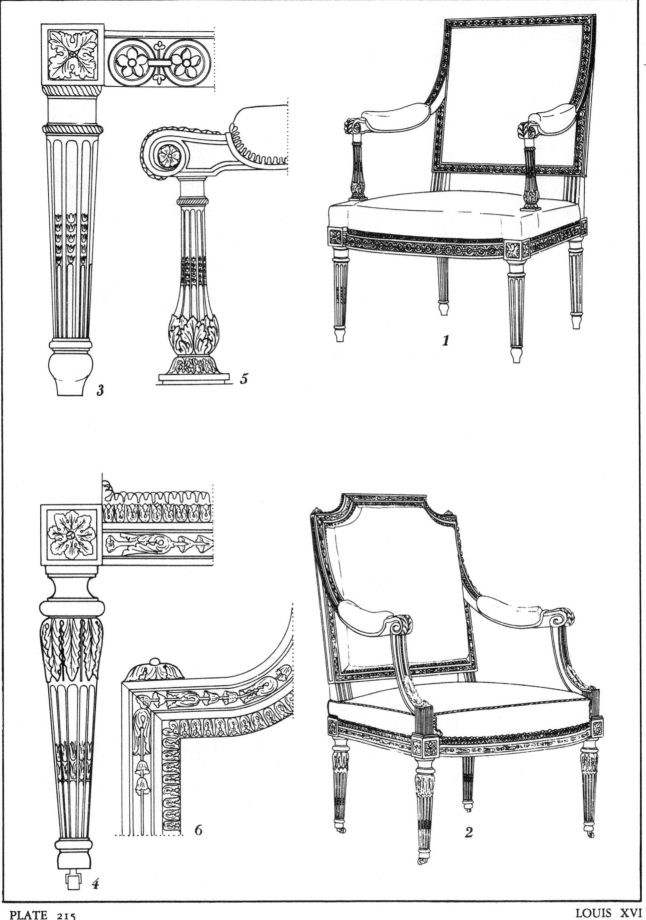

PLATE 215

LOUIS XVI

1 and 2. Carved wooden armchairs by G. Jacob. The upper one is painted and covered in silk. The lower one is gilt and covered with Beauvais tapestry. 3 and 4. Legs. 5. Arm support. 6. Back moulding.

*Louvre*

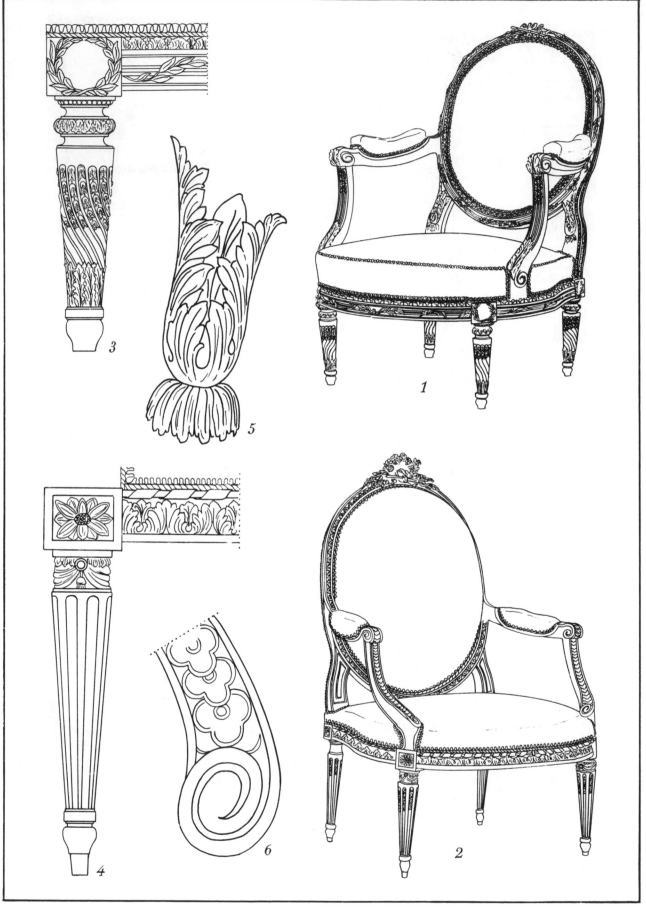

PLATE 216

1 and 2. Carved wooden armchairs by J. Nadal L'Aine and Ph. Poirie (around 1760), covered with Beauvais tapestry.
The lower chair is gilt.    3 and 4. Detail of legs.    5 and 6. Details of arm support and back.

*Louvre*

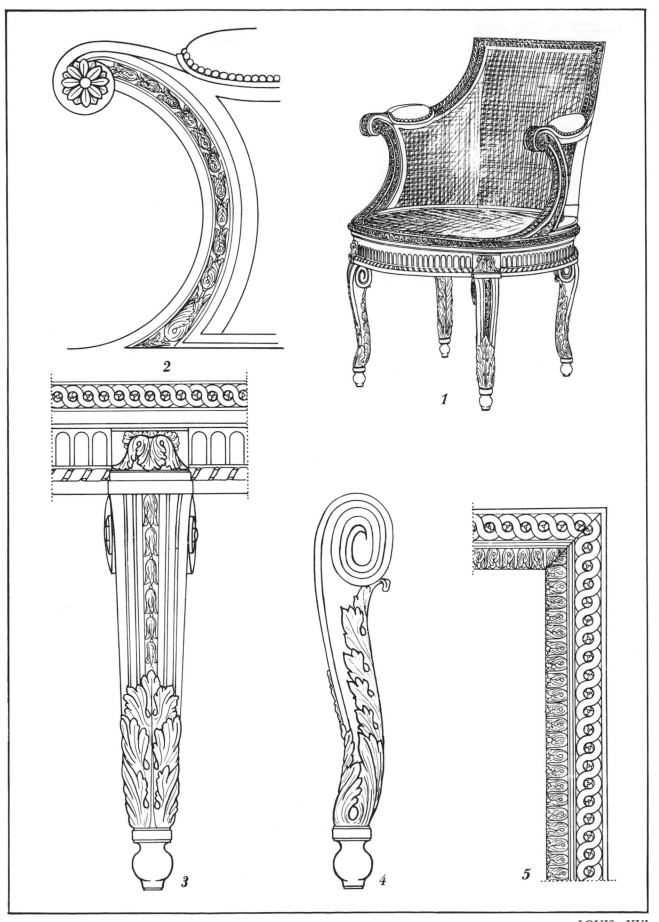

PLATE 217

LOUIS XVI

1. Desk chair made of gilt carved wood and cane, by G. Jacob.   2. Detail of arm support.   3 and 4. Front and side views of leg.   5. Detail of moulding.

*Louvre*

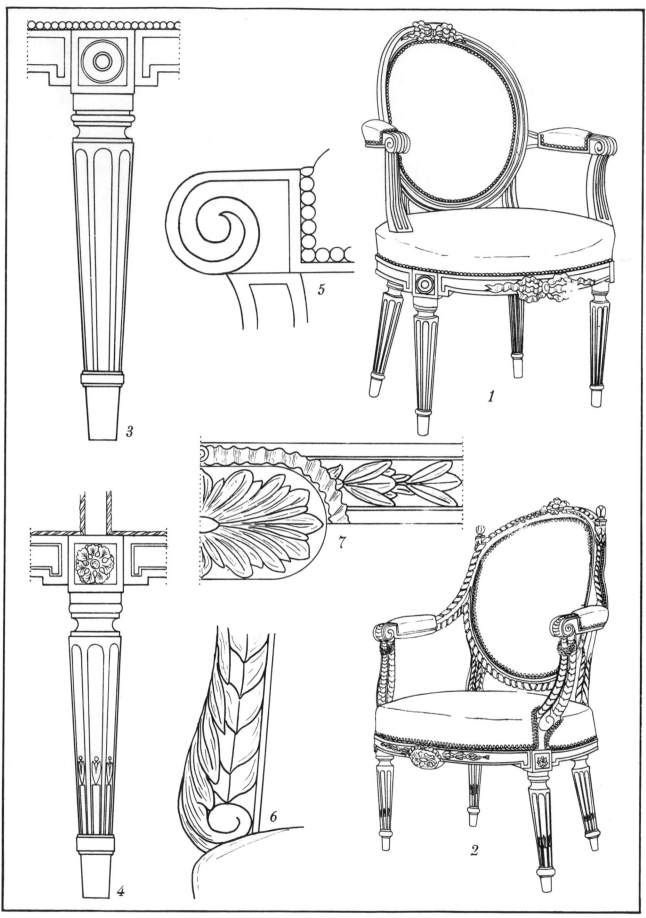

PLATE 218                                                                                              LOUIS XVI

1 and 2. "Carriage" armchairs with medallion backs. The first chair is of walnut, the second of gilt wood. 3 and 4.
Legs. 5 and 6. Arm support. 7. Decoration.

*Private collections*

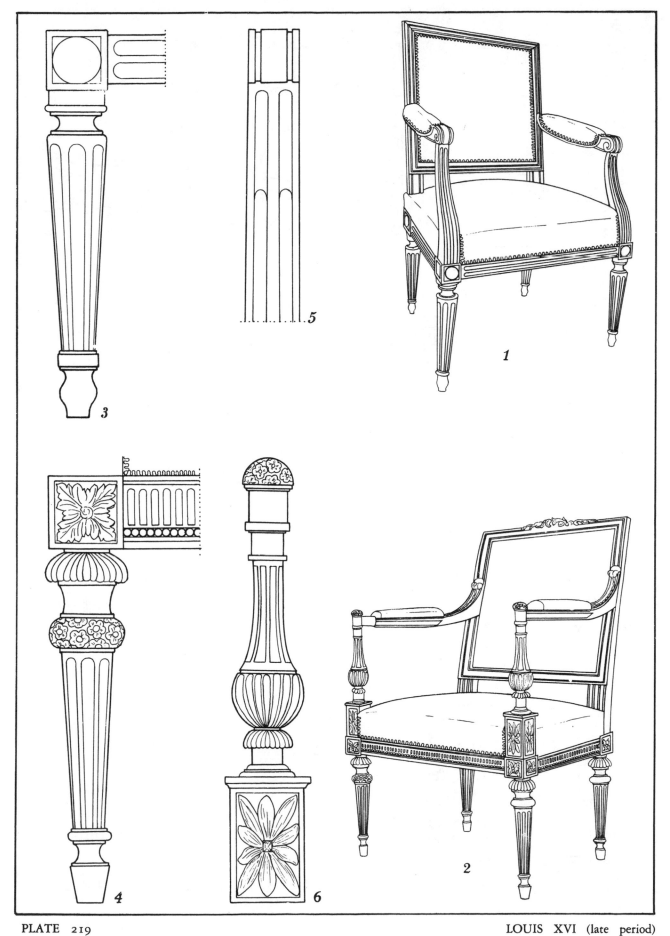

PLATE 219                                                    LOUIS XVI (late period)
1 and 2. Armchairs with square backs. The first chair is of walnut, the second of gilt wood.   3 and 4. Legs.   5. Arm support.   6. Arm support in the form of baluster.

*Private collection*

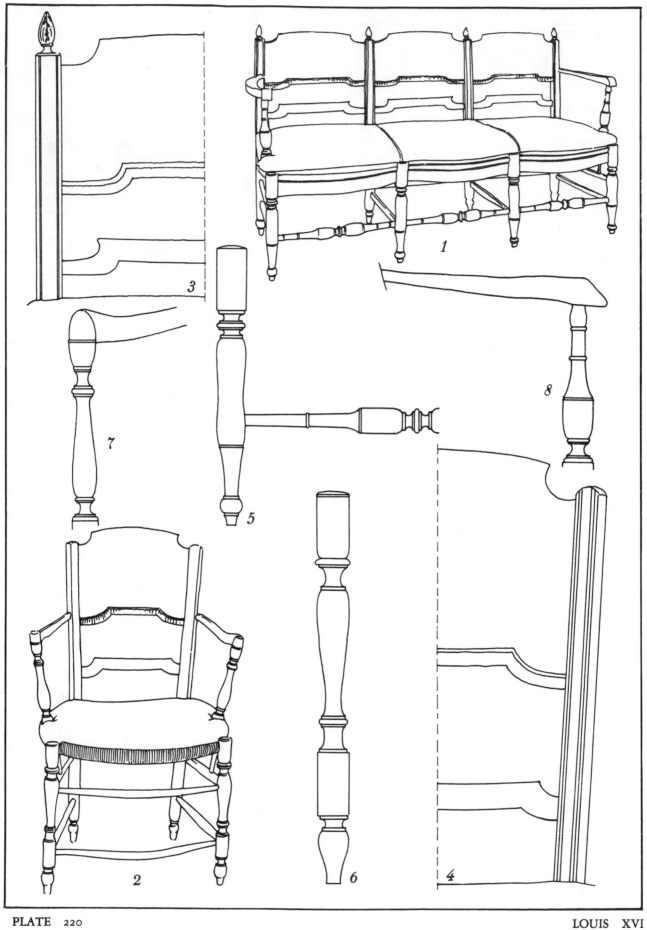

PLATE 220

LOUIS XVI

1 and 2. Provençal sofa and armchair with straw seat, covered with cushions.   3 and 4. Backs.   5 and 6. Legs.   7 and 8. Arm supports.

*Private collection*

224

PLATE 221

1. Sofa.  2. Leg.  3. Detail of arm.  4. Detail of end of arm support.

LOUIS XVI (late period)

*Private collection*

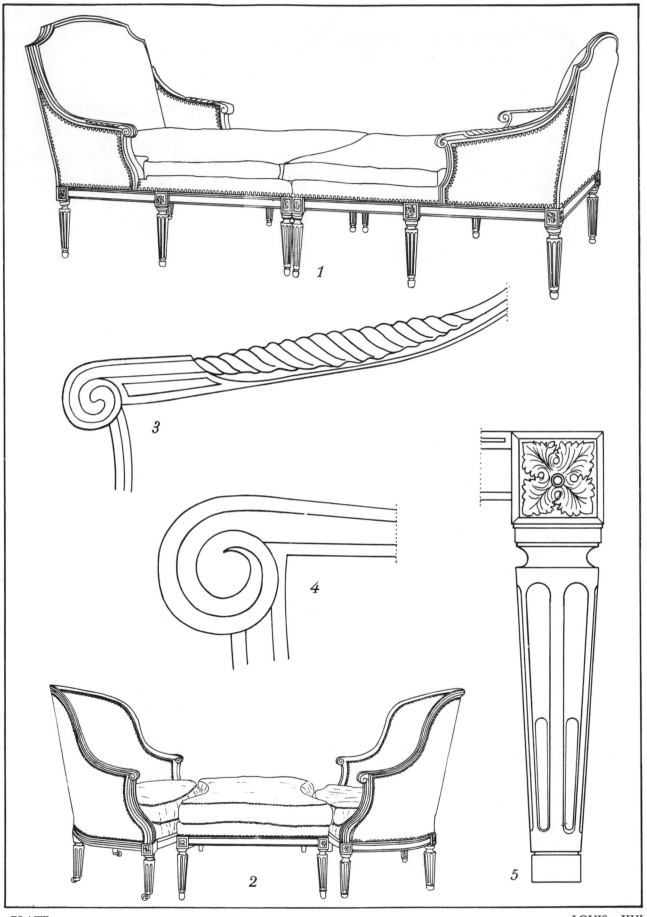

PLATE 222

LOUIS XVI

1 and 2. Chaise longues: sectional furniture for reclining. The first one has two identical sections, the second one has three sections.   3 and 4. Detail of the arms.   5. Leg.

*Private collections*

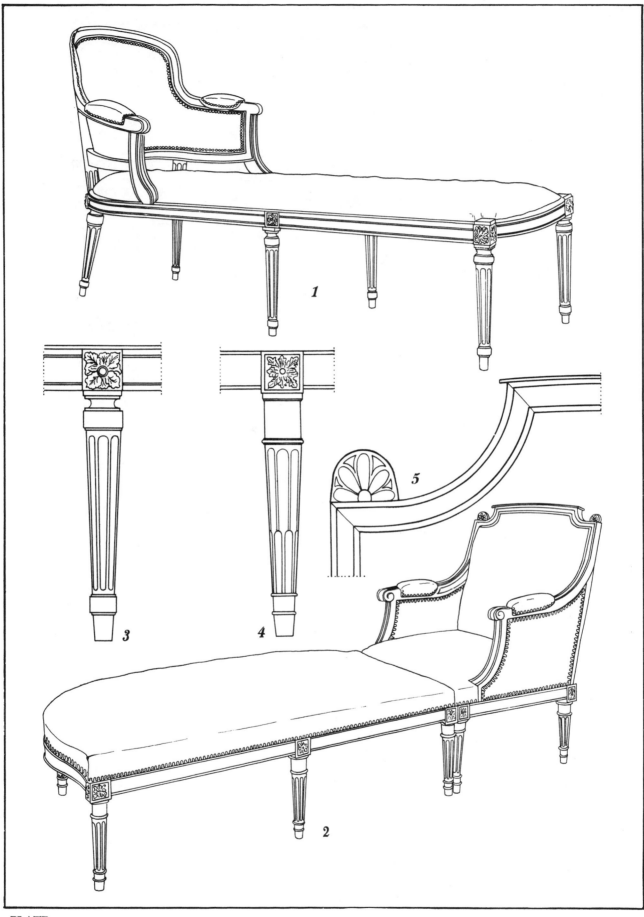

PLATE 223                                                                LOUIS XVI

1 and 2. Chaise longues. The first one is called a "gondola," the second one has two sections.   3 and 4. Legs.   5.
Back.

*Private collections*

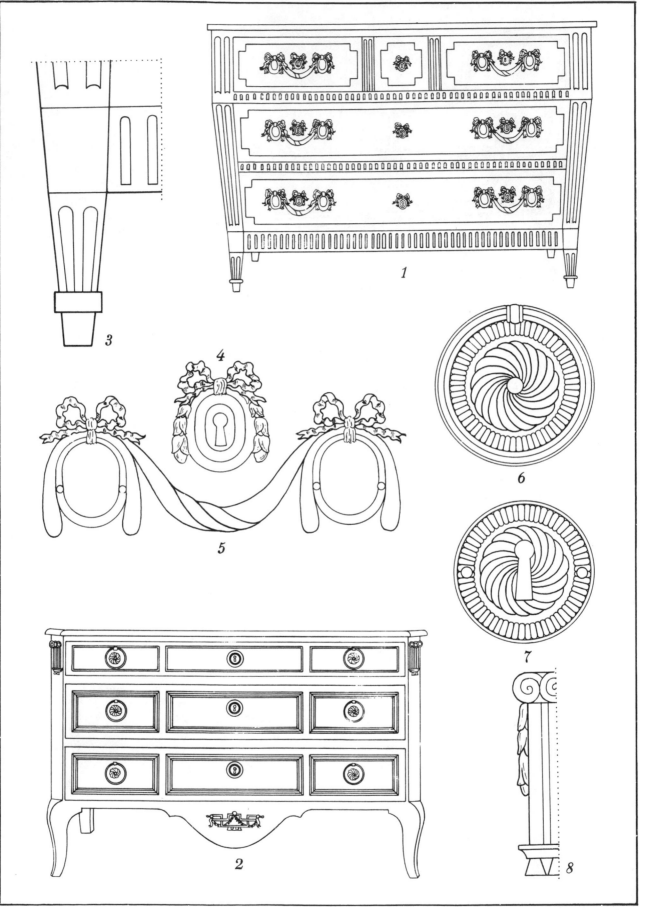

**PLATE 224**

LOUIS XVI (transition from Louis XV period)

1 and 2. Commodes. The first one, rustic style (from the southwest of France), is of walnut, the second one is of Brazilian rosewood and lemon.  3. Leg.  4, 5, 6 and 7. Escutcheon plates and drawer pulls.  8. Detail of decoration on upright.

*Private collections*

**PLATE 225**  LOUIS XVI (early period)

1, 2 and 3. Commodes with diverse characteristics within the style. The first one has some characteristics of Louis XV style; the second has escutcheon plates showing foreign influence; the third has curved legs, a transition from Louis XV.  4, 5, 6, 7 and 8. Escutcheon plates and drawer pulls.

*Private collections*

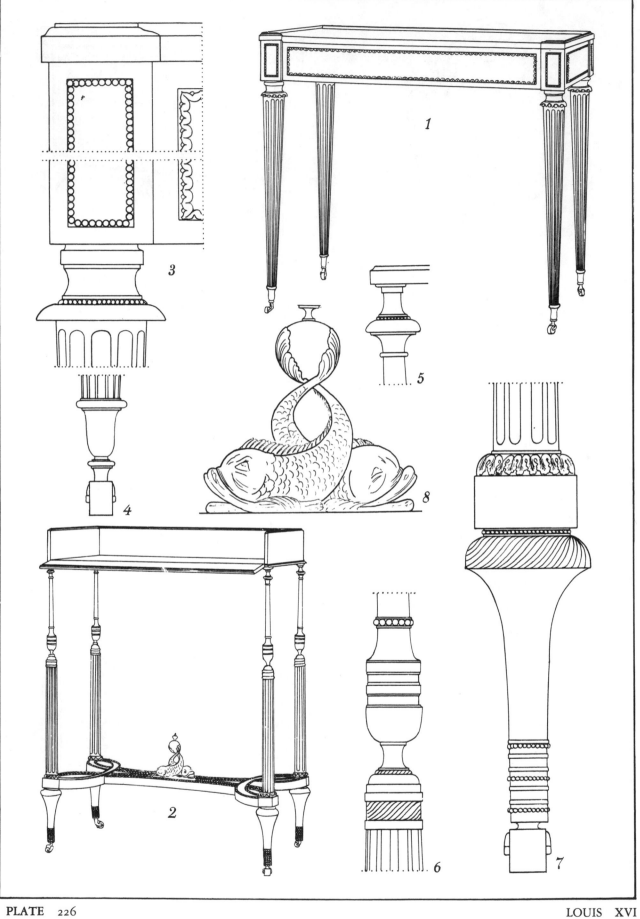

PLATE 226

1. Mahogany lady's desk.   2. Mahogany sewing desk. The two gilt bronzes are by J. H. Riesener.   3 and 4. Leg and
foot.   5, 6 and 7. Details of leg.   8. Bronze dolphins.

*Louvre*

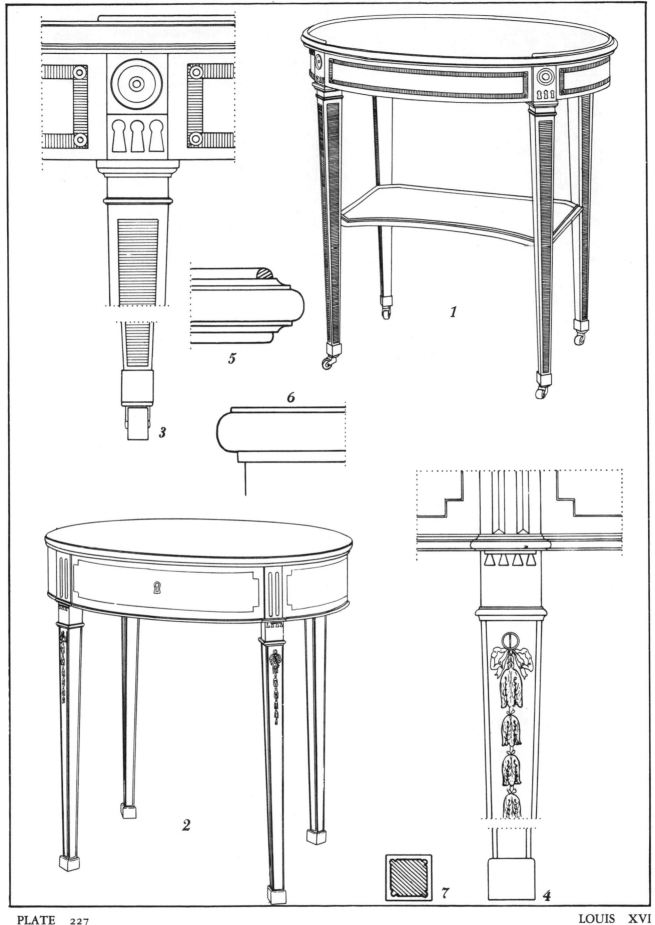

PLATE 227

LOUIS XVI

1 and 2. Oval pedestal tables with some bronze decorations and marquetry.   3 and 4. Details of legs.   5 and 6.
Upper mouldings.   7. Leg section.

*Versailles Palace*

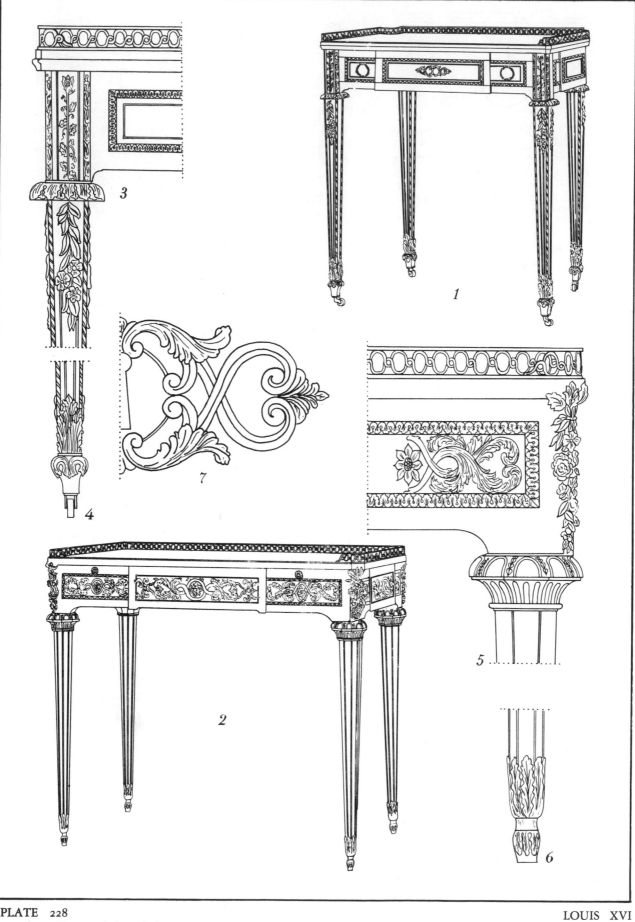

**PLATE 228**                                                                                                   LOUIS XVI

1 and 2. Riesener ladies' desks with marquetry and gilt bronzes.   3, 4, 5 and 6. Details of uprights and legs.   7.
Escutcheon plate.

*Louvre*

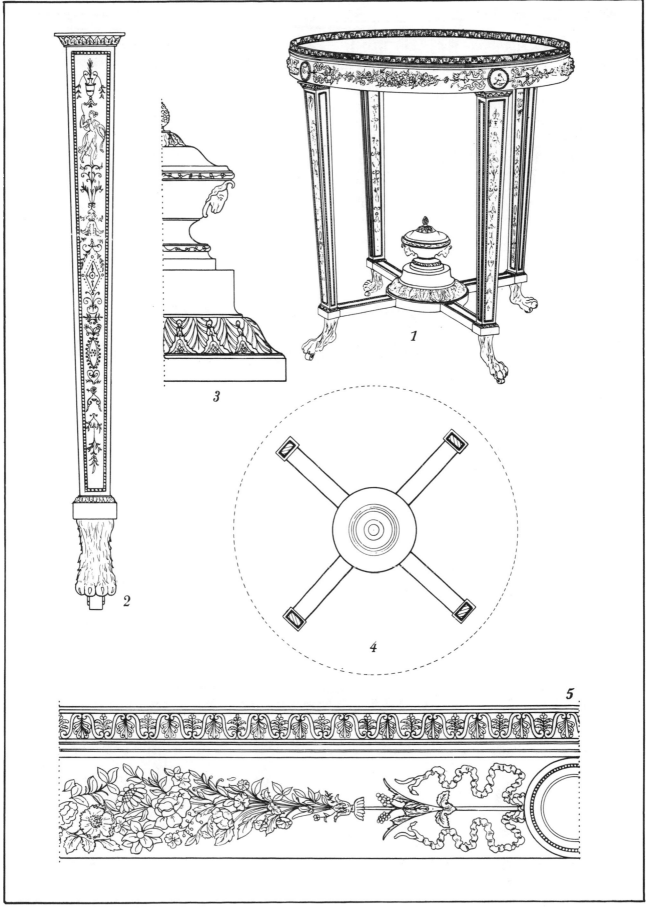

PLATE 229

LOUIS XVI

1. Oval mahogany pedestal table, decorated with bronzes and uprights with delicate paintings in cameos; glass bottom with marble top. Used by Queen Marie Antoinette.   2. Detail of legs.   3. Central urn.   4. Position of the base.   5. Detail of decoration and upper edge.

*Petit Trianon*

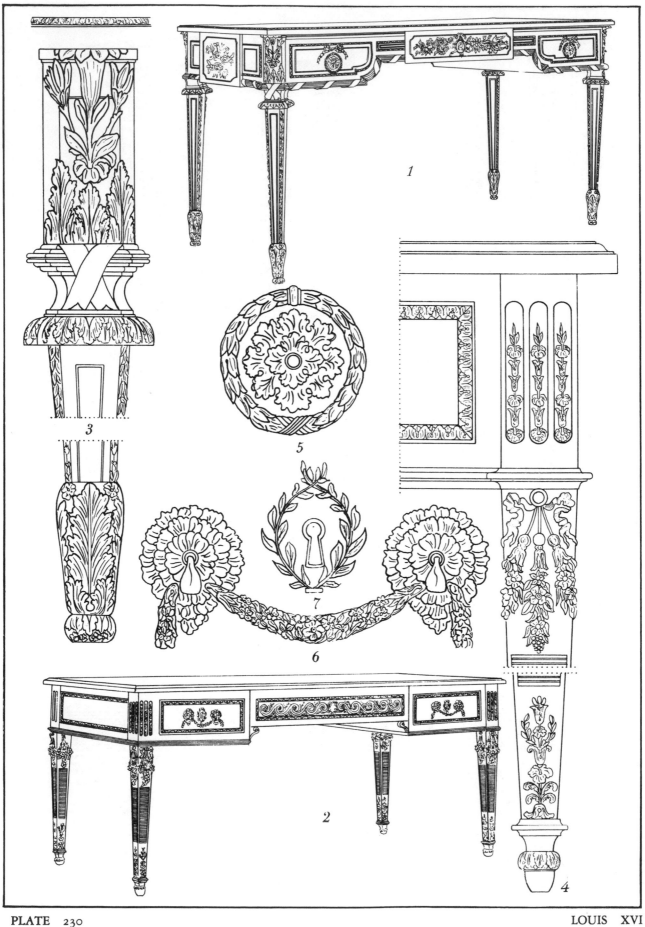

**PLATE 230**

1 and 2. Desks with gilt bronzes. The upper one has marquetry and the lower one is of mahogany.  3 and 4. Details of the uprights and legs.  5 and 6. Drawer pulls.  7. Escutcheon plate.

LOUIS XVI

*Louvre*

PLATE 231

1. Rolltop desk, Louis XVI transition style.  2. Louis XV transition style desk.  3, 4 and 5. Details of bronzes.  6 and 7. Sketch of the panel that trims the upper part.  8. Upright and moulding on leg.

*Fleury-en-Bière Castle and private collection*

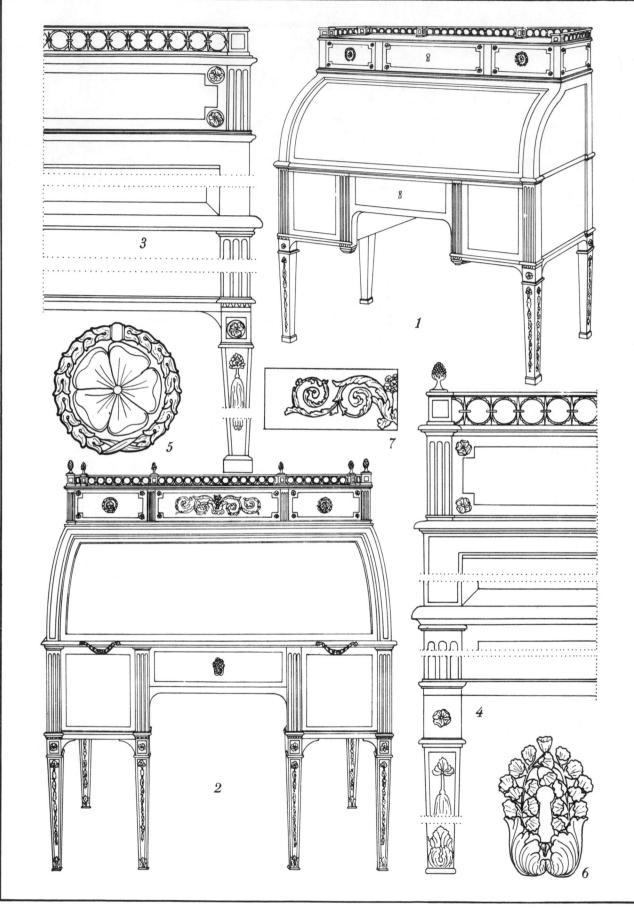

PLATE 232                                                                                                                LOUIS XVI
1 and 2. Rolltop desks with marquetry and gilt bronzes (by David Roentgen).    3 and 4. Details of uprights and legs.    5, 6 and 7. Drawer pull, escutcheon plate and decoration.

*Poles and Arnold Seligmann collections*

**PLATE 233**

1 and 2. Mahogany desks with carved gilt bronzes. The second desk is by J. H. Riesener.   3, 4, 5 and 6. Details of the upright and leg of the second desk.   7 and 8. Upright and leg of the first desk.   9 and 10. Details of the decoration on middle front drawers.   11. Knob.

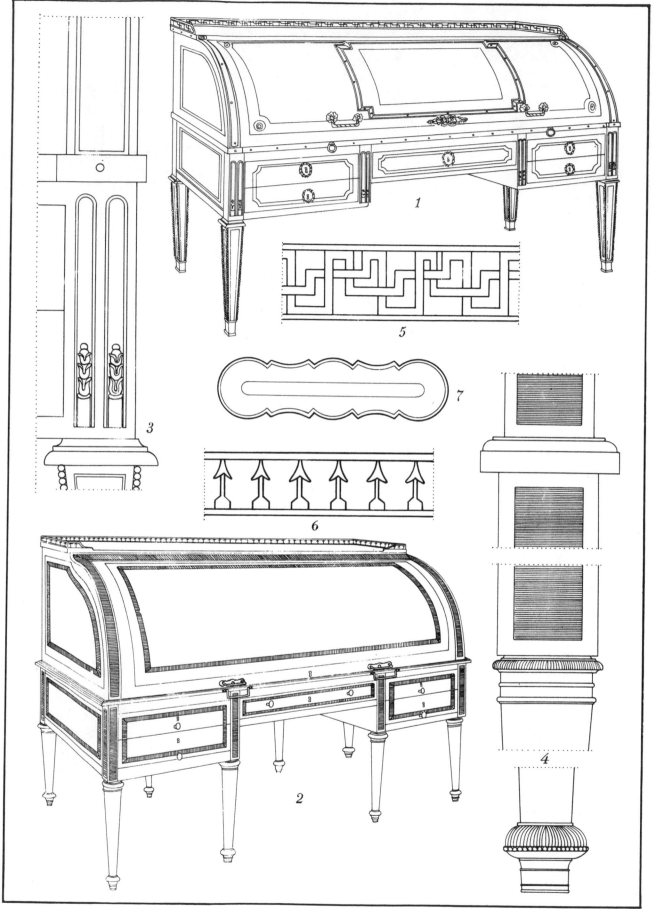

PLATE 234

LOUIS XVI

1 and 2. Desks, the first one in marquetry, the second one in mahogany.   3 and 4. Details of uprights.   5 and 6. Sketches of the trim that skirts the upper edge.   7. Handle.

*Private collection and Ministry of Foreign Affairs, Paris*

**PLATE 235**

LOUIS XVI

1. Ebony lady's desk, black Japanese lacquer with gilt bronzes.   2. Detail of leg.   3. Sketch of moulding at top.   4,
5 and 6. Details of the bronzes.

*Louvre*

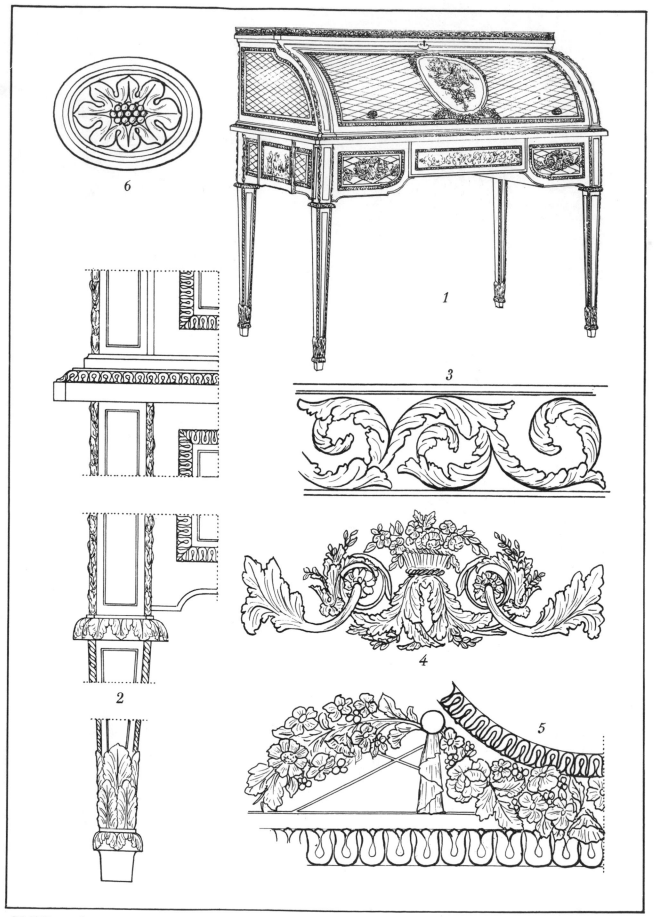

PLATE 236

1. Lady's desk of marquetry (by J. H. Riesener, 1784). 2. Uprights. 3, 4 and 5. Details of the moulding, very elaborate escutcheon plate and central motif. 5. Knob.

*Louvre*

**PLATE** 237

1. Mahogany lady's desk in shape of commode, with gilt bronzes.  2 and 3. Detail of bronze on upright.  4. Upper moulding.  5. Detail of lower decoration.  6. Frieze decoration.  7 and 8. Escutcheon plate and decoration.

*Louvre*

PLATE 238

1. Ebony lady's desk with gilt bronzes.   2. Detail of upright.   3. Moulding on panel.   4. Detail of the frieze and mouldings.

*Louvre*

PLATE 239                                                        LOUIS XVI

1. Mahogany desk adorned with gilt bronzes by E. Lavasseur.   2. Detail of upright.   3. Bronze motif.   4. Moulding on panel.   5. Upright and trim at top.

*Louvre*

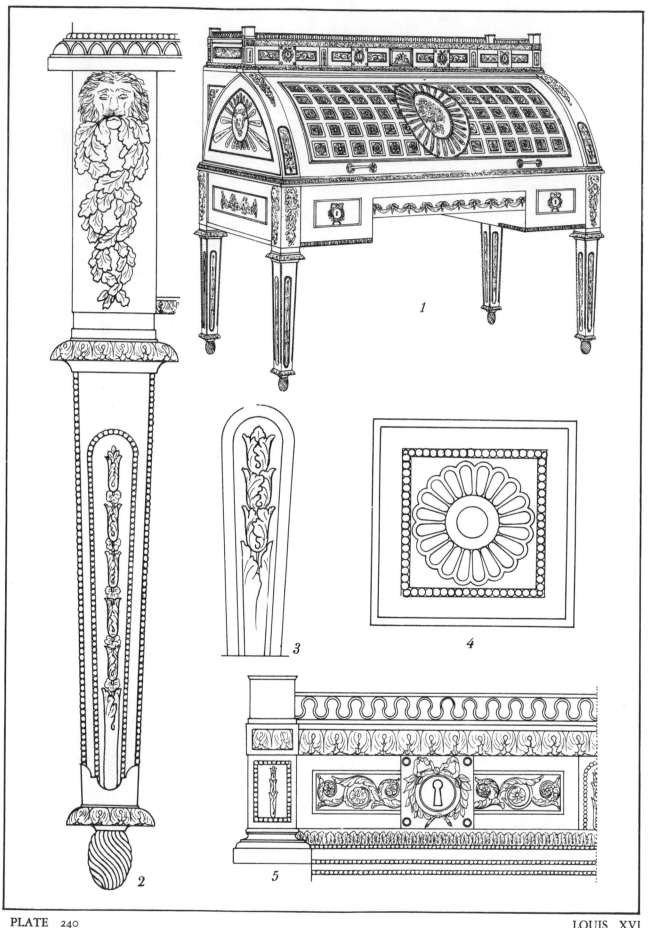

PLATE 240                                                                    LOUIS XVI

1. Desk of marquetry with gilt bronzes (by Roentgen, 1785).    2. Detail of leg.    3 an 4. Detail of bronzes.    5. Detail of upper body and the trim that skirts the top.

*Louvre*

PLATE 241

LOUIS XVI

1. Desk with marquetry of rosewood and lemonwood. Carved gilt bronzes. Marble top with trim. 2 and 3. Top of upright. 4. Lower detail of upright and foot. 5. Frieze decoration. 6. Escutcheon plate.

*Museum of Decorative Arts, Paris*

245

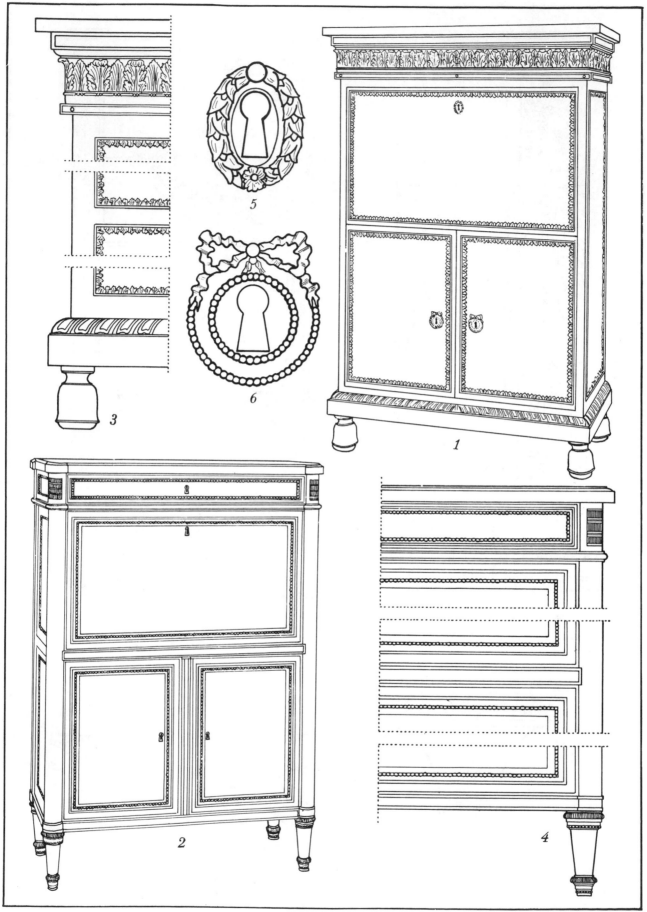

PLATE 242                                                          LOUIS XVI

1 and 2. Desks of mahogany and of lemonwood and amaranth, respectively. The first desk has carved gilt bronzes; the second desk has gilt bronze and a marble top.    3 and 4. Details of uprights and legs.    5 and 6. Escutcheon plates.

*Versailles Palace*

**PLATE** 243                                                    LOUIS XVI (second half of 18th century)

1. Small secretary of marquetry.    2. Detail of upright.    3 and 4. Moulding and sketch of frieze marquetry.

*Private collection*

PLATE 244

LOUIS XVI

1. Secretary with marquetry of colored woods and gilt bronzes.    2. Corner cabinet with marquetry.    3 and 4. Escutcheon
plate and detail of frieze from secretary.    5. Detail of upright.    6. Sketch of frieze.    7. Escutcheon plate.

*Private collections*

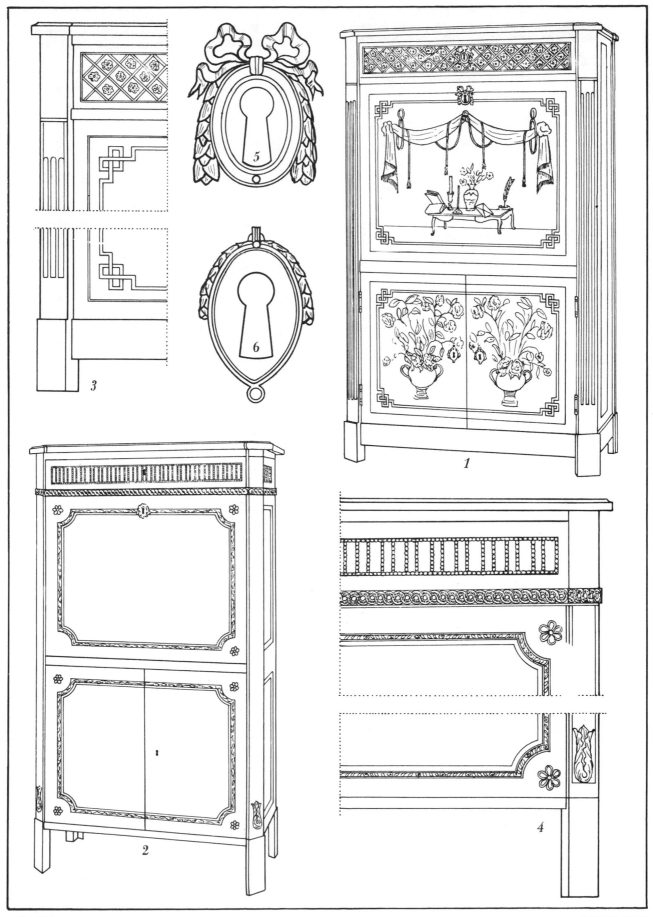

**PLATE 245**

LOUIS XVI

1 and 2. Small desks. The first one has decorations in marquetry of violet wood, rosewood and lemonwood, with decorative lines of boxwood and amaranth. The second desk is of satined rosewood and violet wood. 3 and 4. Detail of upright. 5 and 6. Escutcheon plates.

*Mobilier National de France*

PLATE 246                                                                                          LOUIS XVI

1 and 2. Mahogany desks. The first one has a trim that skirts the top. The second desk has gilt bronzes, carved bronzes and a slab of marble.    3 and 4. Details of desks.

*Versailles Palace and Mobilier National de France*

PLATE 247

LOUIS XVI

1. Mahogany desk commode with bronzes. 2 and 3. Reliefs on upper middle panel. 4. Detail of trim at top. 5. Leg. 6, 7 and 8. Drawer pull, escutcheon plate and bronze decoration.

*Private collection*

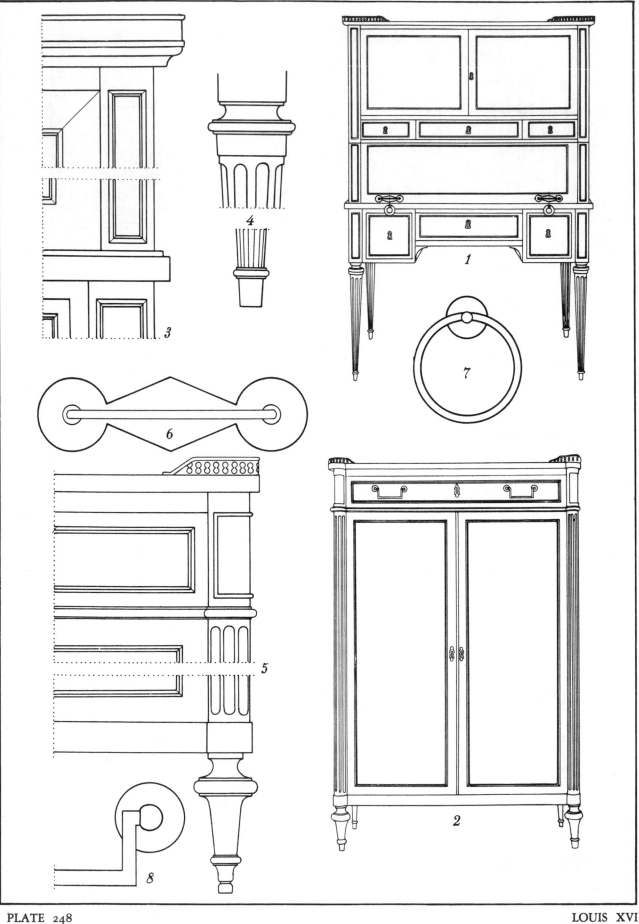

PLATE 248

1. Cylindrical mahogany "bonheur-du-jour" (desk with paper cabinet), with decorative lines of copper and trim skirting the top.   2. Mahogany and copper showcase.   3, 4 and 5. Details of uprights and legs.   6, 7 and 8. Drawer pulls.

*Private collection*

PLATE  249
1 and 2. Secretaries with marquetry of colored woods.    3. Apron of second secretary.    4, 5 and 6. Escutcheon plate.

*Private collections*

PLATE 250                                                                                              LOUIS XVI

1. Office paper cabinet of black wood with decorative lines of copper and bronze decorations.   2 and 3. Details of uprights.   4. Detail of drawer decorations.   5. Rosette.

*Private collection*

**PLATE 251**                                          LOUIS XVI (transition from Louis XV)

1. Commode with five drawers. The pilaster arches, mouldings, friezes and decorations are in bronze.    2. Commode with five drawers with marquetry of different colored woods.    3 and 4. Legs.    5 and 6. Central decorations.    7 and 8. Escutcheon plate and drawer pull.    9. Profile of marble top.

*Private collections*

PLATE 252                                                    LOUIS XVI (transition from Louis XV)

1. Commode with five drawers, with marquetry of amaranth, maple and other woods, carved gilt bronzes, white marble top.    2 and 3. Details of upright and leg.    4, 5 and 6. Detail of the decorations.    7. Corner rosettes.

*Mobilier National de France*

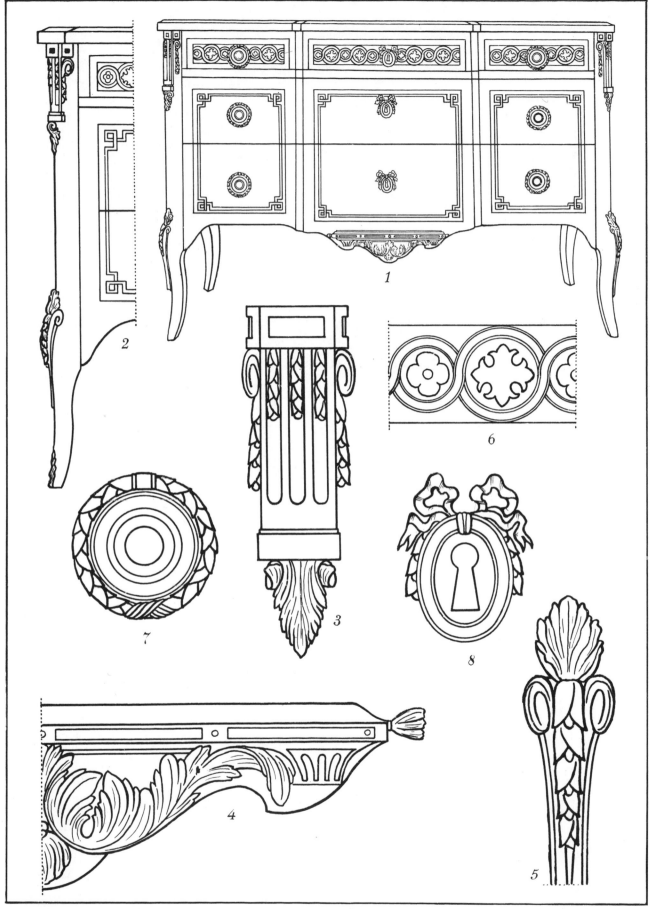

PLATE 253

LOUIS XVI (transition from Louis XV)

1. Commode with three drawers, with marquetry of rosewood, plane tree and lemonwood, gilt carved bronzes and a marble top. 2. Detail of upright and leg. 3, 4 and 5. Details of the decorations. 6. Detail of marquetry border. 7 and 8. Drawer pull and escutcheon plate.

PLATE 254                                            LOUIS XVI (transition from Louis XV)

1 and 2. Commodes with gilt carved bronze decorations and marble tops. The first commode has five drawers and marquetry of rosewood and amaranth. The second one has two drawers and marquetry of rosewood and lemonwood.   3 and 4. Details of uprights.   5. Detail of frieze.   6, 7 and 8. Drawer pulls and escutcheon plate.

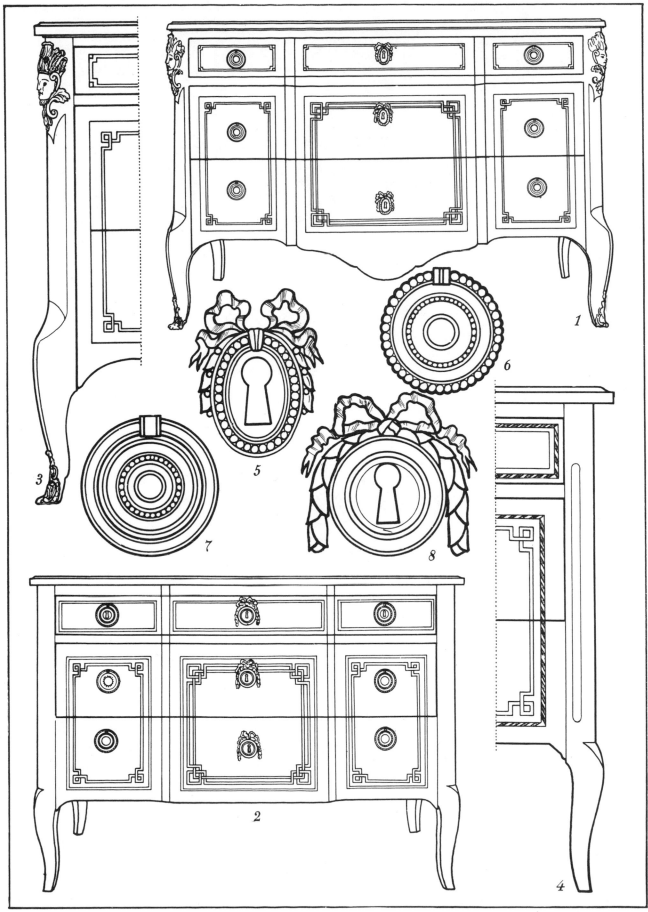

PLATE 255                                                    LOUIS XVI (transition from Louis XV)

1 and 2. Commodes with marble tops. The first one has three drawers, marquetry of rosewood, amaranth and other woods, and carved bronzes. The second one has marquetry of violet wood, rosewood and amaranth.    3 and 4. Details of uprights and legs.    5, 6, 7 and 8. Drawer pulls and escutcheon plates.

*Mobilier National de France*

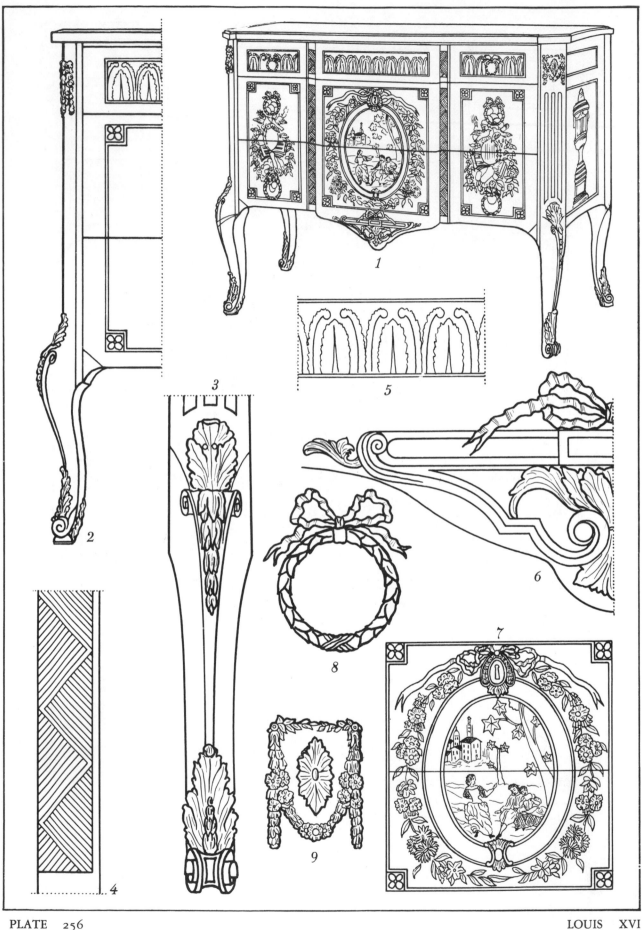

PLATE 256

1. Commode with five drawers and marquetry of rosewood, amaranth and lemonwood with gilt bronze decorations and a marble top. 2. Detail of leg and upright. 3. Front view of leg. 4. Alternation of different woods. 5. Sketch of upper marquetry. 6. Sketch of lower part. 7. Sketch of central marquetry. 8 and 9. Drawer pull and decoration.

*Museum of Decorative Arts, Paris*

PLATE 257                                                                                                    LOUIS XVI

1. Commode with five drawers and marquetry of amaranth, lemonwood and maple, gilt carved bronzes (influence of Louis XV style on legs), and marble top.   2 and 3. Details of upright and legs.   4, 5, 6 and 7. Details of decorations.   8. Drawer pull.

PLATE 258                                                                              LOUIS XVI

1. Commode with two drawers and marquetry of lemonwood and amaranth.   2. Commode with three drawers and
marquetry of walnut, Brazilian rosewood and with decorative lines of boxwood.   3 and 4. Details of uprights and legs.   5,
6 and 7. Drawer pulls and escutcheon plate.

PLATE 259                                                          LOUIS   XVI

1. Desk commode in the early style.    2. Very ornate console table.    3. Small table in the early style.    4. Chiffonier.    5 and 6. Escutcheon plate and detail of moulding.    7. Detail of frieze decoration on console table.    8. Moulding.

*Private collections*

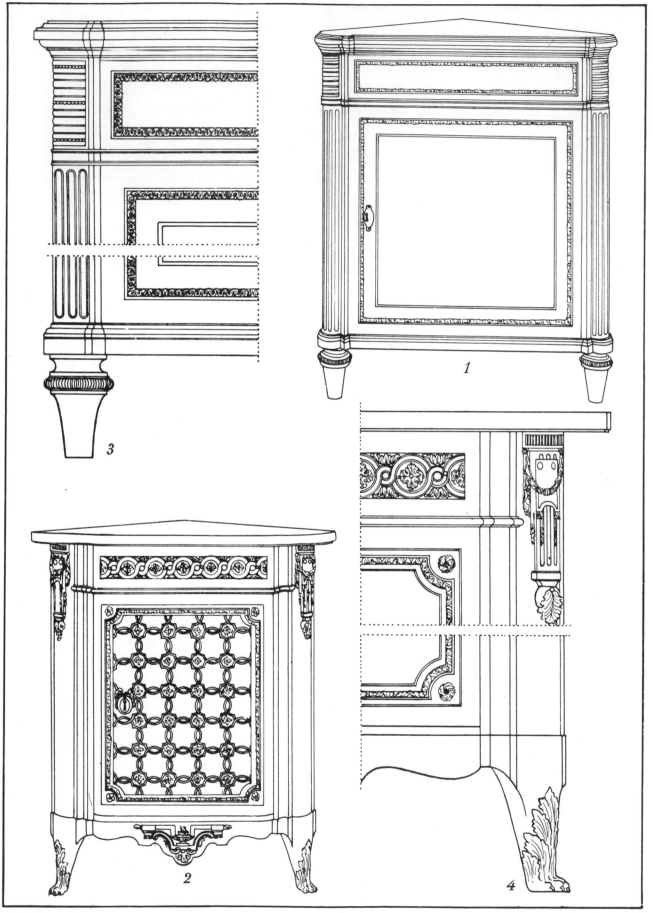

PLATE 260

1 and 2. Mahogany corner cabinets. The first one has mouldings of gilt bronze and white marble. The second cabinet has marquetry of rosewood and amaranth with decorative lines of boxwood and ebony, and gilt carved bronzes.   3 and 4. Details of uprights and legs.

*Champs-Élysée Palace*

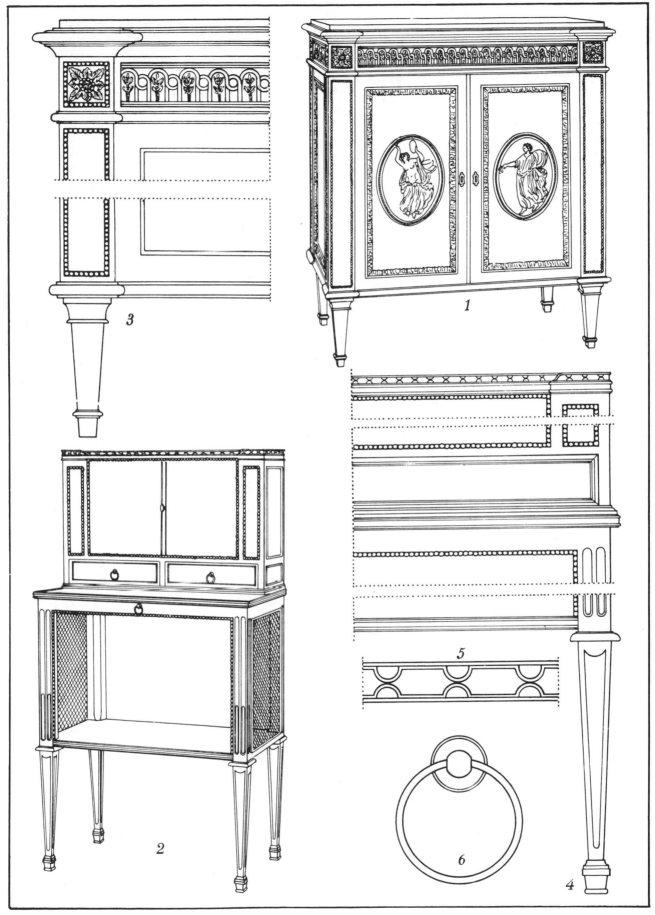

PLATE 261                                                                LOUIS XVI

1. Small mahogany commode with medallions of Sèvres porcelain, gilt carved bronzes and marble top.    2. Small mahogany desk—paper cabinet with moulding and trim of gilt bronze.    3 and 4. Details of uprights and legs.    5. Sketch of bronze trim skirting top.    6. Drawer pull.

PLATE 262                                                                LOUIS XVI

1 and 2. Commodes of three and five drawers, satined wood and mahogany, respectively. Both have gilt carved bronzes and marble tops.   3 and 4. Details of uprights.   5 and 6. Drawer pull and escutcheon plate.

*Versailles Palace*

PLATE 263                                                         LOUIS XVI

1 and 2. Mahogany commodes with five drawers, gilt carved bronzes and marble tops. The second one has trim skirting the top.   3 and 4. Details of uprights and legs.   5, 6 and 7. Drawer pull and escutcheon plates.

*Mobilier National de France and Champs-Élysée Palace*

PLATE 264                                                          LOUIS XVI

1. Mahogany commode with nine drawers.    2. Mahogany commode with swinging doors, with three drawers at the top.
Both numbers one and two have gilt bronze mouldings and marble tops.    3 and 4. Details of uprights and legs.    5 and
6. Escutcheon plate and drawer pull.

**PLATE 265**

LOUIS XVI

1 and 2. Small commodes with marquetry of rosewood and amaranth, decorative lines of boxwood and marble tops. The first commode has two drawers and curved doors. The second one has five drawers.   3 and 4. Details of uprights and legs.   5, 6 and 7. Escutcheon plates and drawer pull.

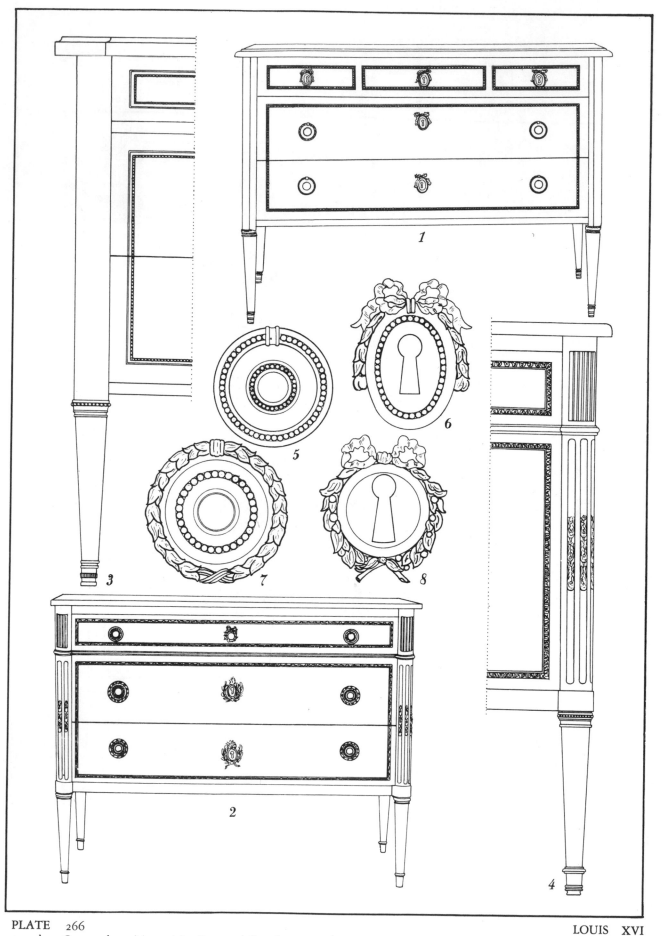

PLATE 266

1 and 2. Commodes with straight lines and five drawers. The upper one has wood veneer; the lower one is of moulded mahogany.  3 and 4. Details of uprights and legs.  5, 6, 7 and 8. Drawer pulls and escutcheon plates.

*Private collection*

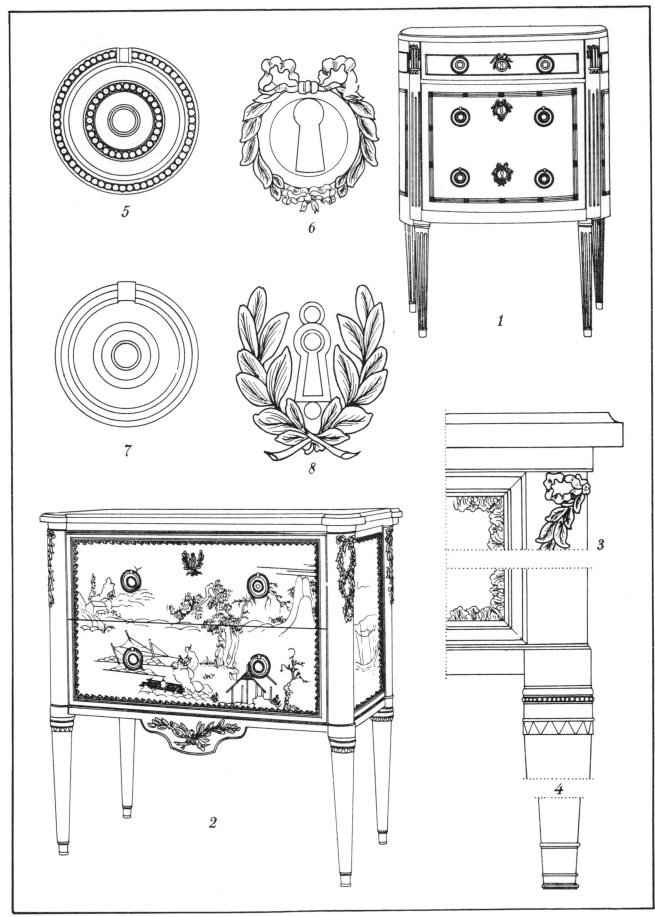

**PLATE** 267

1 and 2. Small commodes. The first one has three drawers and is of wood veneer. The second one has two drawers and is of black lacquer and gold. 3 and 4. Details of the uprights. 5, 6, 7 and 8. Drawer pulls and escutcheon plates.

*Private collections*

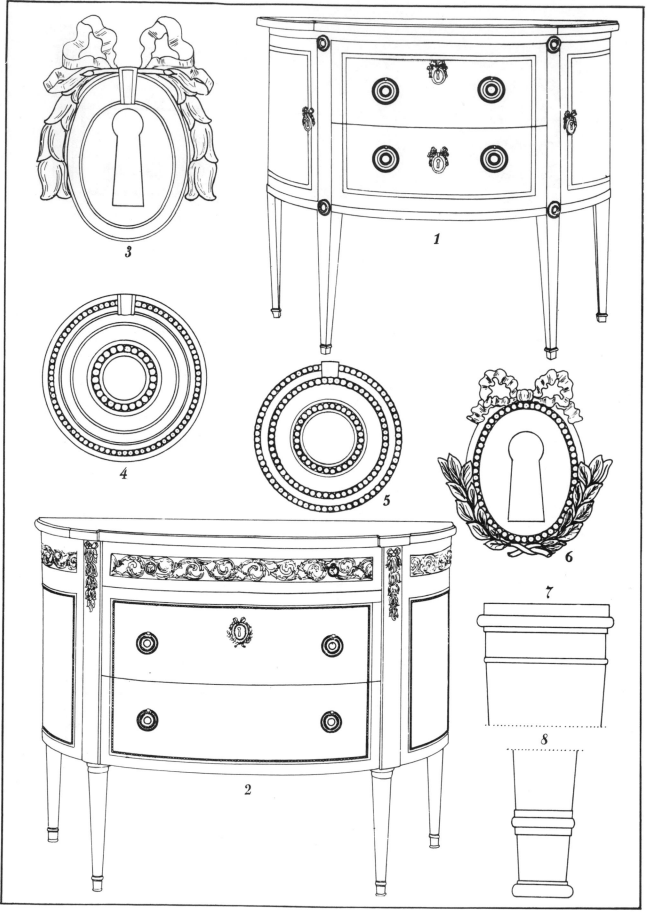

PLATE 268

LOUIS XVI

1 and 2. Circular commodes with long legs, two drawers in front and swinging doors on the sides, with two kinds of wood. The decorations, drawer pulls and escutcheon plates are of carved copper on the upper commode, of bronze on the lower commode.   3, 4, 5 and 6. Escutcheon plates and drawer pulls.   7 and 8. Details of leg.

PLATE 269                                                       LOUIS XVI

1 and 2. Mahogany commodes with three drawers, gilt bronze mouldings and marble tops. The second one has pieces of carved bronze.   3 and 4. Details of uprights and legs.   5 and 6. Drawer pull and escutcheon plate.

*Versailles Palace*

PLATE 270                                                          LOUIS XVI

1. Small commode with three drawers and marquetry of amaranth, holly, rosewood, lemonwood and sycamore.   2. Mahogany corner commode. Both commodes have carved gilt bronzes and marble tops.   3 and 4. Details of uprights and legs.

PLATE 271                                                                                                    LOUIS XVI

1. Commode with four drawers, Chinese lacquer over a black base, carved gilt bronze mounts.    2. Commode with nine
drawers, red marquetry, carved gilt bronze mounts, white marble top.    3 and 4. Details of posts and legs.    5, 6,
7 and 8. Drawer pulls and escutcheons.

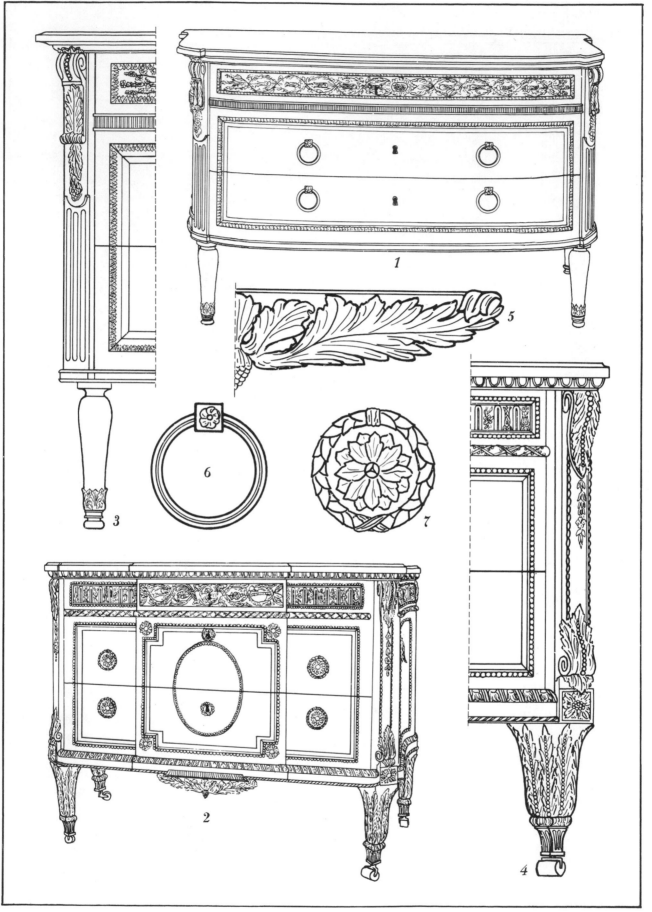

PLATE 272 LOUIS XVI

1 and 2. Commodes with three and five drawers, and marquetry of rosewood, amaranth and other woods. The lower one is of amaranth and stained banana wood and has carved gilt bronzes. The first commode has a turquoise blue marble top. 3 and 4. Details of uprights and legs. 5. Decorations. 6 and 7. Drawer pulls.

PLATE 273           LOUIS XVI

1 and 2. Commodes with five drawers. The upper one has mahogany veneer, the lower one is of rosewood. 3 and 4. Legs. 5 and 6. Profiles of marble tops. 7, 8 and 9. Drawer pull and escutcheon plates.

*Private collection and Ministry of War, Paris*

277

PLATE 274                                                                                    LOUIS XVI

1 and 2. Straight-line commodes with five drawers. The upper one has satined wood and amaranth veneer. The lower one has marquetry on uprights and wood veneer.   3 and 4. Legs.   5 and 6. Details of lower middle decorations.   7 and 8. Profiles of marble tops.   9, 10, 11 and 12. Drawer pulls and escutcheon plates.

*Poles collection and private collection*

**PLATE 275**

1 and 2. Corner commodes of ebony, black Japanese lacquer, gilt bronzes and marble tops (M. Carlin, 1782).   3 and 4. Details of uprights and legs.   5 and 6. Details of moulding and central motif from lower apron.   7 and 8. Details of mouldings.

PLATE 276                                                                LOUIS XVI

1. Mahogany commode with gilt bronzes and marble top (Riesener, 1786).   2. Detail of upright and leg.   3. Front of upright.   4. Escutcheon plate.   5. Drawer pull.   6. Rosette.   7. Detail of frieze decoration.

*Louvre*

PLATE 277

1. Commode with marble top (Riesener, 1782).   2. Detail of upright and leg.   3. Detail of bronze decorations of frieze.   4. Escutcheon plate and trim on central decoration.   5. Bronze design, middle lower apron.   6. Drawer pull.

*Louvre*

PLATE 278

1. Light mahogany and amaranth commode with hinged doors, carved gilt bronzes. There are two drawers at top, and three inside. White marble top.   2 and 3. Details of upright and leg.   4, 5 and 6. Sketches of the decorations.

*Fontainebleau Palace*

PLATE 279                                                                                    LOUIS XVI

1. Mahogany commode with gilt bronzes attributed to Gouthieri (G. Benaman, 1786).    2. Detail of upright and leg.    3.
Rosette on curved panels.    4 and 5. Mouldings.

*Louvre*

PLATE 280

1. Cabinet of inlaid ebony, decorated with gilt bronzes.   2. Detail of leg.   3 and 4. Details of the bronzes.   5. Border moulding.

*Louvre*

PLATE 281

1. Small office wardrobe with marquetry of copper on shell.   2. Detail of front.   3. Central detail.   4. Detail of bottom.

*Private collection*

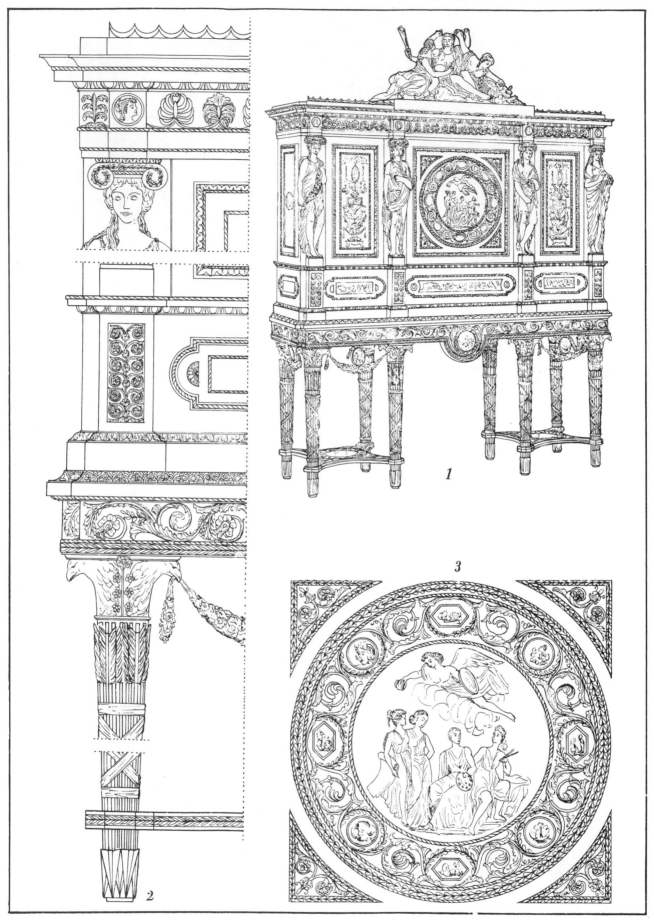

PLATE 282

LOUIS XVI

1. Marie-Antoinette's mahogany jewelry cabinet, with gilt carved bronzes, paintings and cameos.   2. Detail of upright and leg.   3. Detail of central design.

*Versailles Palace*

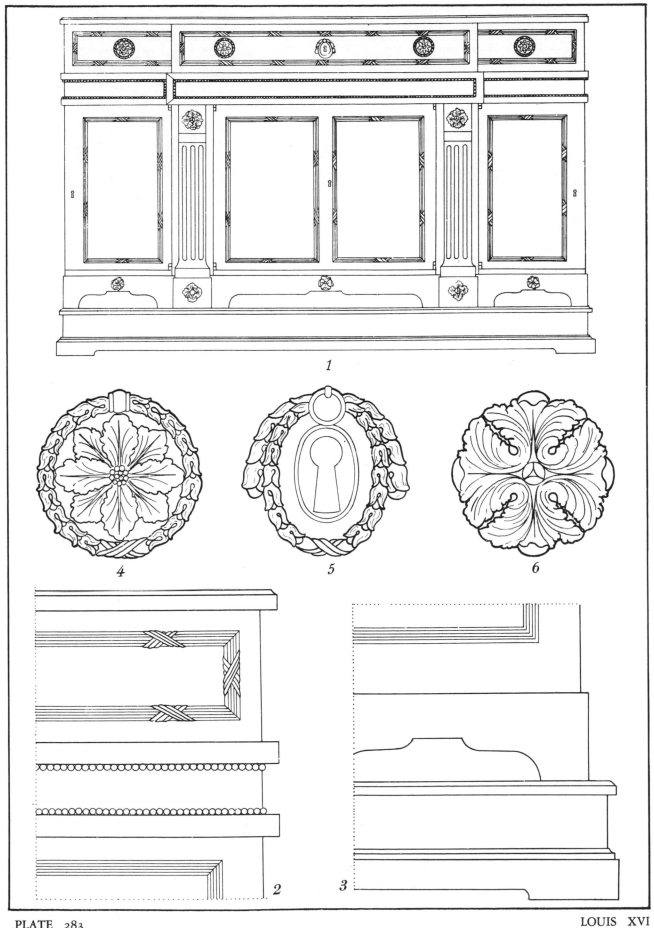

1

4          5          6

2          3

PLATE 283                                                                LOUIS XVI
1. Dining-room sideboard.    2 and 3. Upper and lower details of upright.    4, 5 and 6. Drawer pull, escutcheon
plate and rosette.

*Dutasta collection*

PLATE 284

1. Mahogany-paneled cabinet (J. H. Riesener).    2. Detail of upright and leg.    3, 4 and 5. Decorations.

LOUIS XVI

*Poles collection*

PLATE 285

1 and 2. Dining-room sideboard, of black Japanese lacquer, with gilt bronzes (M. Carlin).    3 and 4. Detail of uprights and legs.    5 and 6. Sketches of the bronzes.

*Louvre*

PLATE 286                                                                LOUIS XVI

1. Mahogany dining-room sideboard, with gilt bronzes and Sèvres porcelains (G. Beneman, 1787).   2. Detail of the graceful design on the front.   3 and 4. Foot and border moulding.

*Louvre*

PLATE 287          LOUIS XVI

1. Dining-room sideboard of mahogany and ebony, with gilt bronzes (Hauri and G. Beneman, 1786–1787).    2. Detail of upright.    3. Detail of foot.    4 and 5. Mouldings.

*Louvre*

PLATE 288                                                          LOUIS XVI

1. Brazilian rosewood sideboard with gilt bronzes and painting on glass.  2. Detail of upright.  3. Detail of frieze decoration.  4 and 5. Bronzes on the legs.  6. Detail of panel moulding.

*Louvre*

**PLATE 289**

1 and 2. Mahogany sideboards with gilt bronzes.   3 and 4. Details of uprights and legs.   5 and 6. Sketch of moulding, bordering central panel of frieze.

*Louvre*

PLATE 290

LOUIS XVI

1. Corner console table of ebony and black Japanese lacquer, with gilt bronzes and marble top (M. Carlin, 1785). 2. Detail of corner post. 3. Detail of frieze. 4. Sketch of lower bronze decoration.

*Louvre*

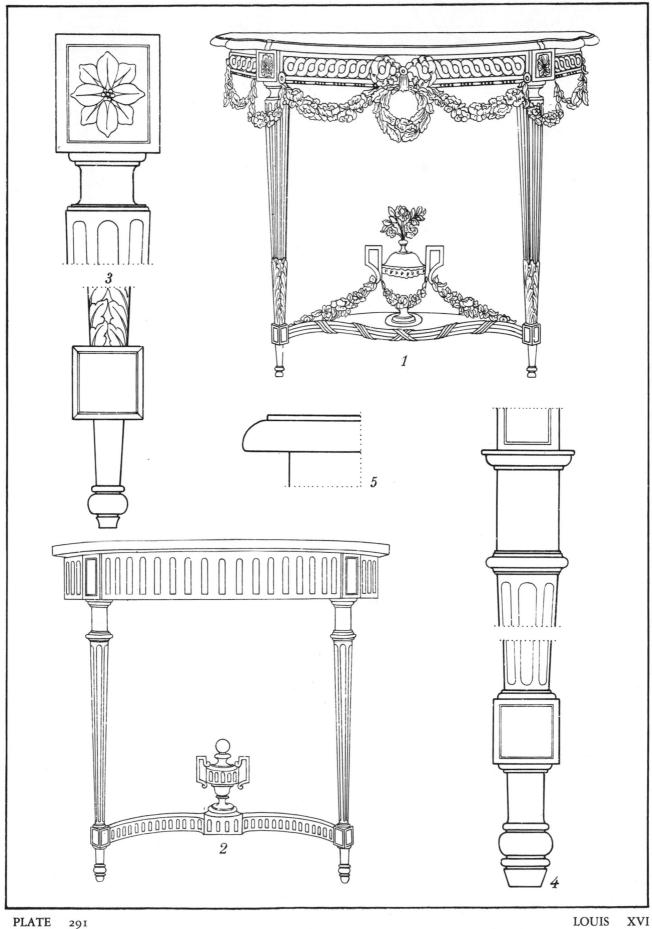

PLATE 291

LOUIS XVI

1 and 2. Two-legged console tables of painted wood and walnut.  3 and 4. Legs.  5. Profile of top.

*Private collections*

295

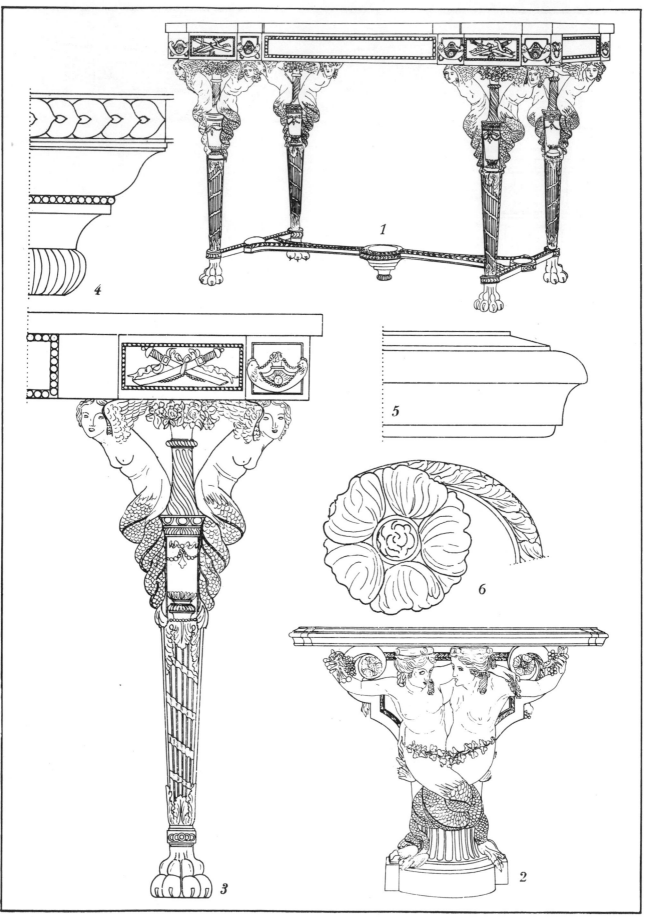

PLATE 292

1 and 2. Carved wooden console tables (J. Jacob). 3. Detail of leg. 4. Detail of middle foot of lower crosspiece. 5. Moulding at top of console table. 6. Detail of large flower at top.

*Louvre*

PLATE 293

LOUIS XVI

1. Console table of gilt carved wood.   2. Detail of foot.   3. Detail of frieze carving.   4. Profile of frieze.   5. Detail of piece joining the legs.

*Louvre*

**PLATE 294**  LOUIS XVI (end of style)

1. Mahogany commode, decorated with Wedgewood plaques and gilt bronzes.  2. Mahogany commode, decorated with gilt bronzes.  3 and 4. Details of uprights and legs.  5 and 6. Escutcheon plate and drawer pull.

*Louvre*

PLATE 295

LOUIS XVI (towards end of style)

1. "Bonheur-du-jour," document case of ebony black Chinese lacquer and gilt bronzes (B. Molitor).    2. Detail of uprights and legs.    3. Upright sculpture.

*Louvre*

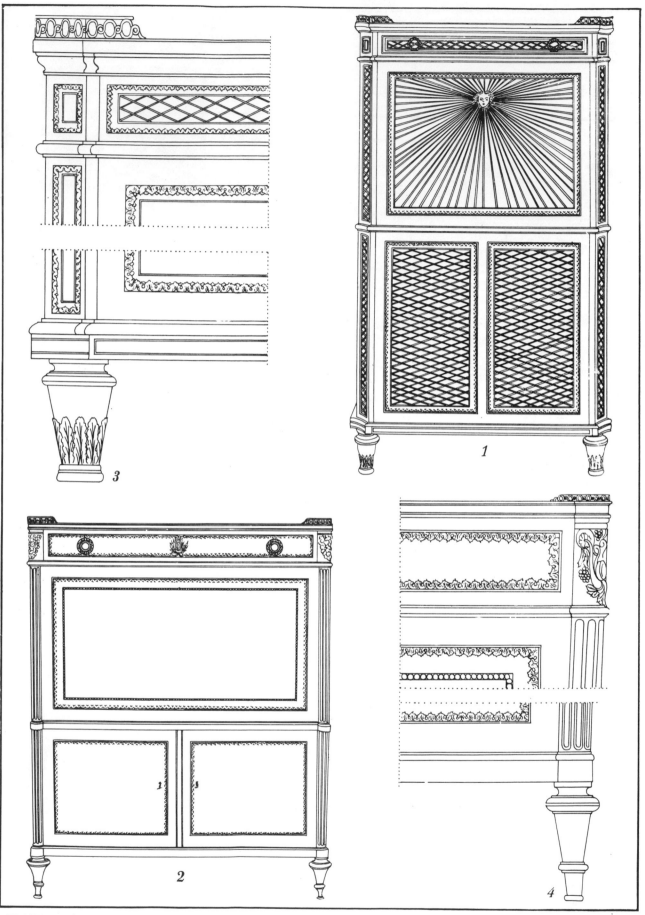

PLATE 296                                                        LOUIS XVI (towards end of style)

1. Marquetry secretary.   2. Mahogany secretary. Both secretaries have bronzes and copper trim skirting the top.   3 and 4. Details of uprights.

*Poles collection and private collection*

PLATE 297

1. Carved wooden bed in the Renaissance tradition.   2. Post.   3. Cornice.   4. Top of the headboard.

*Private collection*

PLATE 298

LOUIS XVI

1. Gilt carved wooden bed, upholstered in velvet.   2. Detail of leg.   3, 4 and 5. Details of carved motifs.

*Louvre*

**PLATE** 299

1. Bed.  2. Upright  3 and 4. Moulding decorations.

*Louvre*

PLATE 300

LOUIS XVI

1. Gilt carved wooden bed, upholstered in silk. 2. Detail of upright. 3. Detail of crest of headboard.

*Louvre*

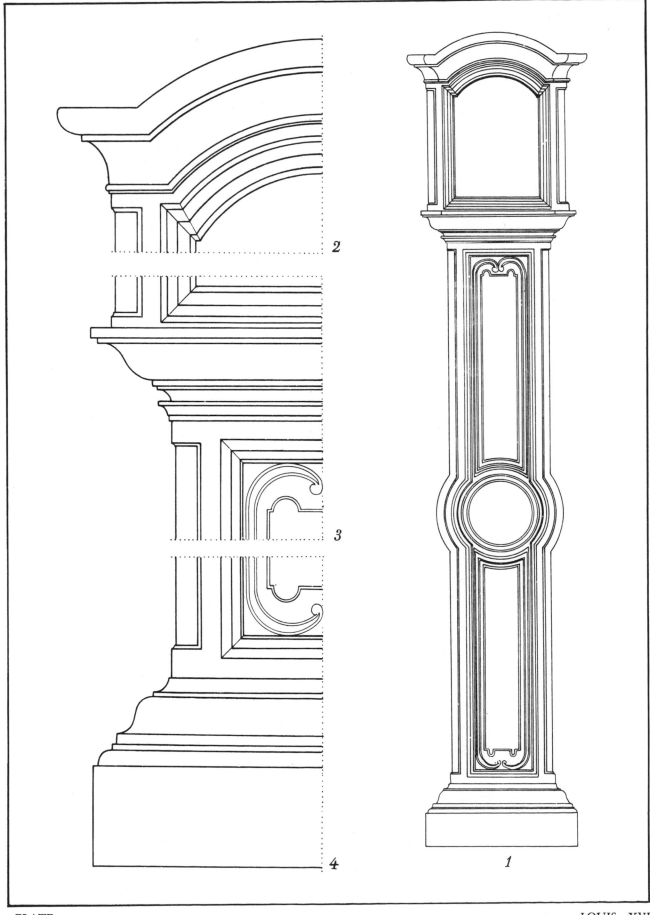

PLATE 301

1. Oak clock cabinet.  2, 3 and 4. Details of front.

LOUIS XVI

*Private collection*

2

1

PLATE 302
1. Oak clock cabinet.  2. Details of the cabinet.

LOUIS XVI

*Private collection*

PLATE 303

LOUIS XVI

1. Clock cabinet with marquetry and gilt bronzes (M. Carlin and Gouthiere).   2. Detail.   3. Leg.   4. Hands.

*Louvre*

PLATE 304
LOUIS XVI
1. Mahogany barometer with gilt bronzes (M. Carlin).    2. Detail of top.    3. Detail of bottom.    4 and 5. Hands.

*Louvre*

PLATE 305

LOUIS XVI

1 and 2. Mahogany and copper chiffoniers.   3, 4, 5 and 6. Details of uprights.   7, 8 and 9. Drawer pulls and escutcheon plate.

*Private collections*

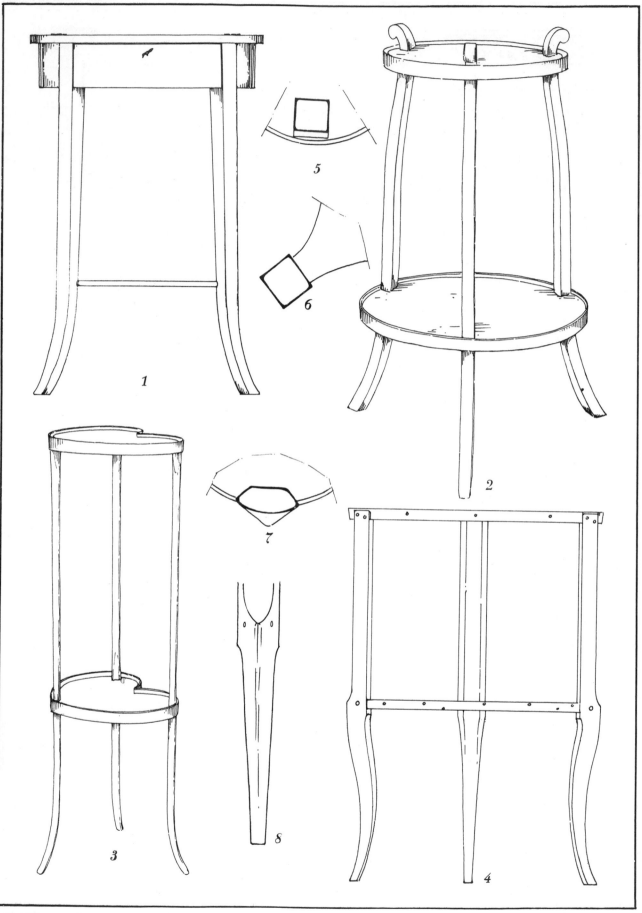

PLATE 306                                                                LOUIS XVI
Simple furniture with some elements of the style: 1. Small worktable. 2. Small stand. 3. Small table with heart-shaped shelves. 4. Small table with shelf. 5, 6 and 7. Leg sections. 8. Leg.

*Private collections*

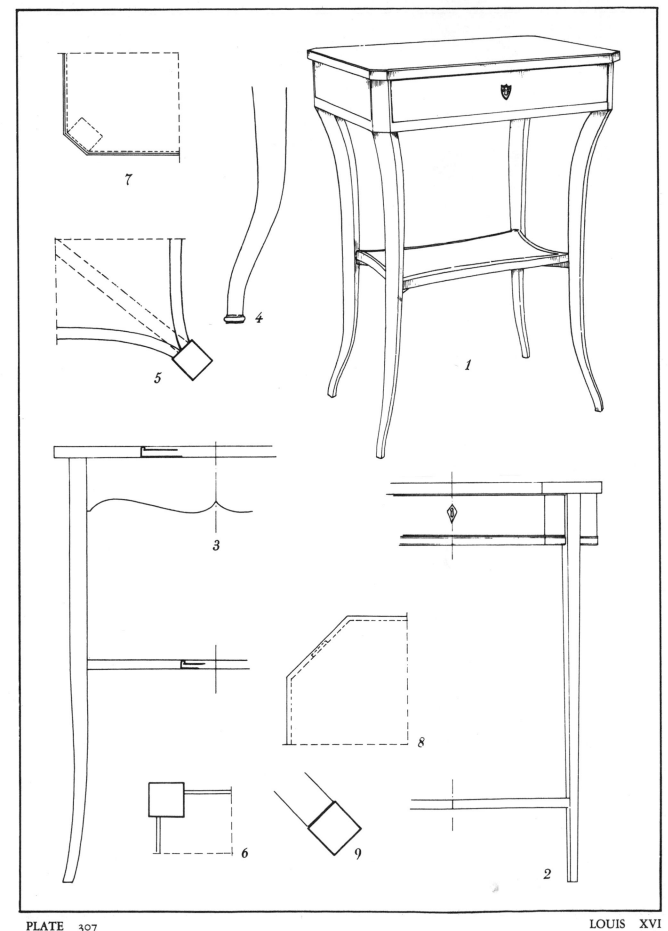

PLATE 307

LOUIS XVI

1 and 2. Small worktables. 3. Small table. 4. Leg. 5 and 6. Shape of lower shelves. 7 and 8. Shape of table corners. 9. Placement of the leg on the diagonal.

*Private collections*

PLATE 308                                                                                LOUIS XVI

1 and 2. Small worktables.    3. Side view (these tables are pushed up against the wall).    4. Leg.    5. Cross section of
the leg.    6. Detail of turned leg.

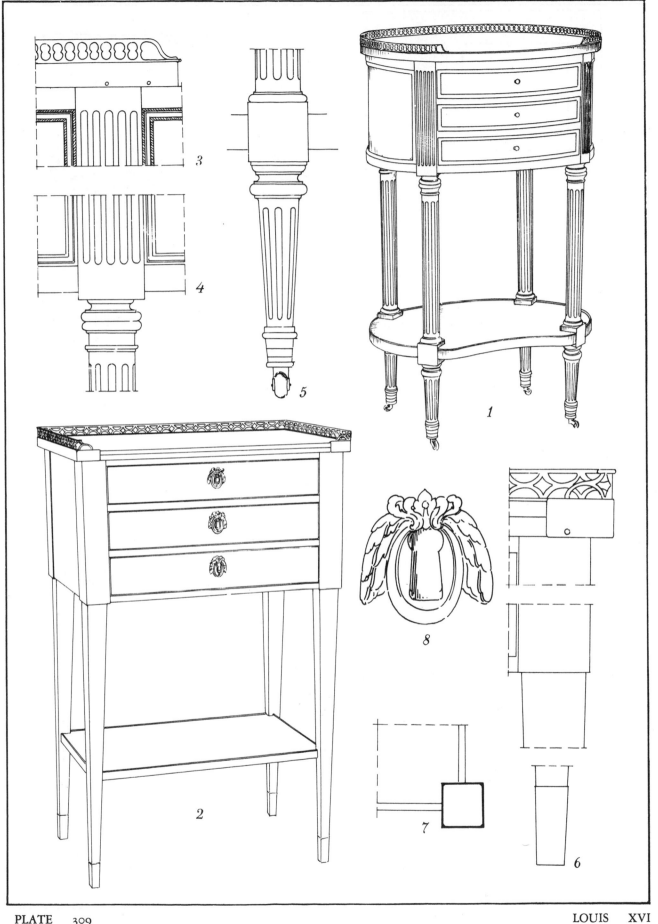

PLATE 309

LOUIS XVI

1 and 2. Small sewing tables.   3, 4 and 5. Details of leg.   6 and 7. Leg of second table.   8. Escutcheon plate.

*Private collections*

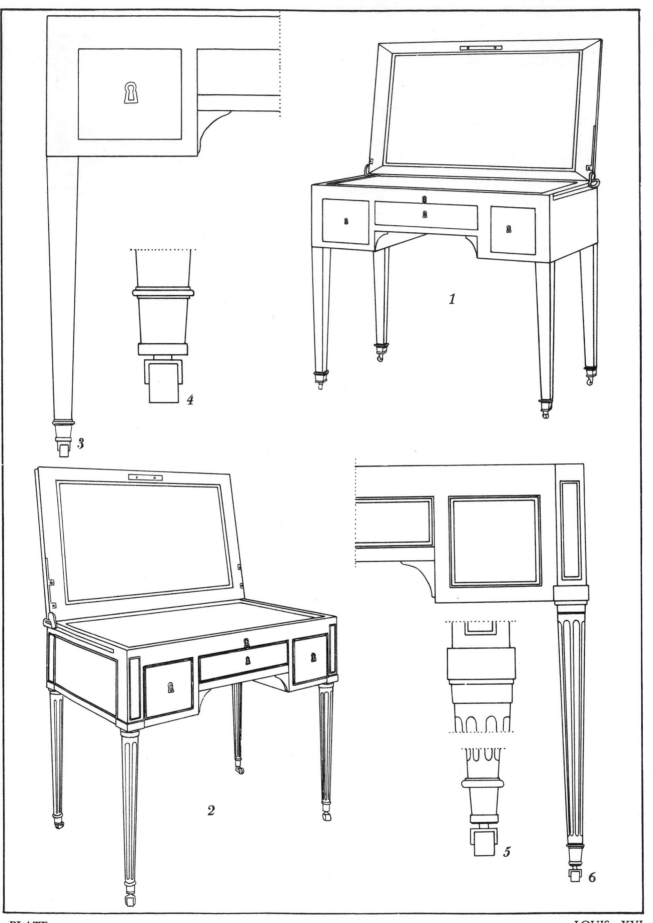

PLATE 310                                                                                              LOUIS XVI
1 and 2. Mahogany vanities with mirrors in movable frames. The second has panels outlined with gilt bronze decorative
lines.    3, 4, 5 and 6. Details of uprights and legs.

*Fontainebleau Palace*

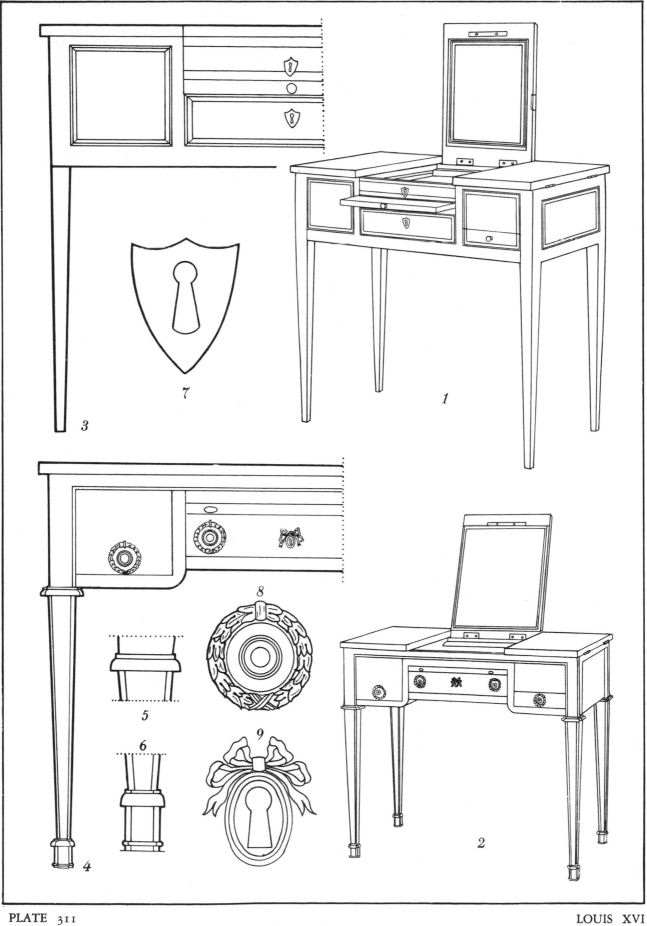

PLATE 311

LOUIS XVI

1. Vanity with marquetry and decorative lines of rosewood.  2. Mahogany vanity with bronzes.  3 and 4. Details of uprights and legs.  5 and 6. Details of moulding.  7, 8 and 9. Escutcheon plates and drawer pull.

*Museum of Decorative Arts, Paris*

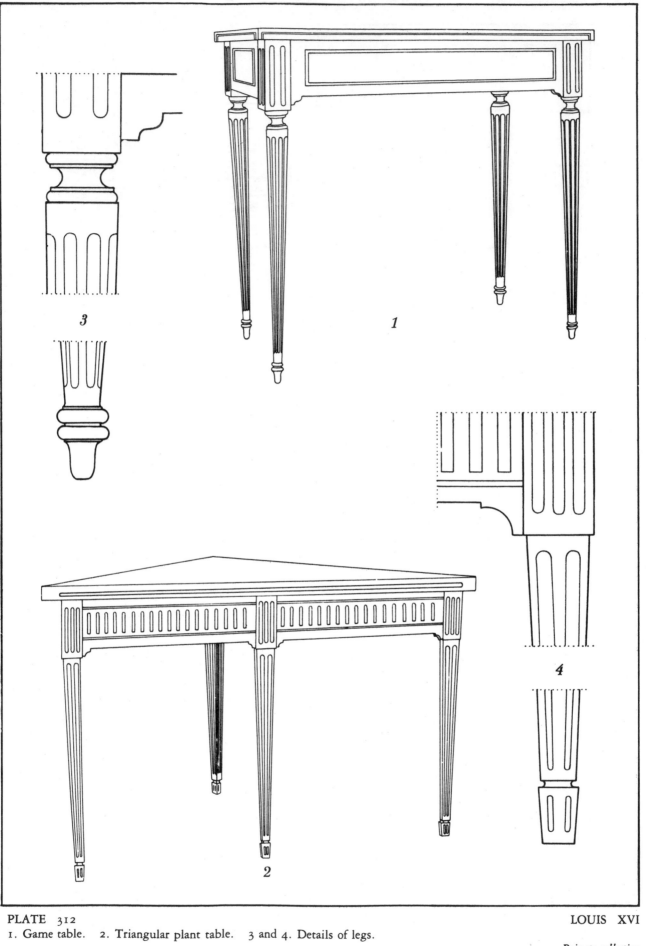

PLATE 312

1. Game table.    2. Triangular plant table.    3 and 4. Details of legs.

LOUIS XVI

*Private collection*

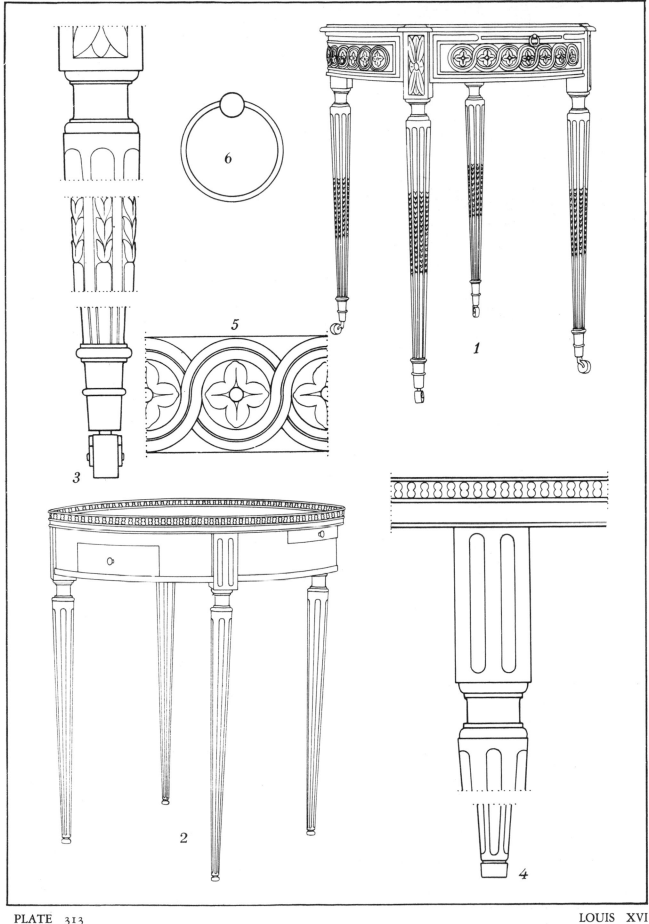

PLATE 313                                                          LOUIS XVI

1 and 2. Small game tables. The first table is of marble and gilt wood. The second one is of mahogany, copper and
marble.   3 and 4. Legs.   5. Decoration.   6. Drawer pull.

*Private collections*

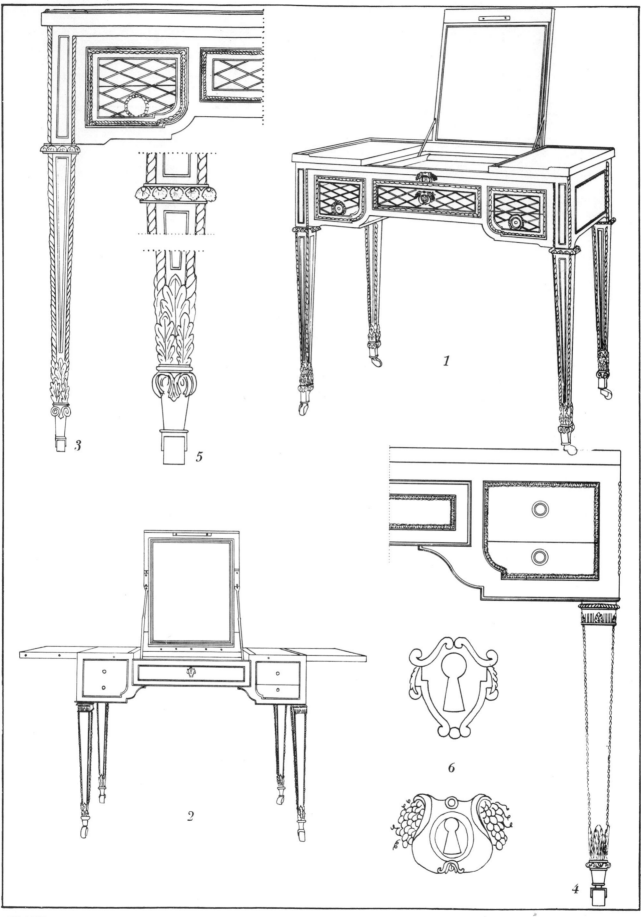

PLATE 314

LOUIS XVI

1 and 2. Mahogany vanities, with ornamented lines. The first one is outlined in gilt bronze, the second in marquetry.   3 and 4. Details of uprights and legs.   5. Detail of leg.   6. Escutcheon plates.

*Mobilier National de France and Petit Trianon*

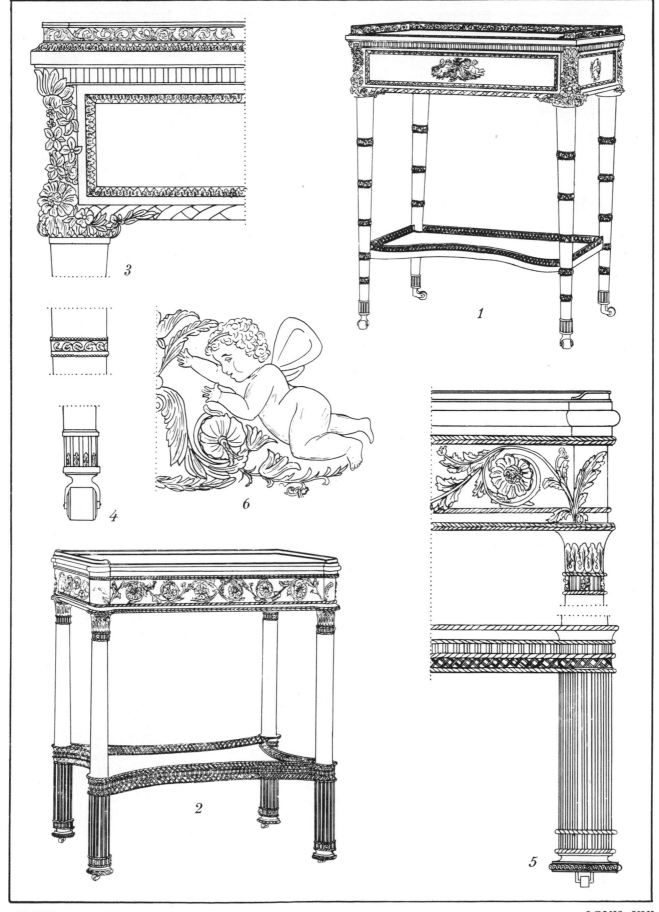

PLATE 315

1 and 2. Worktable and lady's desk, both of mahogany and decorated with gilt bronzes.  3, 4 and 5. Details of uprights.  6. Sketch of escutcheon plate.

*Louvre*

PLATE 316

LOUIS XVI (end of style)

1. Mahogany and ebony desk with carved gilt bronzes and a turquoise blue marble top.   2 and 3. Detail of top of upright and foot.   4, 5, 6 and 7. Bronze decorations.

*Fontainebleau Palace*

PLATE 317                                                                LOUIS XVI

1, 2 and 3. Small framed mirrors with finials of cut and very ornately carved wood.   4 and 5. Details of frames.

*Private collections*

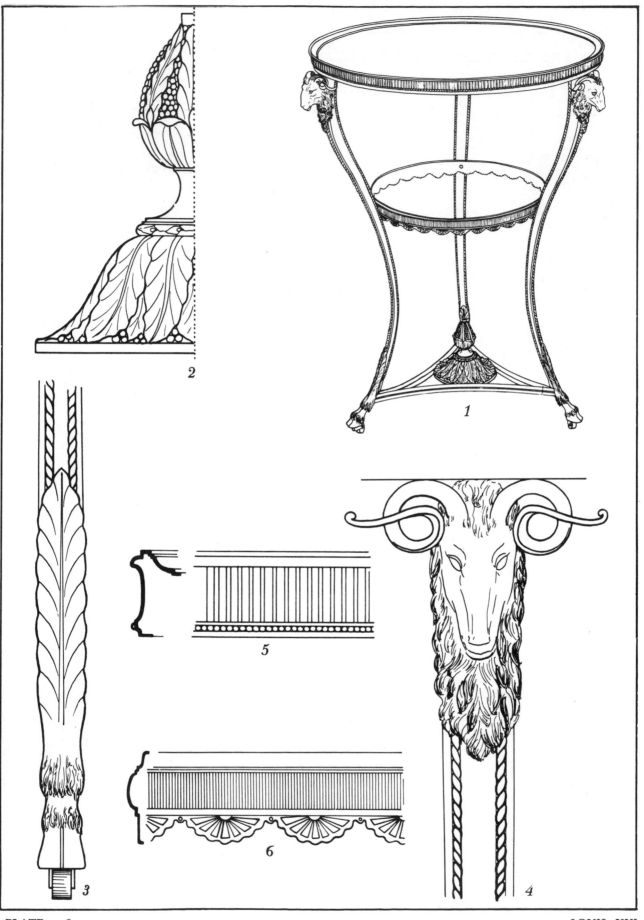

PLATE 318                                                                                    LOUIS XVI

1. Bronze pedestal table.   2. Detail of central finial.   3 and 4. Details of legs.   5 and 6. Mouldings.

*Champs-Élysée Palace*

PLATE 319

LOUIS XVI

1. Small circular pedestal table of mahogany with a marble top and bronze decorations.   2. Detail of wooden middle support and bronze side supports.   3. Lower moulding.

*Versailles Palace*

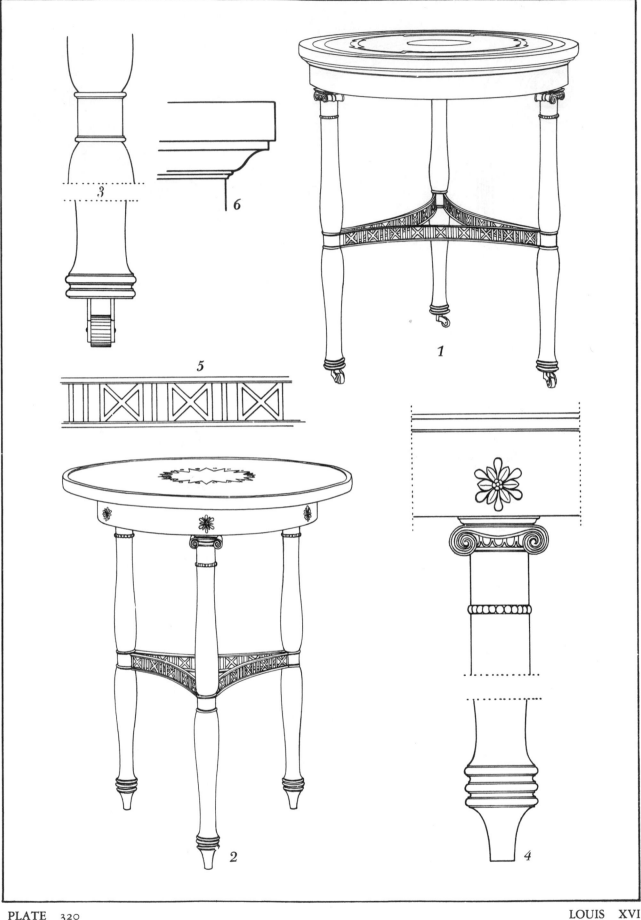

PLATE 320

LOUIS XVI

1 and 2. Small mahogany pedestal tables, with marble tops, bronze decorations and bronze festoons between the legs.  3 and 4. Legs.  5. Detail of festoon.  6. Profile of the moulding.

*Malmaison Castle and Fontainebleau Palace*

PLATE 321

1 and 2. Round mahogany pedestal tables with bronzes.   3 and 4. Details of legs.   5. Detail of upper trim and decorations.   6. Profile of same.

*Versailles Palace and Petit Trianon*

PLATE 322                                                                          LOUIS XVI

1 and 2. Commodes: The first one is characterized by severe lines; the second one, from the region of Provence, by
revolutionary emblems.    3. Detail of upright.    4 and 5. Drawer pulls.    6. Detail of upright.

*Private collections*

PLATE 323

LOUIS XVI (transition to Directoire)

1. Wardrobe with two doors (the escutcheon plate is in the style of Louis XV). 2 and 3. Details of escutcheon plate and hinge. 4 and 5. Cornice and base of leg.

*Private collection*

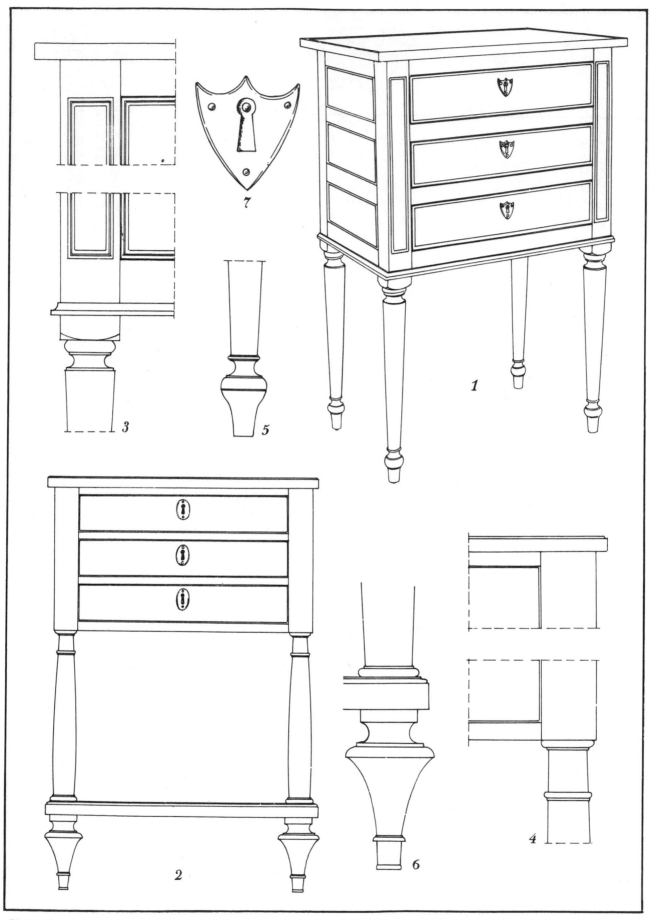

**PLATE** 324      END OF LOUIS XVI AND BEGINNING OF DIRECTOIRE (simplified style)
1. Small commode with three drawers.    2. Small sewing table.    3 and 4. Details of uprights.    5 and 6. Legs.    7. Escutcheon plate.

PLATE 325                    END OF LOUIS XVI AND BEGINNING OF DIRECTOIRE

1 and 2. Small sewing tables with two and three drawers.   3 and 4. Uprights.   5 and 6. Legs.   7 and 8. Cross section of uprights.

PLATE 326

END OF LOUIS XVI AND DIRECTOIRE

1 and 2. Small pedestal tables.    3 and 4. Supports.    5 and 6. Turned posts.    7 and 8. Balusters on lower shelf.

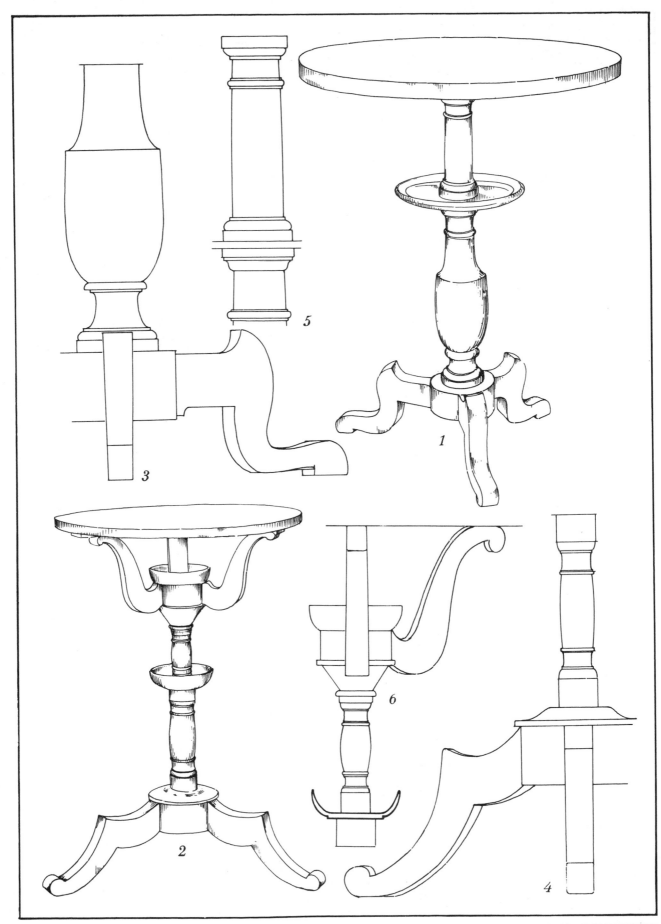

PLATE 327                                    END OF LOUIS XVI AND DIRECTOIRE

1 and 2. Small pedestal tables.    3 and 4. Supports.    5 and 6. Turned central posts.

PLATE 328

END OF LOUIS XVI AND DIRECTOIRE

1 and 2. Small pedestal tables.    3 and 4. Supports.    5 and 6. Turned central posts.

PLATE 329 END OF LOUIS XVI AND DIRECTOIRE

1 and 2. Small pedestal tables called "servantes" (servant girls) with three shelves.   3 and 4. Details of supports.   5 and 6. Turned central posts.

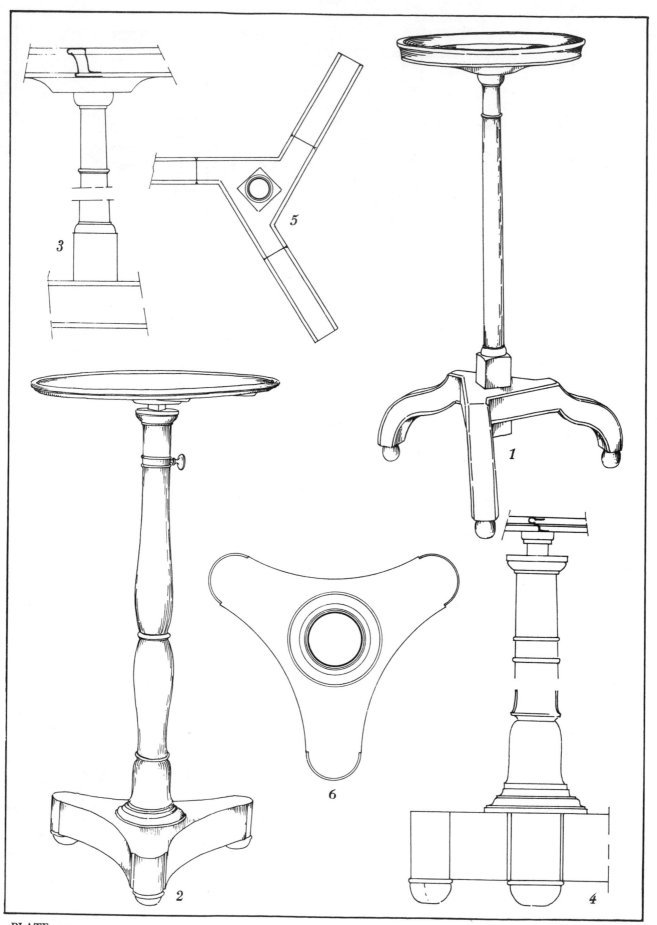

PLATE 330

1 and 2. Small pedestal tables.    3 and 4. Details of the supports.    5 and 6. Base of pedestals.

END OF LOUIS XVI AND DIRECTOIRE

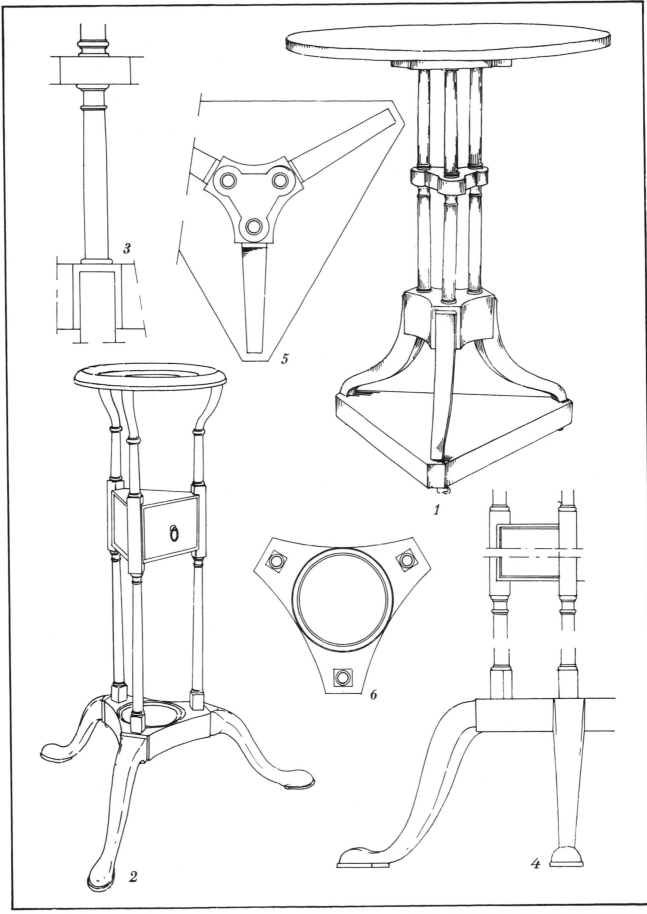

PLATE 331

1 and 2. Small pedestal side tables.    3 and 4. Supports.    5 and 6. Base of pedestals.

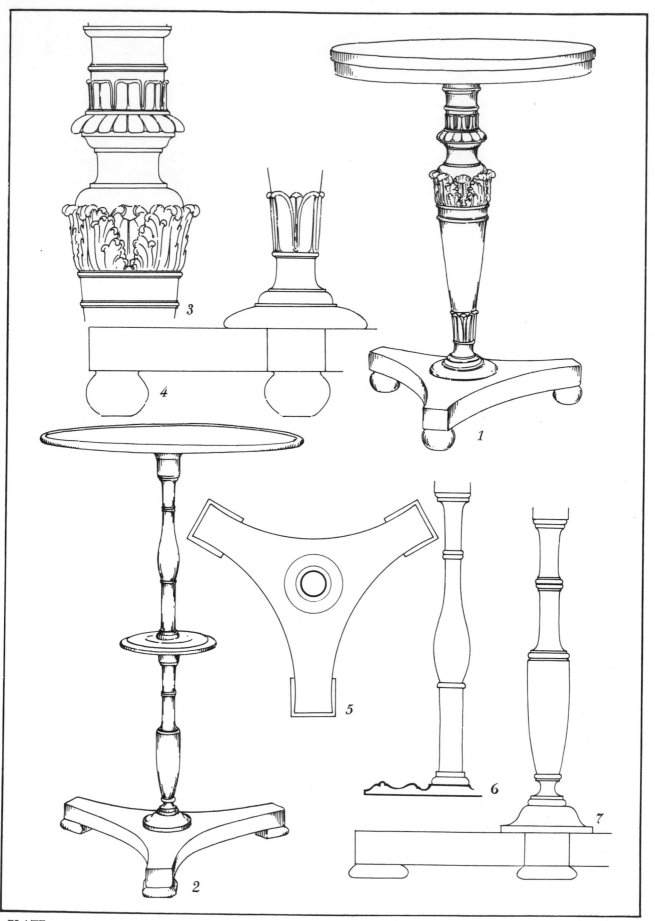

PLATE 332

END OF LOUIS XVI AND DIRECTOIRE

1 and 2. Small pedestal tables.   3 and 4. Details of the support.   5. Base.   6 and 7. Turned posts of second table.

PLATE 333          END OF LOUIS XVI

1. Mahogany and ebony commode with four drawers, carved gilt bronzes and turquoise blue marble.    2. Details of upright and leg.    3 and 4. Decorative drawer pulls.    5 and 6. Very elaborate large escutcheon plates.

*Fontainebleau Palace*

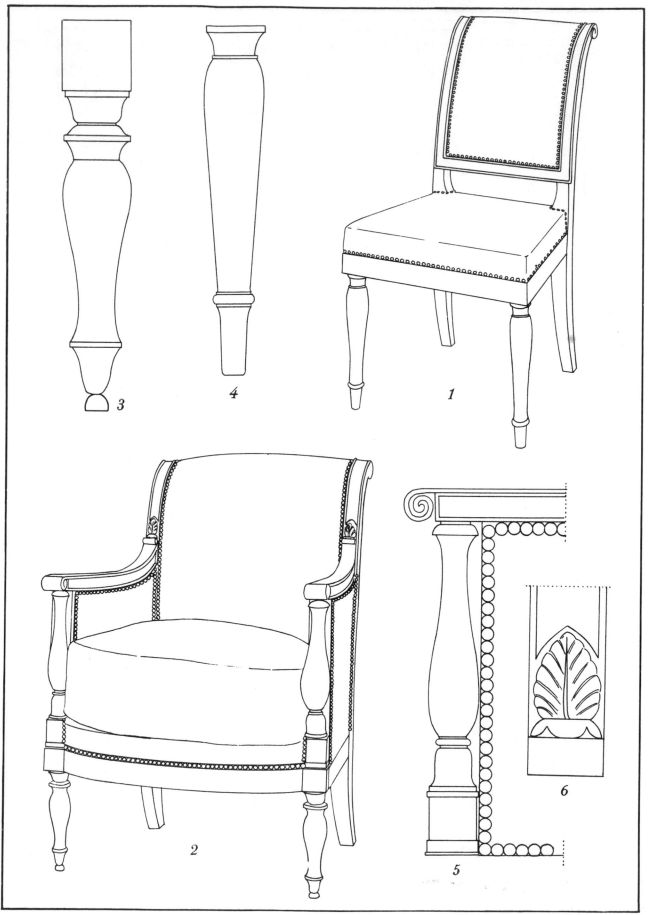

PLATE 334                                                           DIRECTOIRE

1. Mahogany chair with rolled back. Back and seat are covered with cloth and horsehair.   2. Mahogany wing chair.
Back is covered in silk.   3 and 4. Turned legs.   5. Arm support.   6. Detail of carving on upright.

*Malmaison Castle and Compiègne Palace*

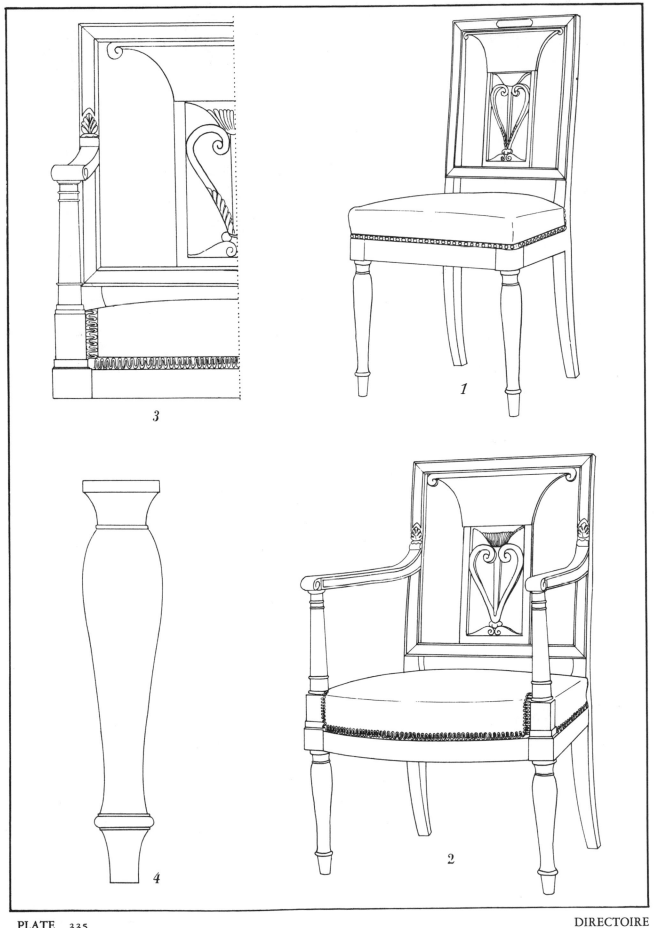

PLATE 335                                                                              DIRECTOIRE

1 and 2. Mahogany chair and armchair with openwork backs. Seat of first one is covered with leather, of second one with velvet.   3. Detail of straight back.   4. Leg.

*Malmaison Castle and Mobilier National de France*

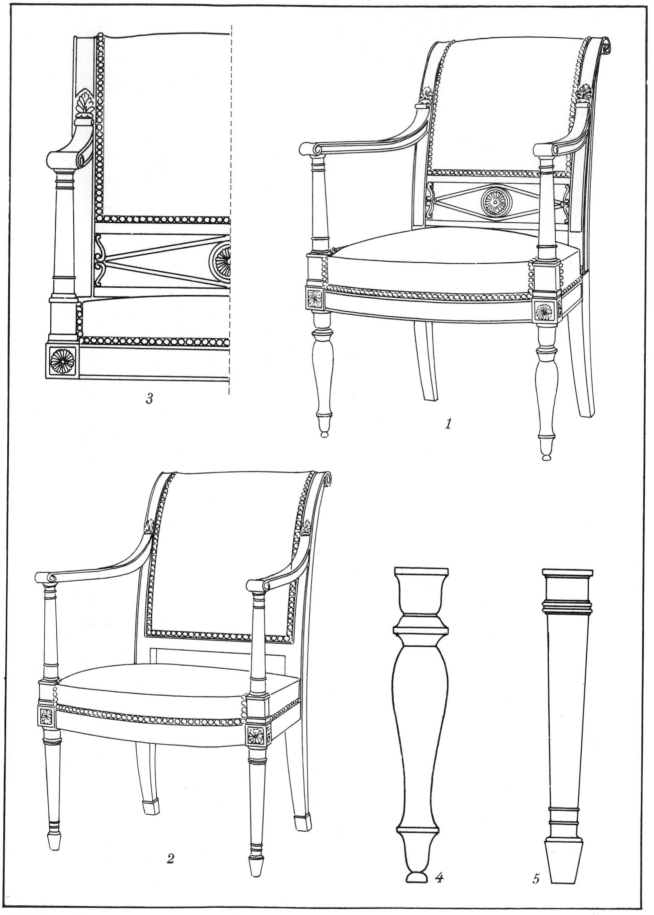

PLATE 336                                                                                                DIRECTOIRE

1 and 2. Mahogany armchairs covered in silk and leather, respectively.   3. Detail of back.   4 and 5. Turned legs in
baluster and conical shapes which define this style.

*Compiègne Palace*

PLATE 337

1. Small mahogany chair with rolled openwork back and silk seat.   2. Mahogany chair with rolled openwork back and low seat, to go next to the fireplace.   3. Leg.   4. Scroll of rolled back.   5. Detail of back.   6. Rosette on rear upright.

*Fontainebleau Palace*

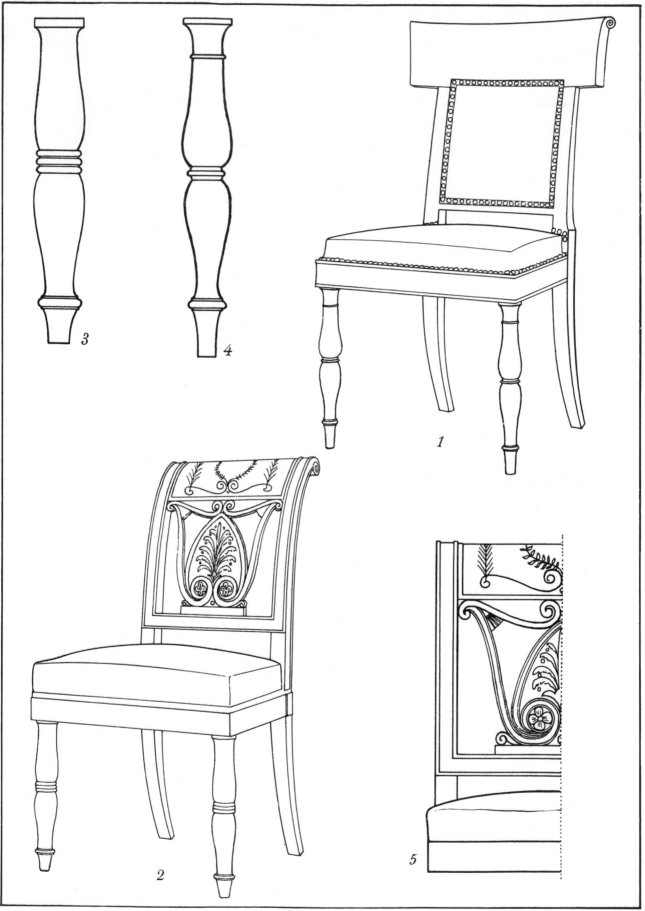

PLATE 338

1 and 2. Mahogany chairs. The first chair has a cylindrical back; the second one has a rolled back.    3 and 4. Legs.    5. Back.

*Fontainebleau Palace*

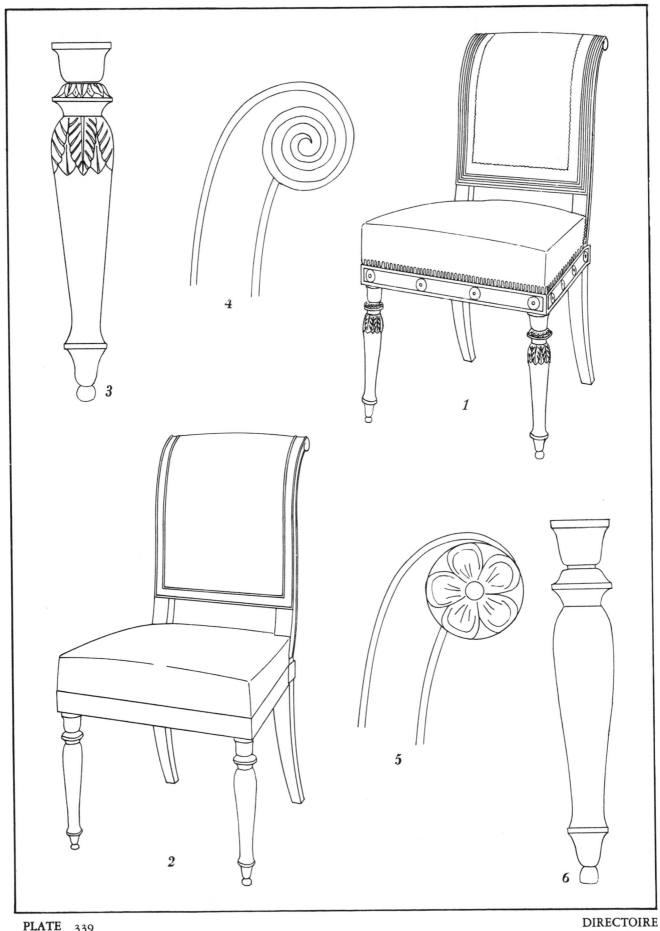

PLATE 339                                                                                                    DIRECTOIRE

1 and 2. Chairs with rolled backs and turned legs.   3 and 4. Leg and scroll on back of first chair.   5 and 6. Leg
and scroll of second chair.

*Malmaison Castle*

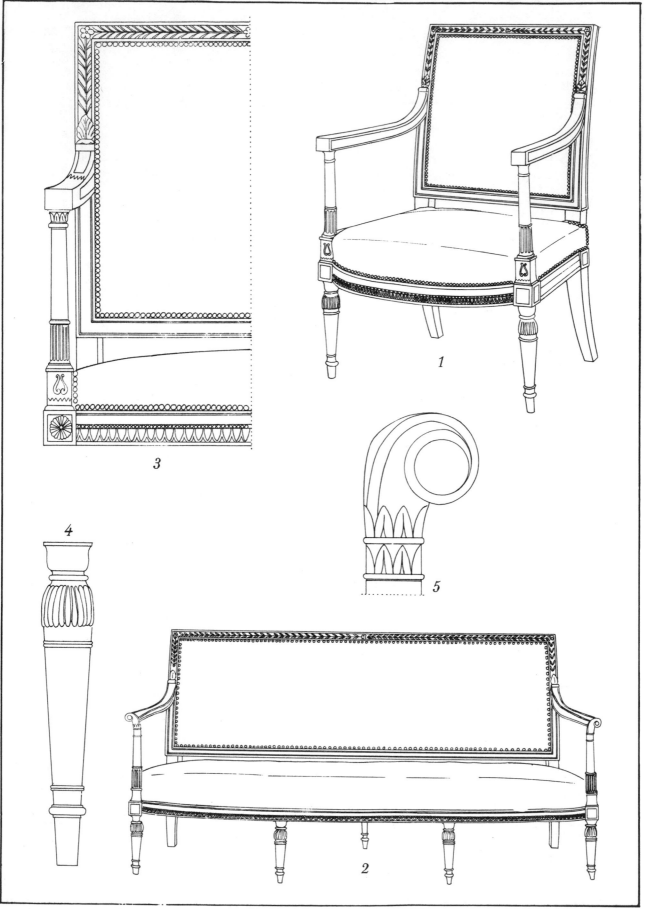

PLATE 340                                                                                    DIRECTOIRE

1 and 2. Carved wooden armchair and sofa, painted grey and covered with Beauvais tapestry.   3. Back.   4. Leg.   5. Scroll at end of arm.

*Fontainebleau Palace*

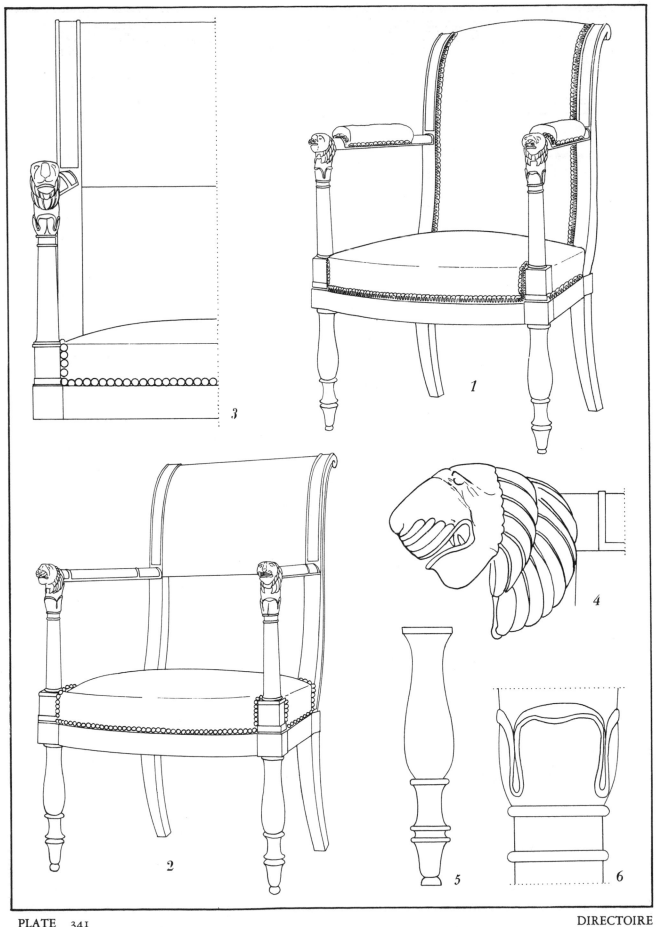

PLATE 341                                                                                  DIRECTOIRE

1 and 2. Mahogany armchairs with rolled backs, arms ending in lions' heads and covered in silk and velvet.   3. Back.   4. End of arm.   5. Turned leg.   6. Detail of arm support.

*Mobilier National de France*

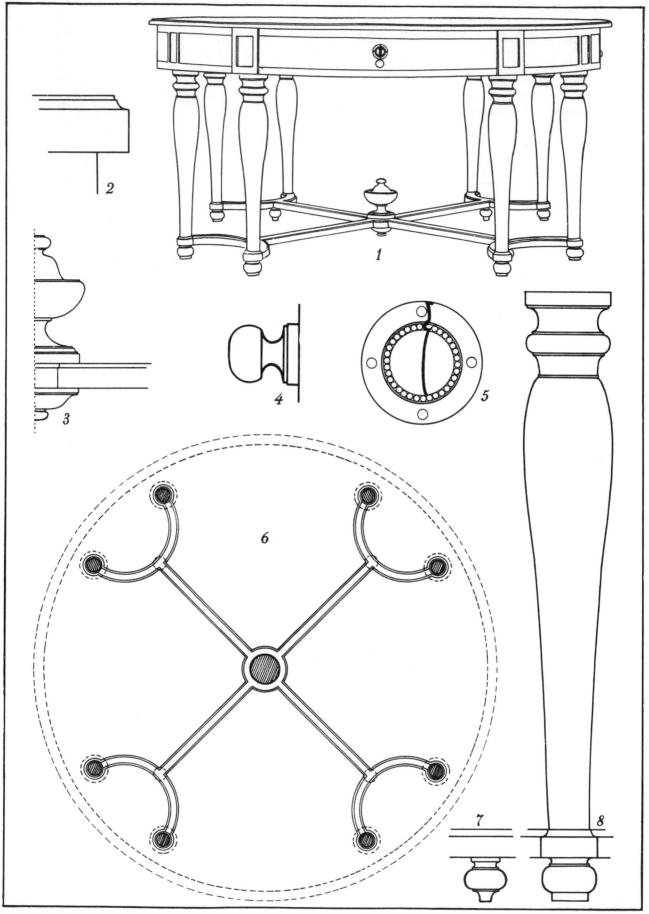

PLATE 342

DIRECTOIRE (beginning of style)

1. Round table of blackened beechwood with eight turned legs.   2. Upper moulding.   3. Central finial.   4 and 5. Drawer pull and escutcheon plate on drawer.   6. Base.   7 and 8. Leg and details of feet.

*National Archive (Spain)*

PLATE 343                                                      DIRECTOIRE (beginning)

1 and 2. Console tables of Brazilian rosewood and pear.   3 and 4. Details of uprights.   5, 6 and 7. Drawer pulls and escutcheon plate.

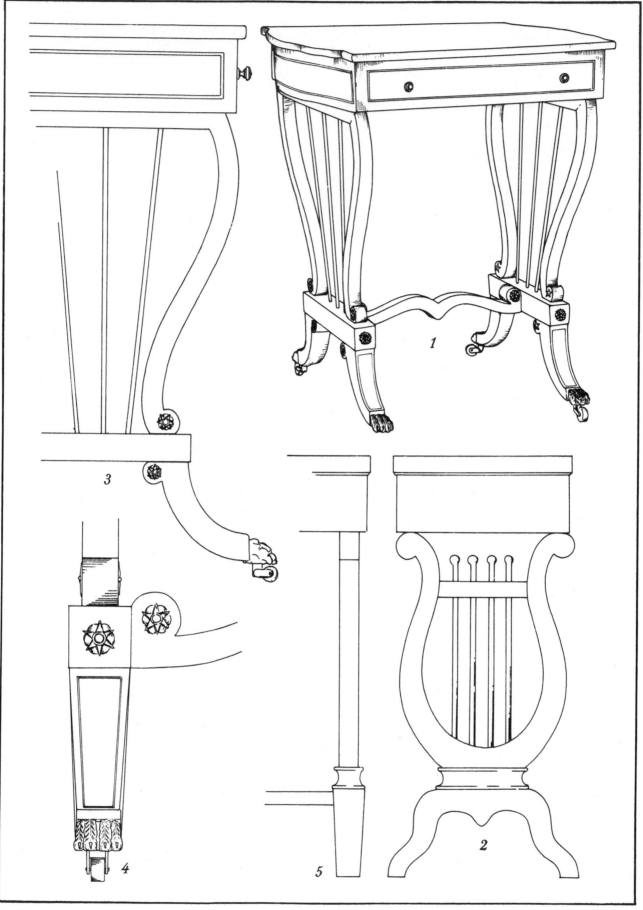

PLATE 344
1 and 2. Small worktables.    3. Side view.    4 and 5. Legs.

DIRECTOIRE

*Private collection*

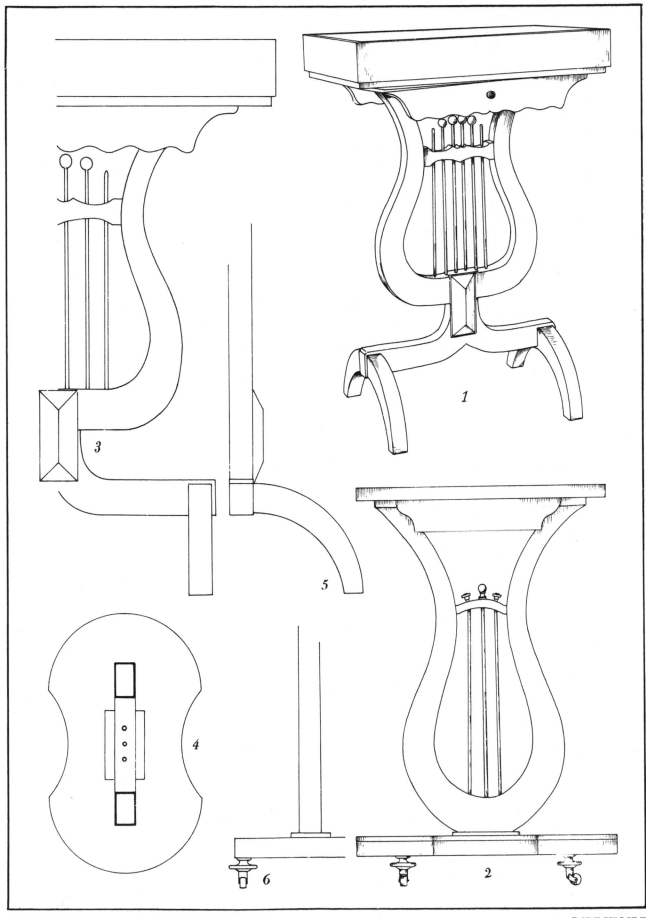

PLATE 345
1 and 2. Small knitting tables called "knitters."   3. Detail.   4. Shape of lower bracket.   5 and 6. Legs.

*Private collection*

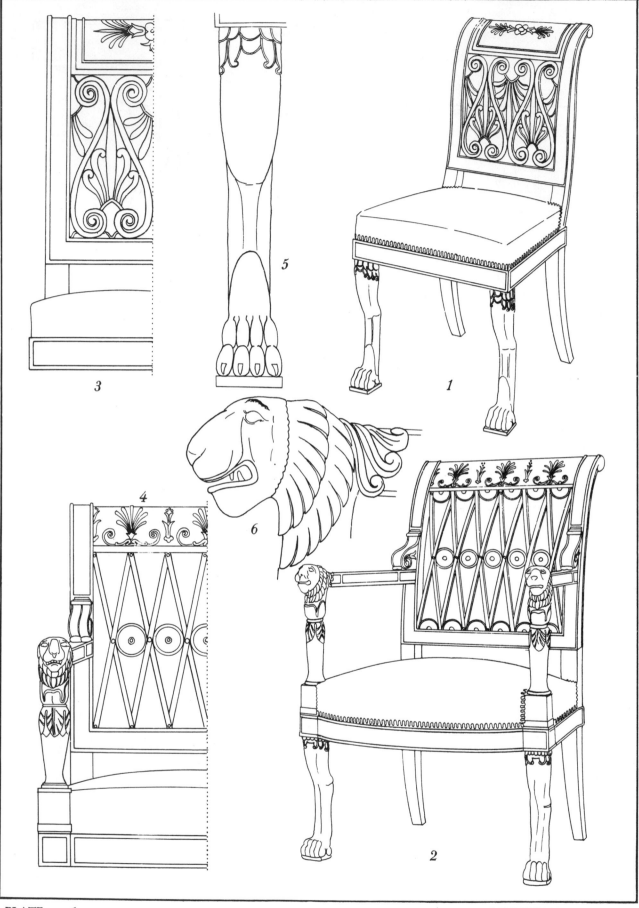

PLATE 346                                                  DIRECTOIRE  (Consulate)

1. Mahogany chair with rolled openwork back and clawed feet.  2. Mahogany armchair with arms ending in lion's head and rolled openwork back.  3 and 4. Backs.  5. Legs.  6. Arm end.

*Malmaison Castle and Mobilier National de France*

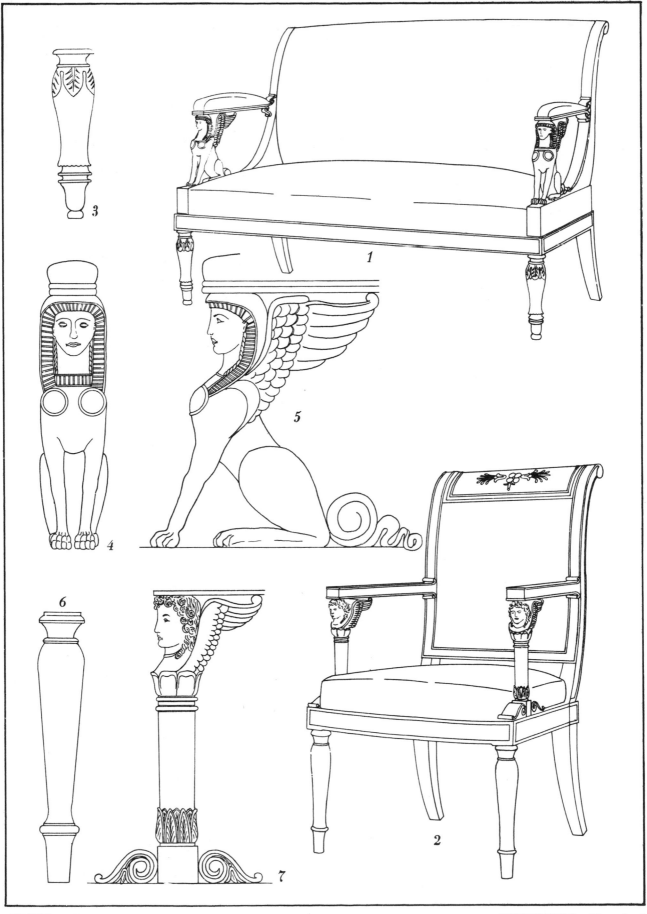

PLATE 347                                                                    DIRECTOIRE   (Consulate)

1 and 2. Sofa and armchair with rolled backs and arm supports in the shape of winged chimeras and women's heads.   3,
4 and 5. Leg and arm support from sofa.   6 and 7. Leg and arm support from armchair.

*Mobilier National de France*

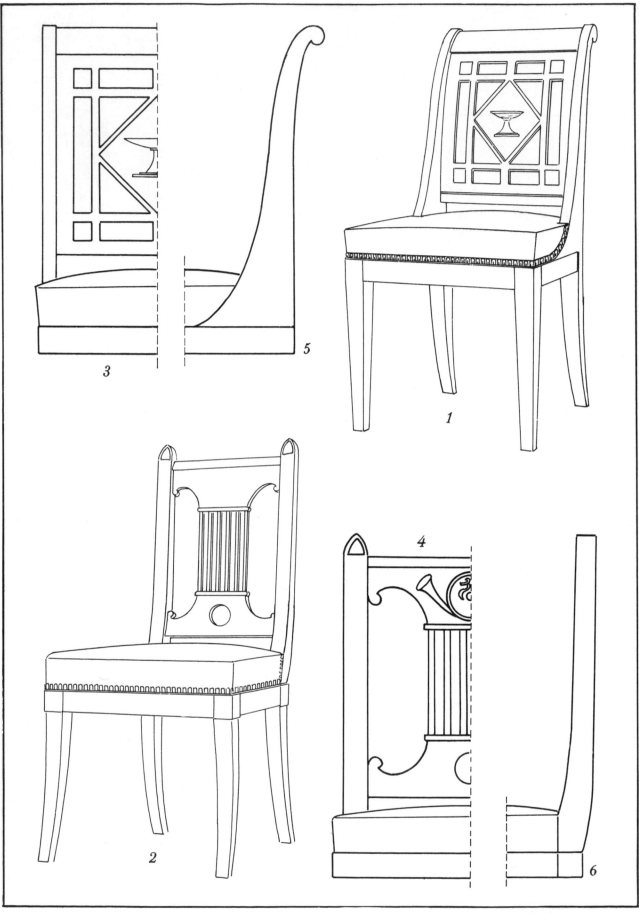

PLATE 348

DIRECTOIRE (Consulate)

1 and 2. Mahogany armchairs with openwork backs and square legs, the rear ones slightly curved. The first chair has a rolled back, the second chair, a straight one. 3 and 4. Backs. 5 and 6. Profile of backs.

*Mobilier National de France and Fontainebleau Palace*

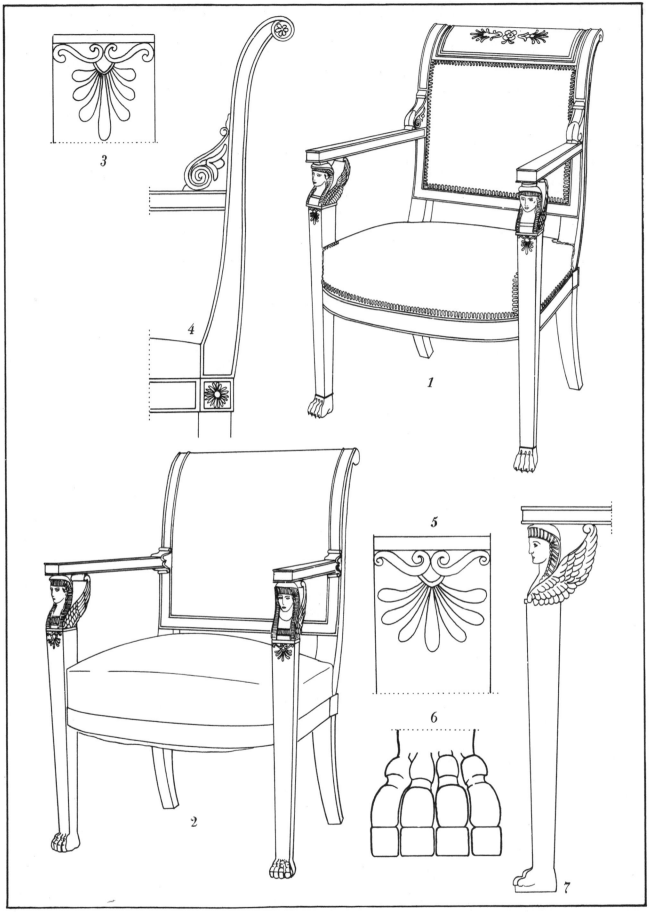

PLATE 349 DIRECTOIRE (Consulate)

1 and 2. Mahogany armchairs, the arms supported by Egyptian heads.   3 and 4. Decoration and back.   5, 6 and 7. Decoration on leg and clawed foot.

*Malmaison Castle and Mobilier National de France*

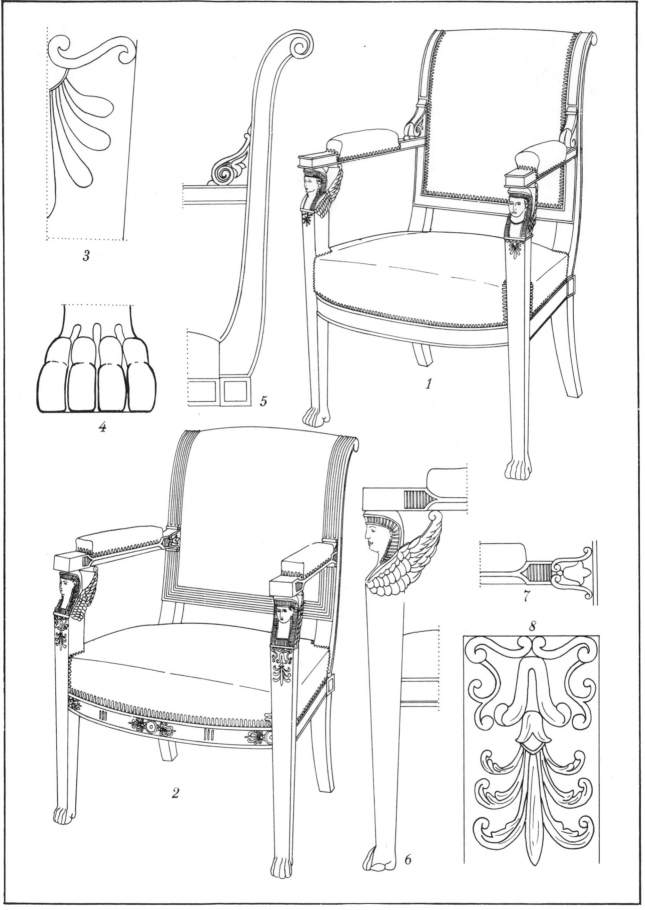

PLATE 350                DIRECTOIRE (Consulate)

1 and 2. Gilt carved wooden armchair, arms supported by Egyptian heads, and rolled backs. 3, 4 and 5. Details of leg ornamentation and back of first chair. 6, 7 and 8. Decorative legs and connection of arms to back.

*Malmaison Castle*

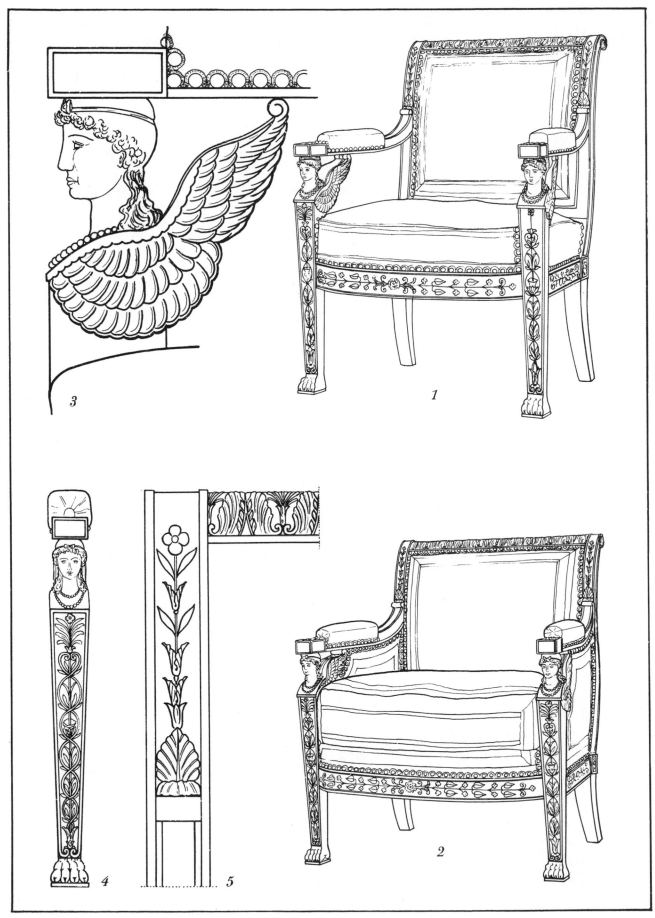

PLATE 351                                                                                        DIRECTOIRE (Consulate)

1 and 2. Armchairs with rolled backs and arms supported by winged Egyptian heads. The second one is a wing chair.   3.
Detail of arm support.   4. Leg.   5. Back upright.

*Mobilier National de France*

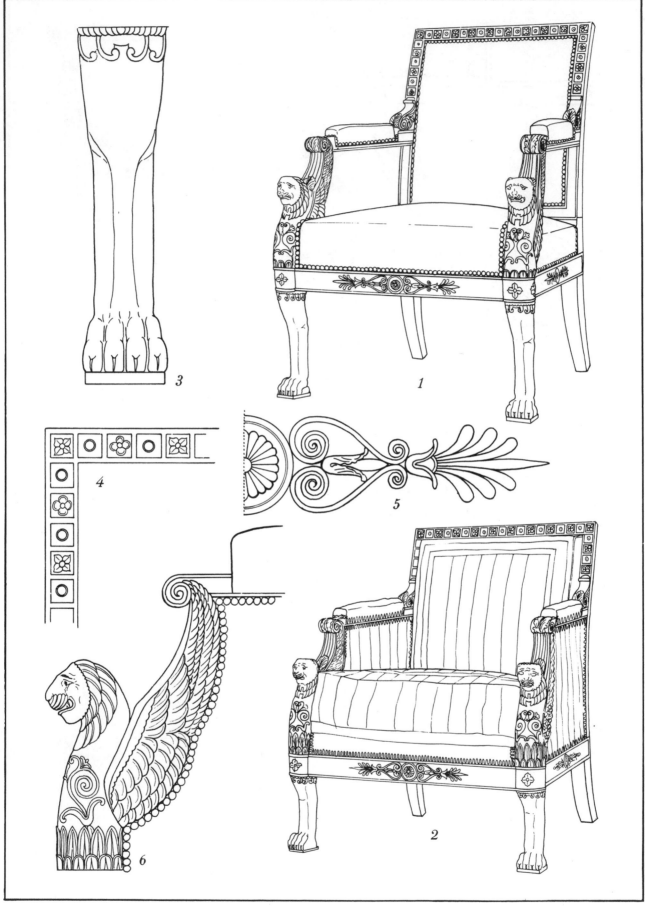

PLATE 352                                                   DIRECTOIRE  (Consulate)

1 and 2. Armchairs with straight backs and arms supported by carved winged leopards' heads. The second one is a wing chair.   3. Leg.   4 and 5. Decorations.   6. Detail of arm support.

*Mobilier National de France*

PLATE 353                                                    DIRECTOIRE (end of Consulate)
1 and 2. Daybeds of gilt carved wood.   3. Side support.   4. Detail of support.   5. Carved design.   6. Clawed
foot.

*Mobilier National de France*

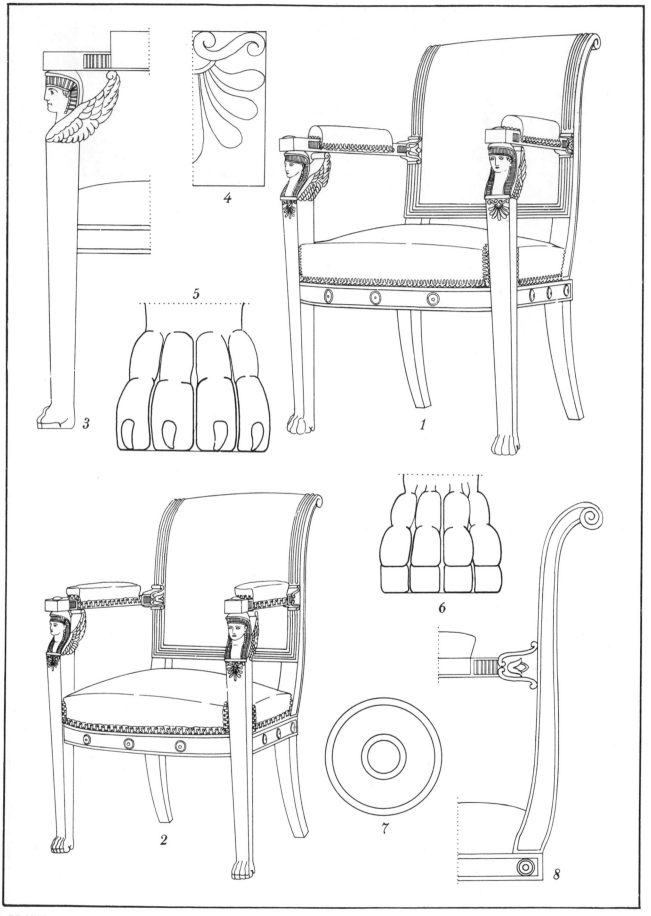

**PLATE 354**  DIRECTOIRE (end of Consulate and beginning of Empire)
1 and 2. Gilt carved wooden armchairs with rolled backs and arms supported by Egyptian heads.  3, 4 and 5. Details of leg, decoration and clawed foot of first chair.  6, 7 and 8. Details of back, foot and decorative disk.

*Fontainebleau Palace and Mobilier National de France*

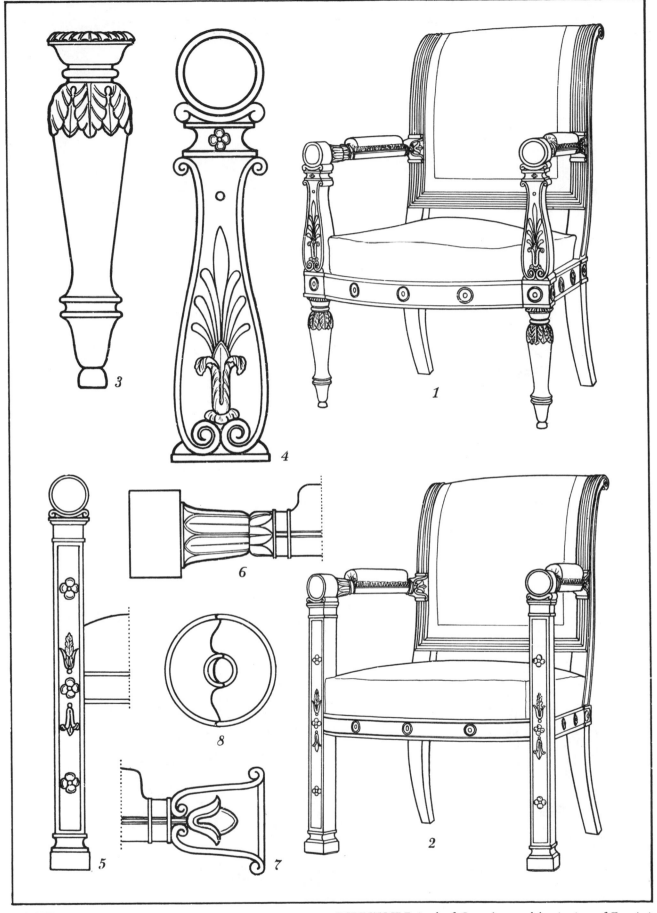

PLATE 355                                     DIRECTOIRE (end of Consulate and beginning of Empire)
1 and 2. Gilt carved wooden armchairs with rolled backs.    3 and 4. Leg and arm support.    5. Leg and support.    6
and 7. Details of connections of arm with support and with back.    8. Decorative disk.

*Mobilier National de France and Fontainebleau Palace*

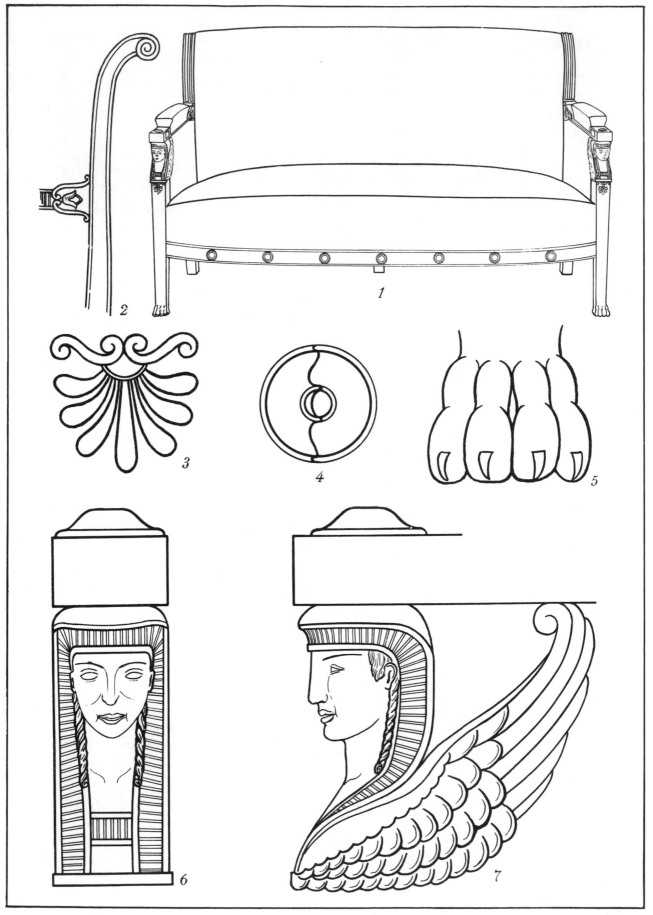

**PLATE** 356 DIRECTOIRE (end of Consulate and beginning of Empire)
1. Gilt carved wooden sofa with rolled back, arm supports end in Egyptian heads. 2. Back. 3, 4 and 5. Decoration, disk and clawed foot. 6 and 7. Details of Egyptian woman's head.

*Mobilier National de France*

PLATE 357

EMPIRE (Consulate period)
1 and 2. Portable mahogany mirrors with bronzes.   3 and 4. Details of uprights.   5. Clawed foot.

*Mobilier National de France and Fontainebleau Palace*

**PLATE** 358          EMPIRE (Consulate period)

1 and 2. Portable mahogany mirrors with bronzes.    3, 4 and 5. Details of uprights of first mirror.    6. Support.    7. Rosette.    8. Decoration.

*Mobilier National de France*

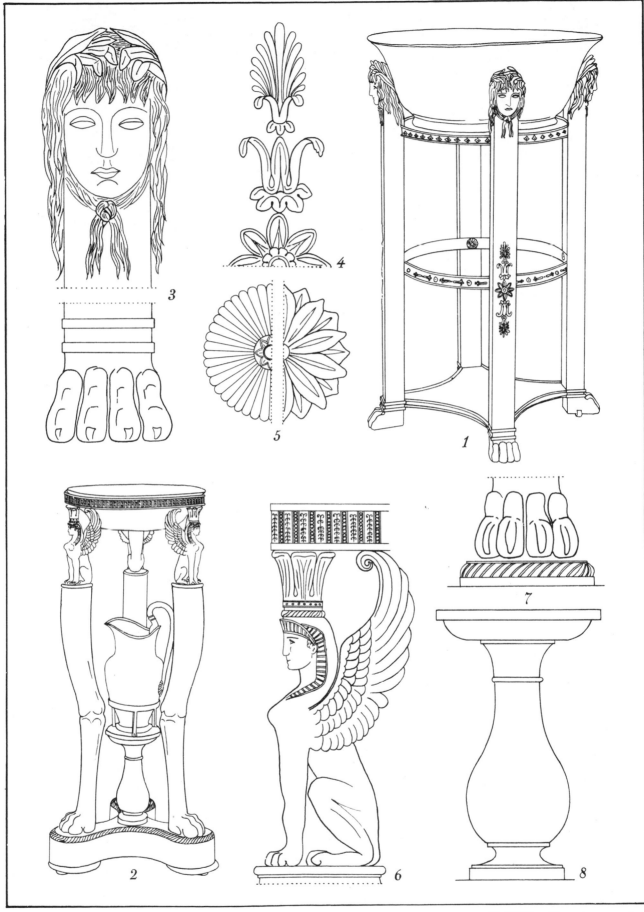

PLATE 359                                                    EMPIRE  (Consulate  period)

1 and 2. "Athenian" mahogany washstands with gilt bronzes, with decorated basins of Sèvres porcelains.   3. Upright and clawed foot.   4 and 5. Details of decorations and rosettes.   6. Detail of upright.   7. Claws.   8. Turned support for pitcher.

*Malmaison Castle*

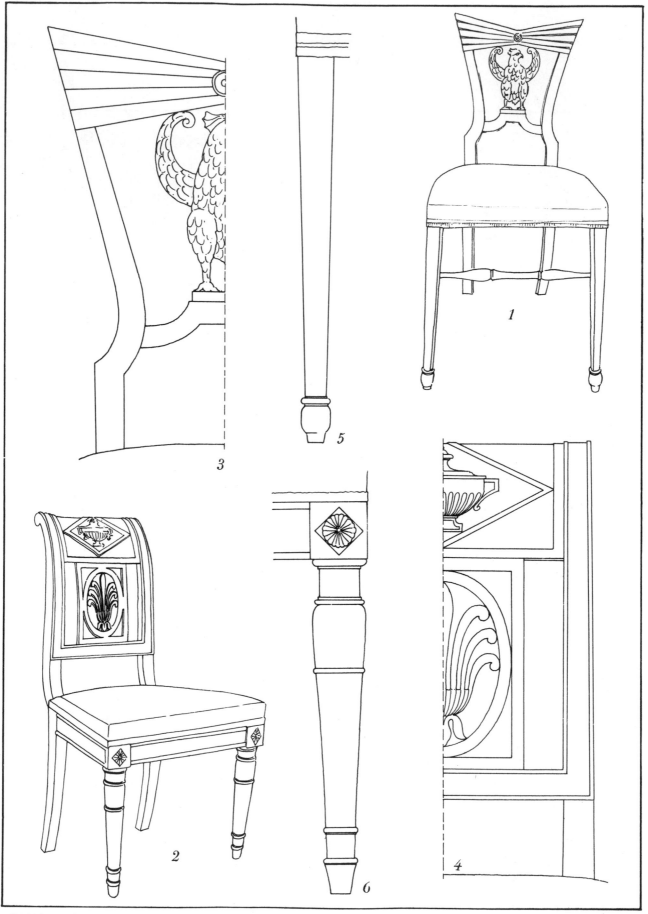

PLATE 360

1. Mahogany chair from time of Revolution.  2. Chair with rolled back.  3 and 4. Details of backs.  5 and 6. Legs.

*Private collections*

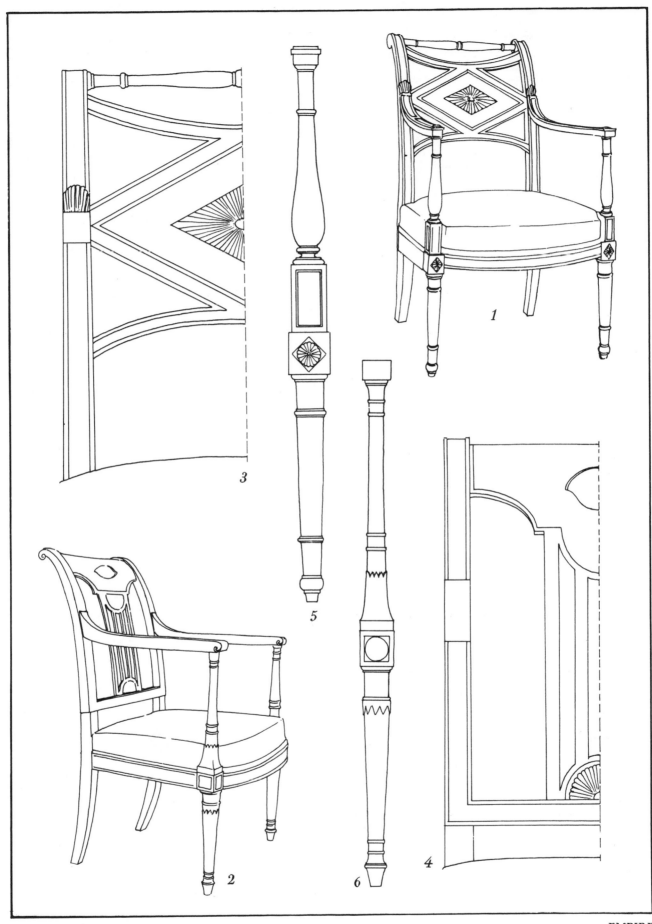

**PLATE** 361

EMPIRE

1 and 2. Painted wooden armchairs with openwork backs, which curve backwards at top.   3 and 4. Details of backs.   5 and 6. Legs and arm supports.

*Private collections*

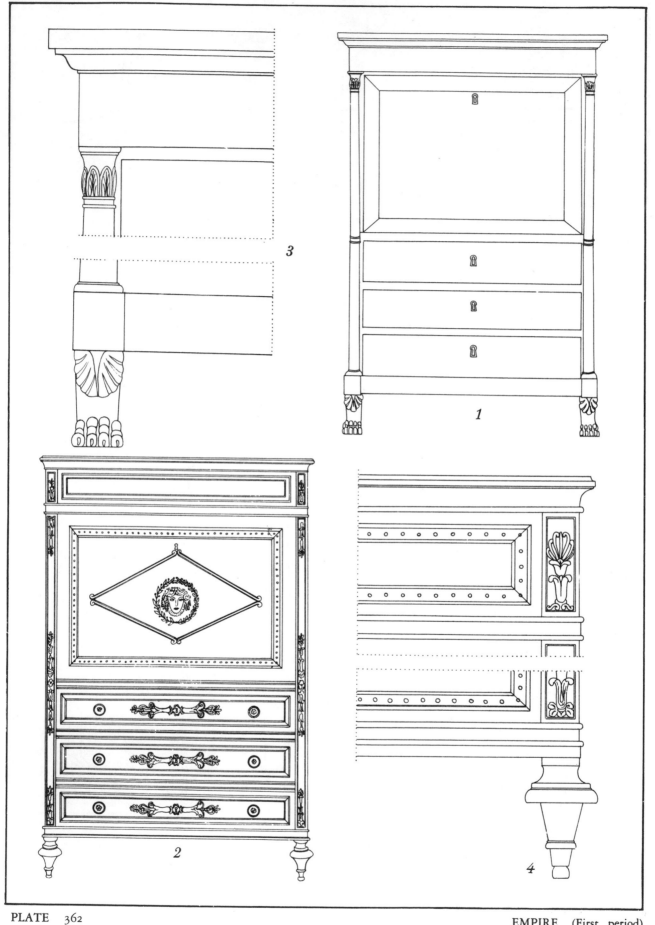

PLATE 362                                                                 EMPIRE   (First period)

1 and 2. Wardrobes of mahogany, and mahogany and lemonwood, respectively, with carved gilt bronzes. The second
one is by Georges Jacob (around 1795).   3 and 4. Details of uprights and legs.

*Mobilier National de France and private collection*

PLATE 363                                                            EMPIRE   (beginning)

1. Mahogany commode with straight lines, three drawers and clawed feet.   2. Mahogany commode with short baluster-
shaped legs and uprights decorated with palm leaves in Consulate style.   3. Marble moulding.   4, 5 and 6. Rosette,
escutcheon plate and bronze drawer pull.   7. Detail of upright.   8 and 9. Copper drawer pull and bronze escutcheon
plate.

*Private collections, Paris and elsewhere*

PLATE 364

1. Straight-line commode on crosspiece ending in clawed feet.   2. Mahogany commode with three drawers, like the previous one, with uprights in the shape of small columns.   3 and 4. Details of uprights.   5 and 6. Escutcheon plate and central decoration of bronze frieze.

PLATE 365

1. Entredeux console, placed between two windows, with two unequal hinged doors and one drawer. 2. Partial view of another entredeux. 3. Detail of thyrsus. 4 and 5. Detail of friezes. 6 and 7. Profiles.

*Ministry of Foreign Affairs and Bardac collection*

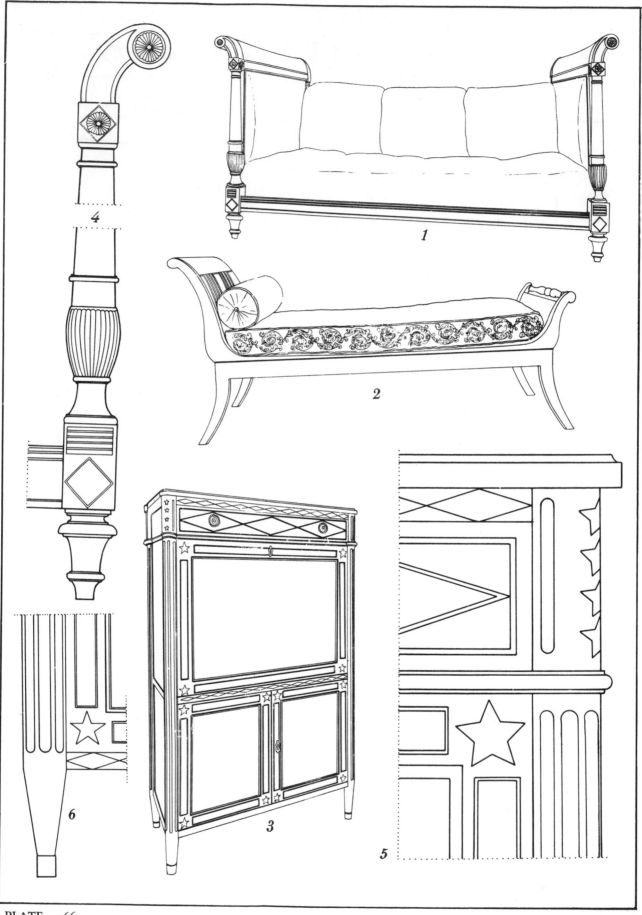

PLATE 366

1. Painted wooden bed with rolled back, from the early period.   2. Chaise longue with unequal ends.   3. Mahogany secretary, with inlaid copper, from the early period.   4. Upright and leg of bed.   5. Upper detail of secretary.   6. Detail of upright and leg of secretary.

*Private collections*

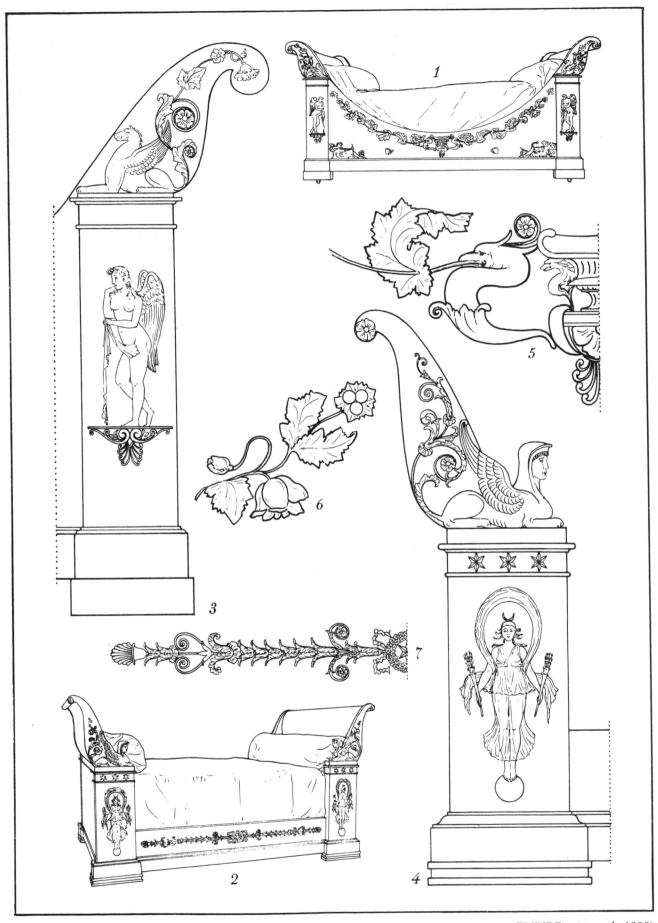

PLATE 367

EMPIRE (around 1800)

1 and 2. Beds. 3 and 4. Details of uprights. 5, 6 and 7. Sketches of the decorations.

*Museum of Decorative Arts, Paris*

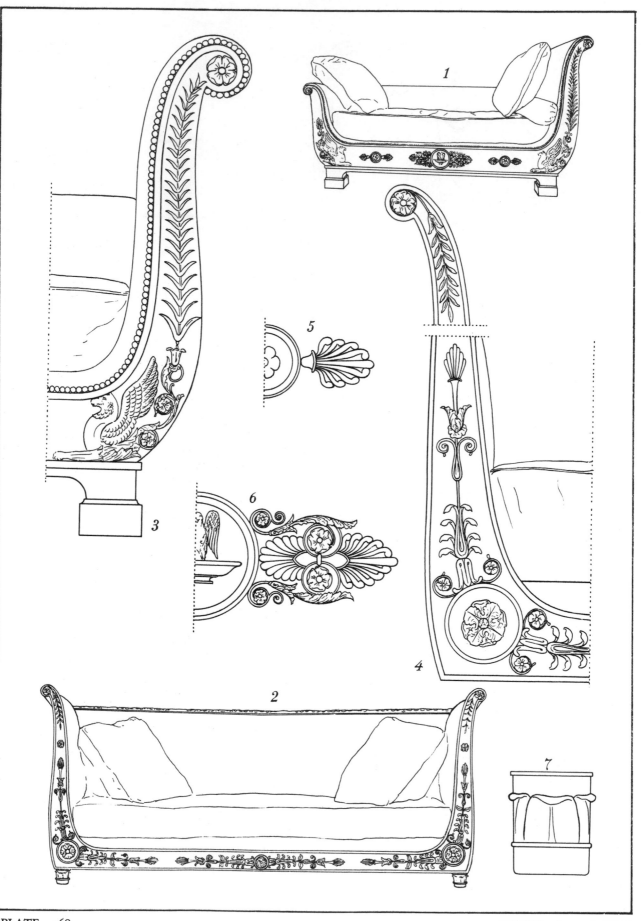

PLATE 368

1 and 2. Sofas or daybeds.    3 and 4. Details of uprights.    5, 6 and 7. Sketches of decorations and foot.

EMPIRE   (around  1800)

*Museum of Decorative Arts, Paris*

372

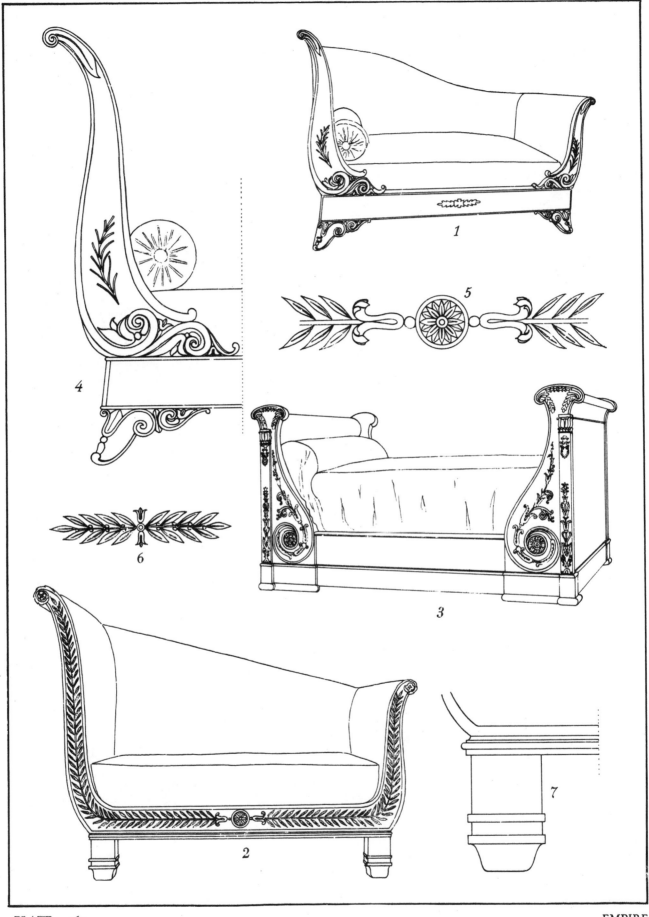

PLATE 369
EMPIRE

1 and 2. Daybeds.    3. Napoleon's bed.    4. Detail of upright.    5 and 6. Details of decorations.    7. Leg.

*Private collection, Compiègne Castle and Grand Trianon*

PLATE 370

EMPIRE

1. Cradle of the King of Rome.   2. Bed designed by Percier and Fontaine.   3. Detail of cradle.   4 and 5. Front and bottom of base.   6. Detail of column.   7. Detail of upright.

*Fontainebleau Palace and album of Percier and Fontaine*

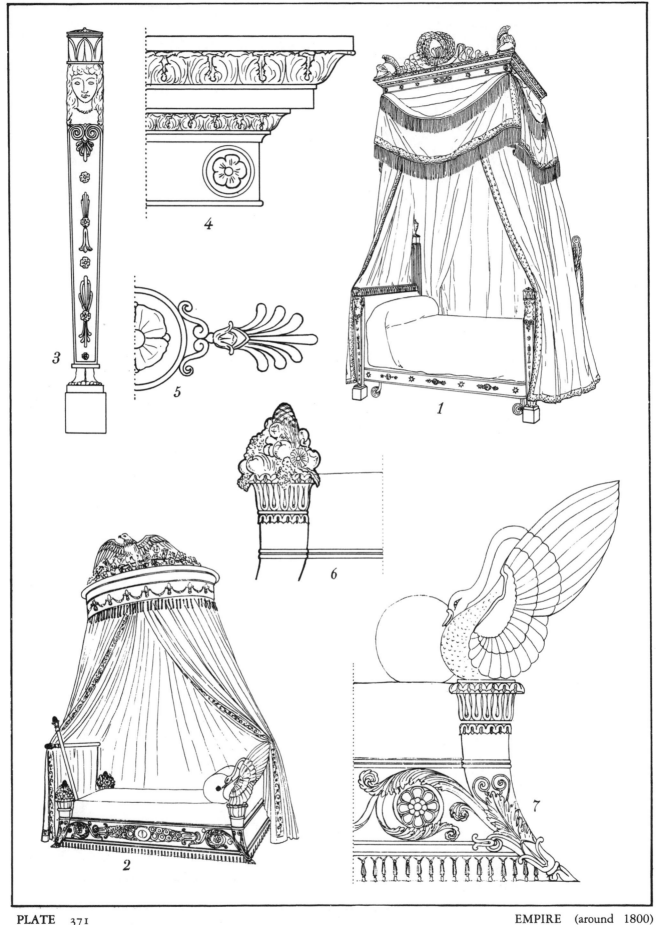

PLATE 371

EMPIRE (around 1800)

1 and 2. Elegant beds (the second one belonged to the Empress Josephine). 3 Detail of upright. 4. Cornice. 5. Decoration. 6 and 7. Details of corner supports.

*Fontainebleau Palace and Malmaison Castle*

375

PLATE 372

EMPIRE (around 1800)

1. Elegant table.  2. Details of uprights.  3. Brace.  4. Profile of moulding.  5. Detail of decorative vase at bottom.

*Grand Trianon*

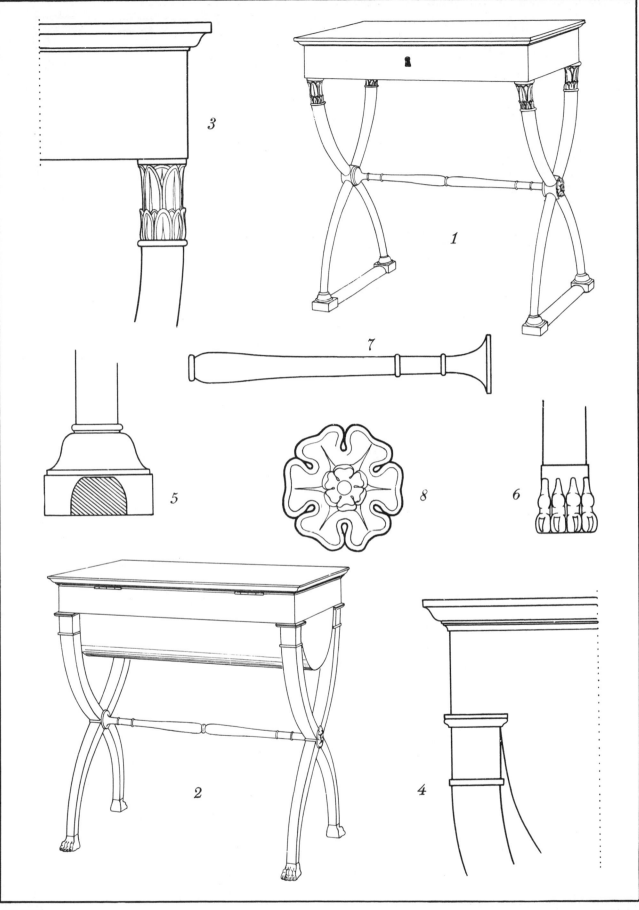

PLATE 373

EMPIRE

1 and 2. Small mahogany worktables with legs in X, carved gilt bronze decorations. 3 and 4. Details of top of legs. 5 and 6. Lower part of legs. 7. Profile of turned crosspiece. 8. Button trim.

*Grand Trianon and Petit Trianon*

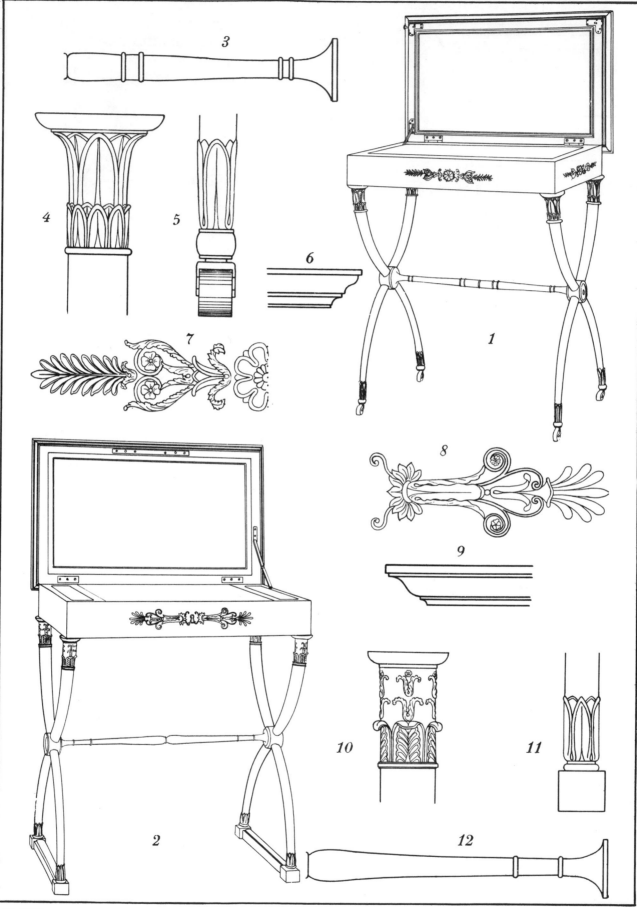

PLATE 374

EMPIRE

1 and 2. Small mahogany worktables with legs in X, with gilt bronze decorations. 3, 4, 5, 6 and 7. Details of upper table. 8, 9, 10, 11 and 12. Details of lower table.

*Fontainebleau Palace and Malmaison Castle*

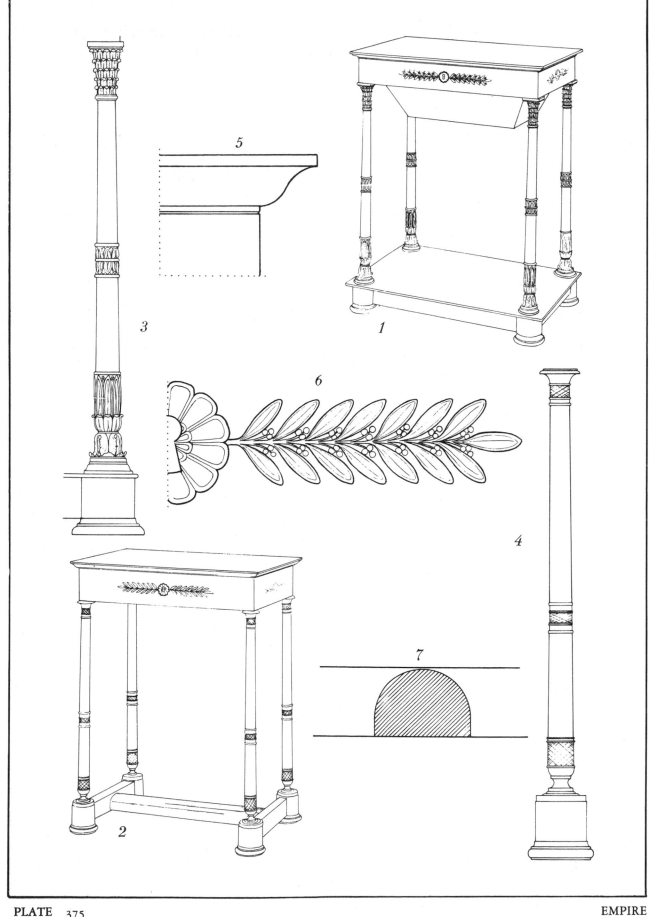

PLATE 375                                                                                                    EMPIRE

1 and 2. Small mahogany worktables with turned uprights and bronzes, used by the Empress Josephine and Marie-Louise.   3 and 4. Details of uprights.   5. Upper moulding.   6. Sketch of bronze escutcheon plate.   7. Cross section of lower crosspiece.

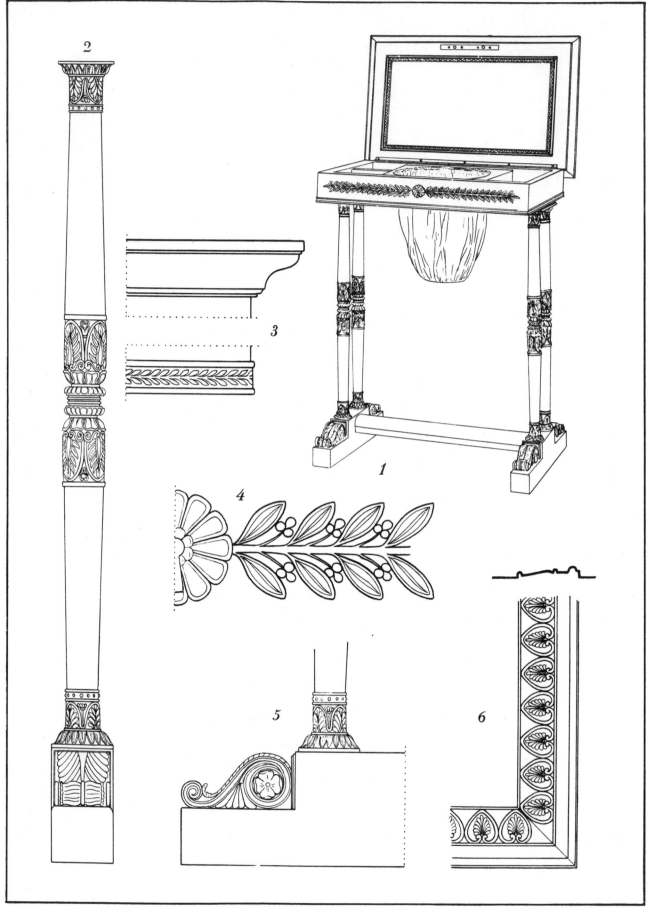

PLATE 376 EMPIRE

1. Small mahogany worktable, decorated with bronzes, which belonged to Empress Josephine.   2. Detail of column.   3. Moulding on lid and front of table.   4. Escutcheon plate.   5. Detail of foot.   6. Moulding on inside of lid.

*Malmaison Castle*

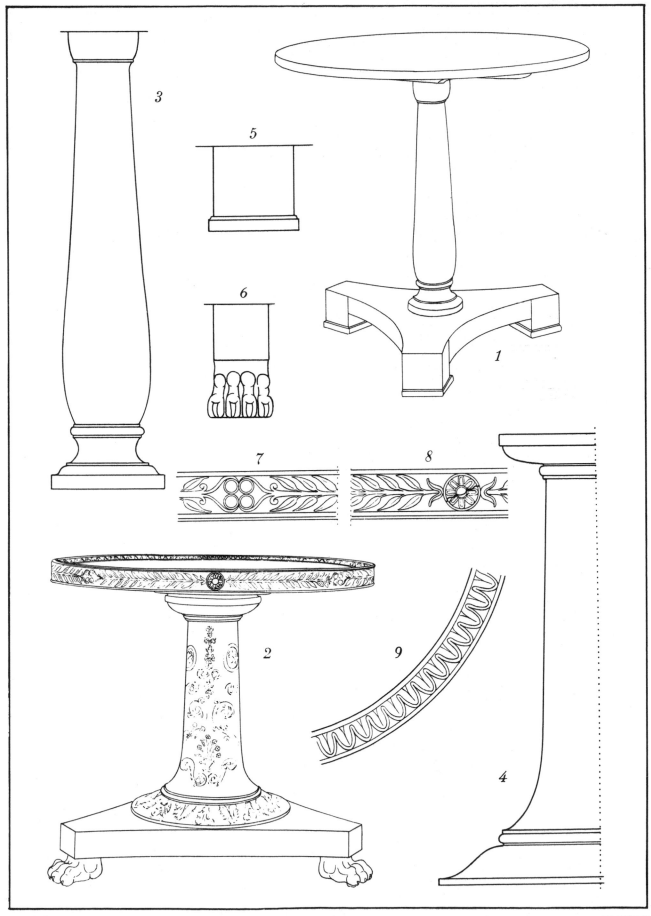

PLATE 377

1 and 2. Round pedestal tables. The first table is of mahogany, the second one of Sèvres porcelain, decorated with gilt bronzes.   3 and 4. Supports.   5 and 6. Feet.   7, 8 and 9. Border decorations.

*Fontainebleau Palace*

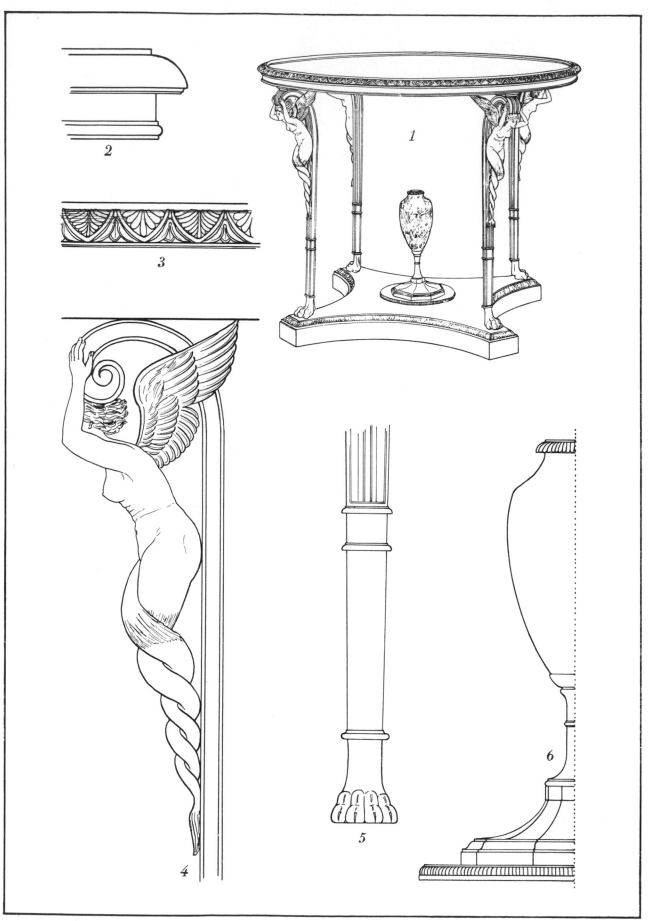

PLATE 378

EMPIRE

1. Small pedestal table made of yew, with bronzes.   2 and 3. Upper moulding.   4. Figure of a siren in black bronze.   5. Clawed foot.   6. Detail of vase.

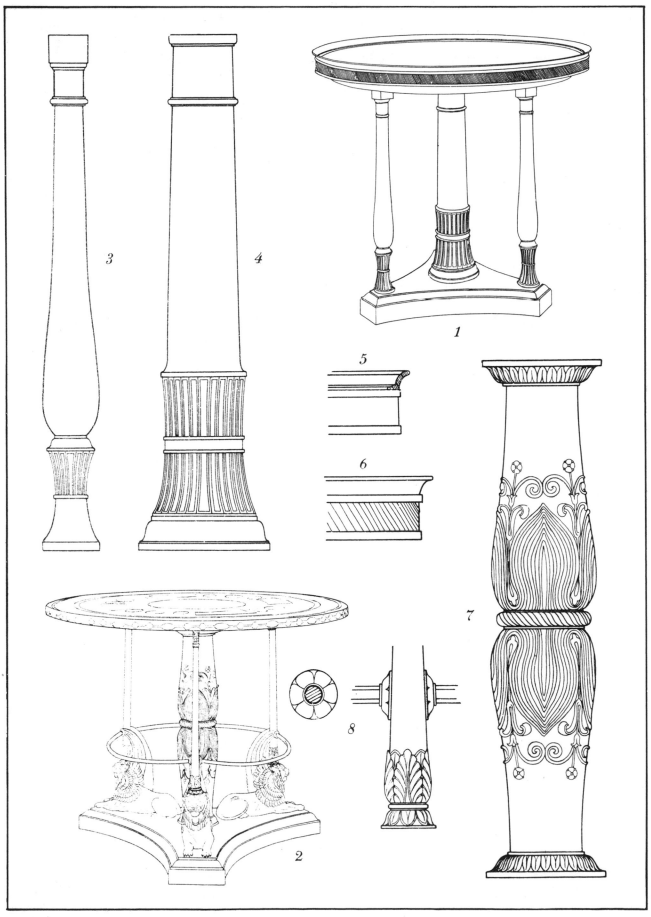

PLATE 379                                                                   EMPIRE

1 and 2. Round mahogany pedestal tables. The first one has a top of red porphyry, the second one of marble.  3 and 4. Detail of leg and central column.  5 and 6. Detail of moulding porphyry top.  7. Middle column of gilt carved wood.  8. Detail of bottom of copper uprights resting on winged lions.

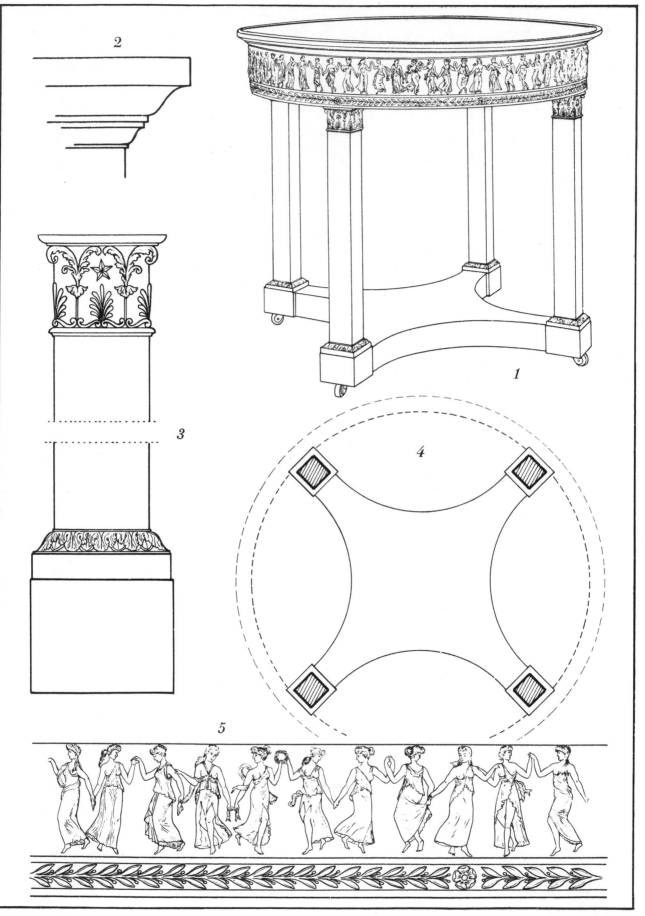

PLATE 380                                                                    EMPIRE
1. Mahogany pedestal table, decorated with bronzes and with a marble top.   2. Marble moulding.   3. Detail of
legs.   4. Bottom of table.   5. Detail of frieze.

*Grand Trianon*

PLATE 381

1 and 2. Small round pedestal tables with tops of marble and mosaic, respectively. 3 and 4. Detail of columns. 5 and 6. Front and cross section of base. 7. Detail of carved wood foot. 8 and 9. Mouldings around top.

*Ministry of War and Grand Trianon*

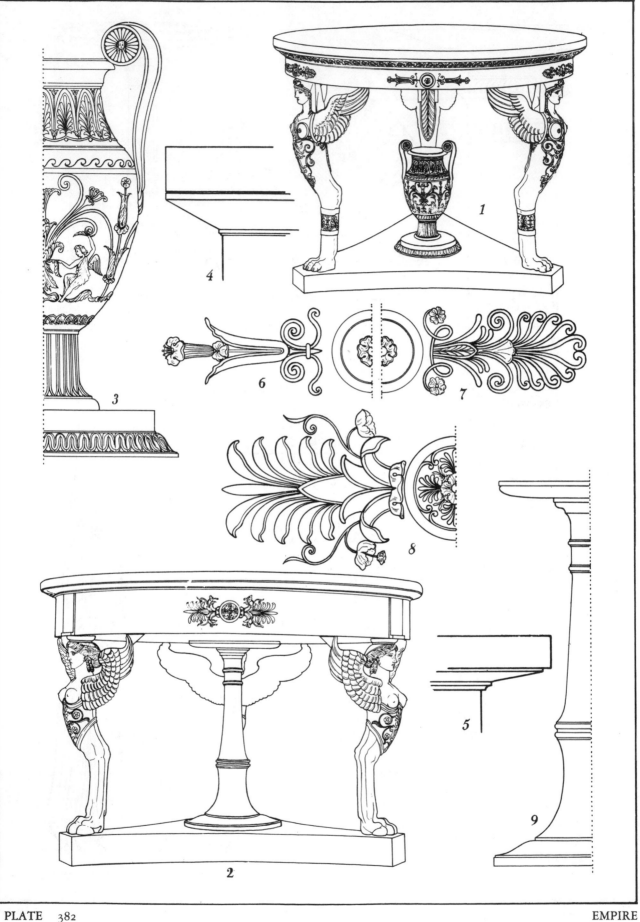

PLATE 382

1 and 2. Mahogany pedestal tables decorated with bronzes and with legs in shape of winged figures (upper one, Egyptian). 3. Detail of vase. 4 and 5. Upper moulding and cross section of marble. 6, 7 and 8. Details of bronzes. 9. Middle support.

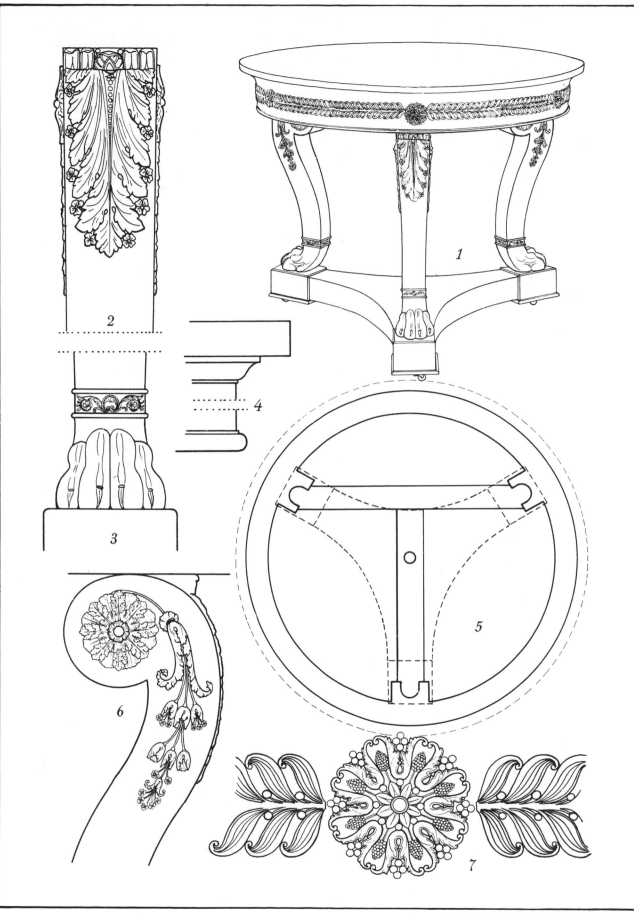

PLATE 383

EMPIRE

1. Round mahogany pedestal table with bronze decorations and clawed feet. 2 and 3. Details of legs. 4. Mouldings. 5. Base. 6. Side view of leg. 7. Bronze decoration.

*Compiègne Palace*

PLATE 384                                                                EMPIRE

1. Round pedestal table.    2. Detail of leg.    3. Sketch of decoration on top.    4. Frieze outlined by lower interlace.    5. Central part of interlace.

*Grand Trianon*

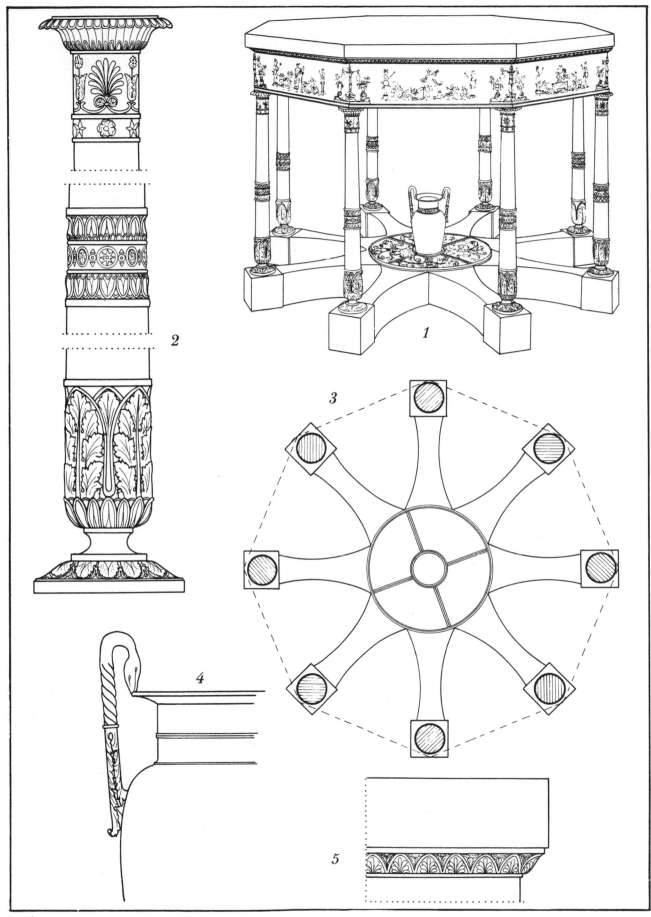

PLATE 385                                                                      EMPIRE

1. Octagonal mahogany table with bronze decorations and marble top supported by eight columns.   2. Detail of column.   3. Base of table.   4. Detail of vase in middle.   5. Upper moulding.

*Malmaison Castle*

PLATE 386

1. Oval elm-root table, legs are decorated with gilt carved sphinxes. 2. Round top with top of colored varnished steel. 3, 4 and 5. Details of sphinx, bronze border and decoration on upright. 6, 7 and 8. Details of vase, leg and decoration.

*Fontainebleau Palace*

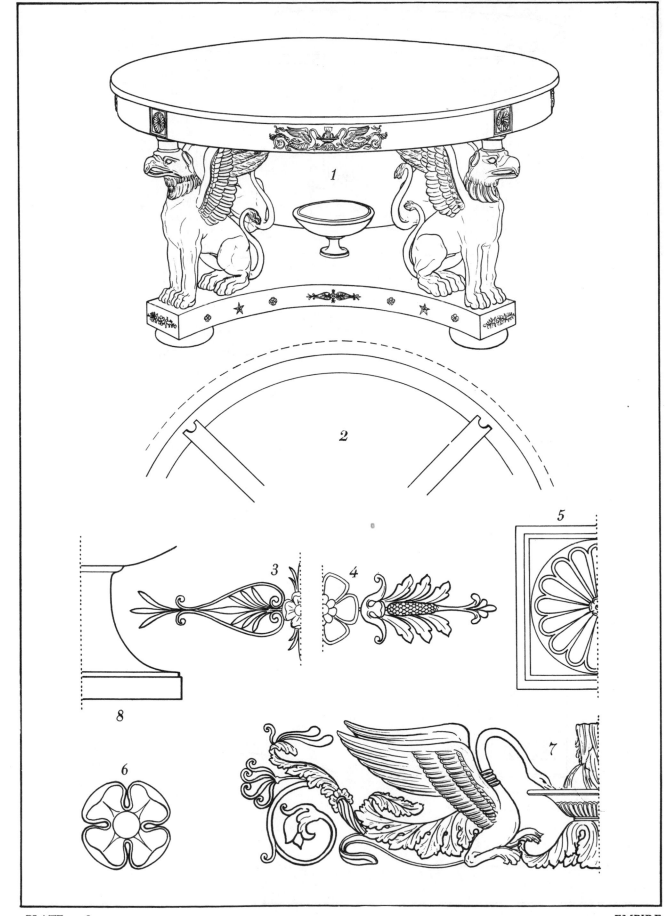

PLATE 387                                                                                    EMPIRE

1. Round mahogany table, supported by winged sphinxes and decorated with gilt bronzes.   2. Table frame.   3, 4, 5,
6 and 7. Details of bronzes.   8. Detail of chalice in middle.

*Compiègne Palace*

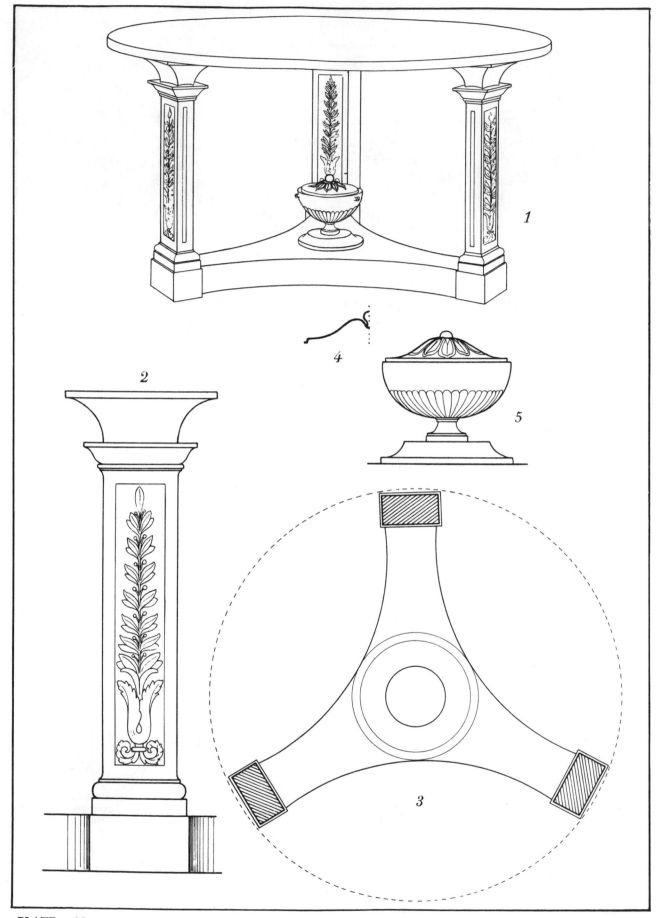

PLATE 388                                                                    EMPIRE
1. Round three-legged table with marquetry.   2. Detail of leg.   3. Placement of legs.   4 and 5. Detail of urn in middle.

*Grand Trianon*

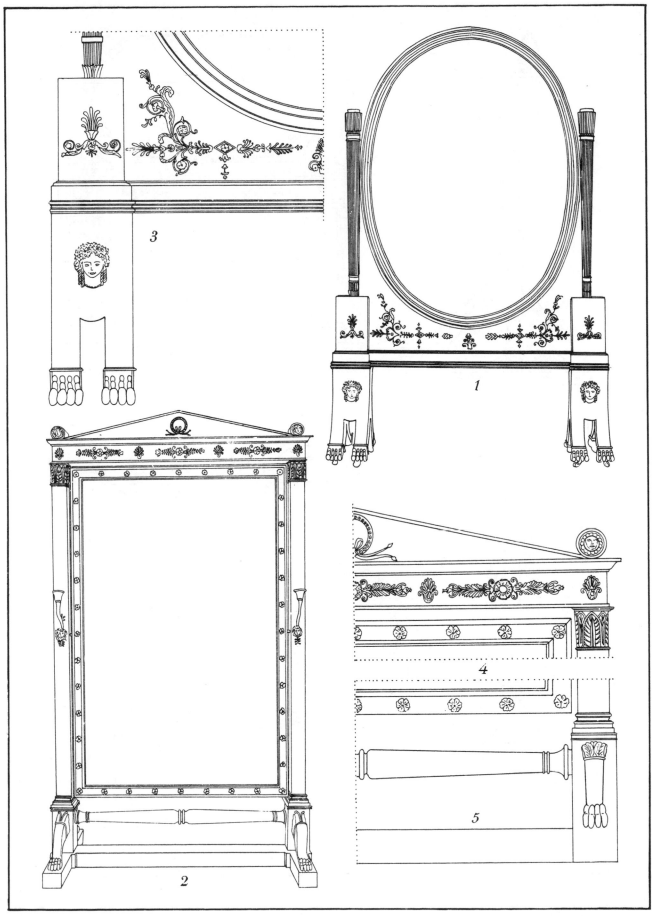

PLATE 389                                                                          EMPIRE  (first  period)
1 and 2. Portable mahogany mirrors with bronzes (the first one belonged to Empress Josephine).   3, 4 and 5. Details
of upright and frame.

*Mobilier National de France and Fontainebleau Palace*

PLATE 390

1. Mahogany dressing table, which belonged to Empress Josephine, decorated with carved gilt bronzes; the legs are in the shape of a lyre.    2. Detail of upright.    3, 4 and 5. Details of bronzes.    6. Detail of base.

*Mobilier National de France*

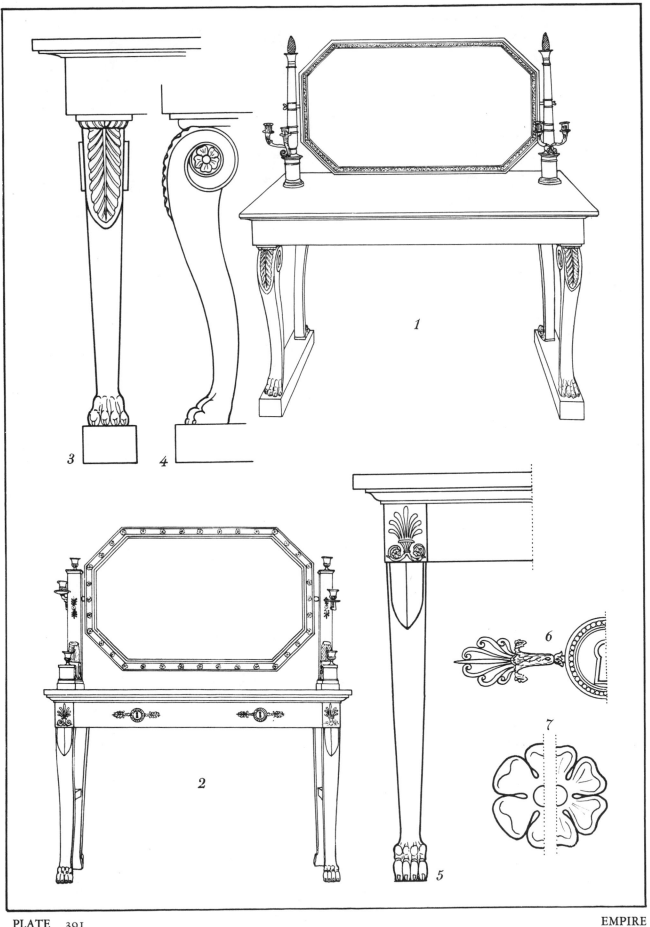

PLATE 391                                                                                   EMPIRE

1 and 2. Mahogany dressing tables, decorated with carved gilt bronze.   3, 4 and 5. Details of legs.   6 and 7.
Details of escutcheon plate and rosette.

*Fontainebleau and Compiègne Palaces*

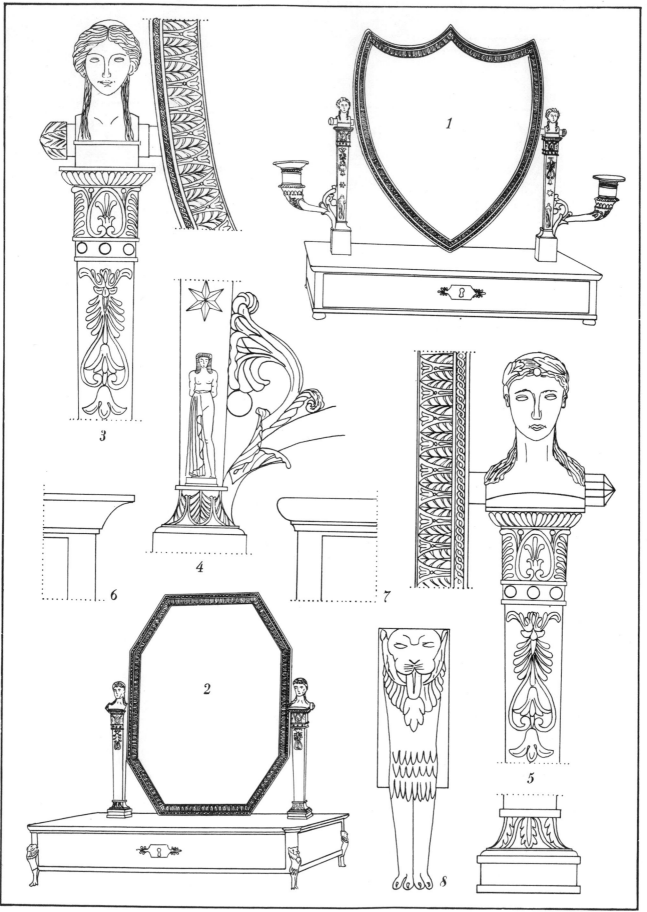

PLATE 392

EMPIRE

1 and 2. Small mahogany dressing tables, decorated with bronzes.   3, 4 and 5. Details of mirror supports.   6 and
7. Mouldings.   8. Leg.

*Malmaison Castle and Fontainebleau Palace*

PLATE 393

1 and 2. Portable mahogany mirrors decorated with gilt copper and bronze.   3, 4, 5 and 6. Details of uprights and clawed foot.   7 and 8. Details of frame.

*Museum of Decorative Arts, Paris and Fontainebleau Palace*

PLATE 394

1. Large ash dressing table decorated with carved gilt bronzes.   2 and 3. Details of legs.   4. Upper crest.   5. Detail of rear pilaster.   6 and 7. Base of mirror frame.

*Fontainebleau Palace*

PLATE  395

1. Elm-root dressing table, decorated with carved gilt bronzes.   2. Mahogany dressing table with clawed feet. The mirror supports are square and end in women's heads of gilt bronze.   3 and 4. Details of uprights and legs.   5 and 6. Decorations.   7. Drawer pull.

*Mobilier National de France*

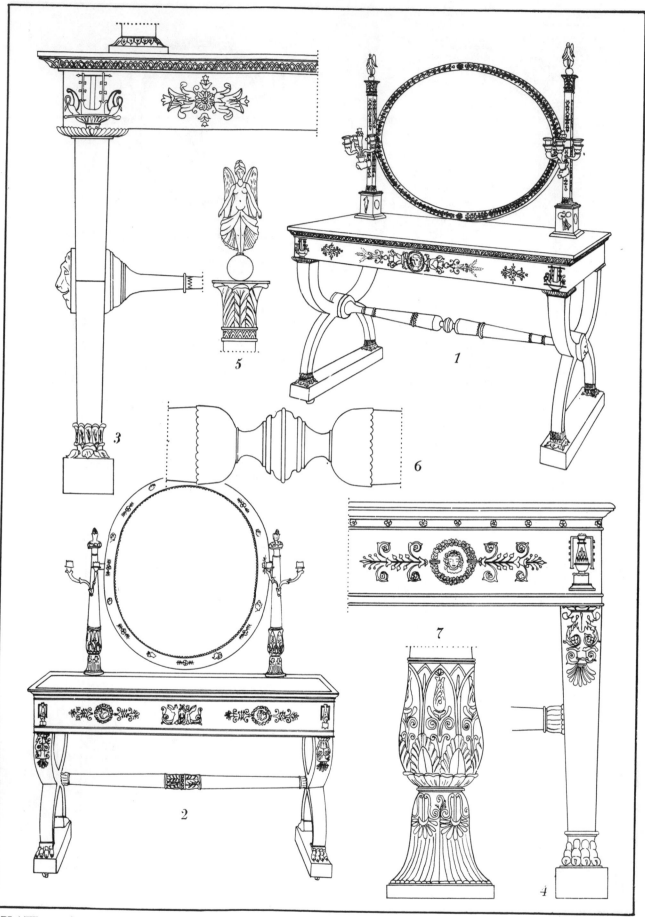

PLATE 396

1 and 2. Mahogany dressing tables, adorned with carved gilt bronzes and decorative legs. 3 and 4. Details of uprights and legs. 5. Finial. 6. Turned lower crosspiece. 7. Base of mirror support.

*Fontainebleau Palace and Malmaison Castle*

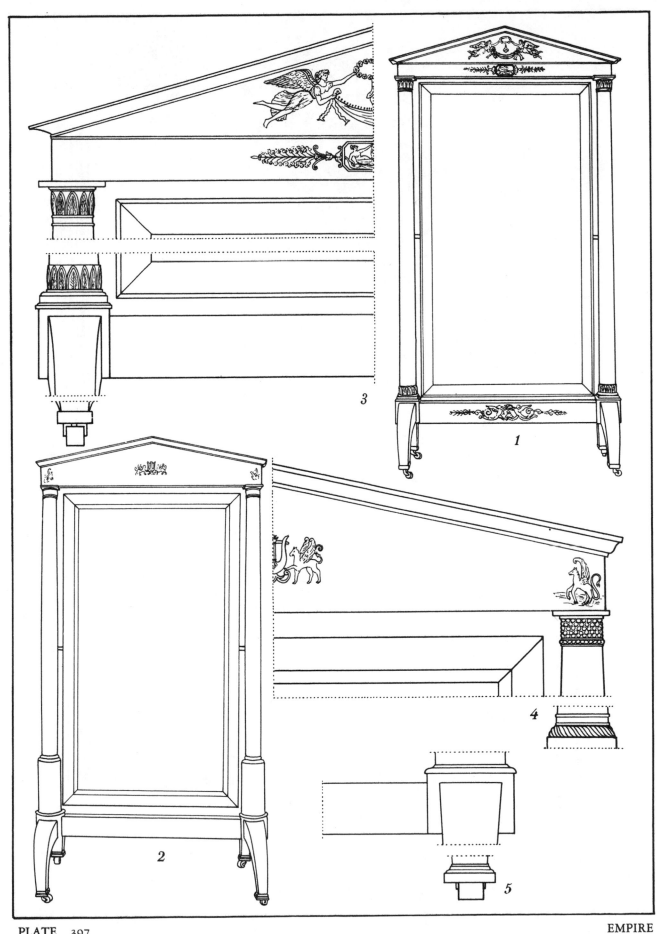

PLATE 397

EMPIRE

1 and 2. Portable mahogany mirrors with bronzes.   3, 4 and 5. Details of uprights and frames or mirrors.

*Mobilier National de France and Ministry of War*

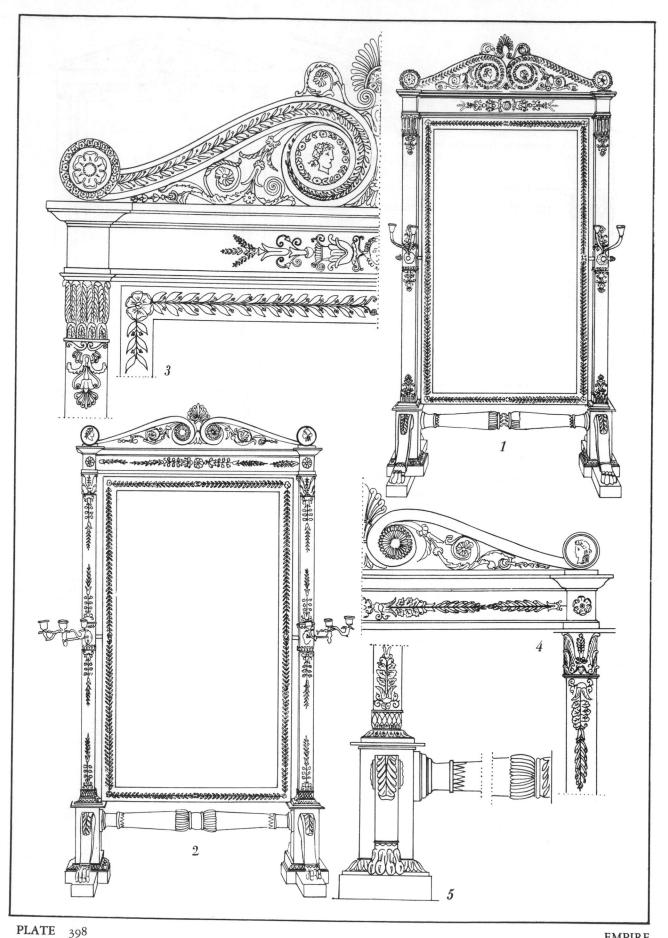

PLATE 398

**1 and 2.** Portable mahogany mirrors with bronzes.     **3, 4 and 5.** Details of uprights, frames and support.

*Fontainebleau and Compiègne Palaces*

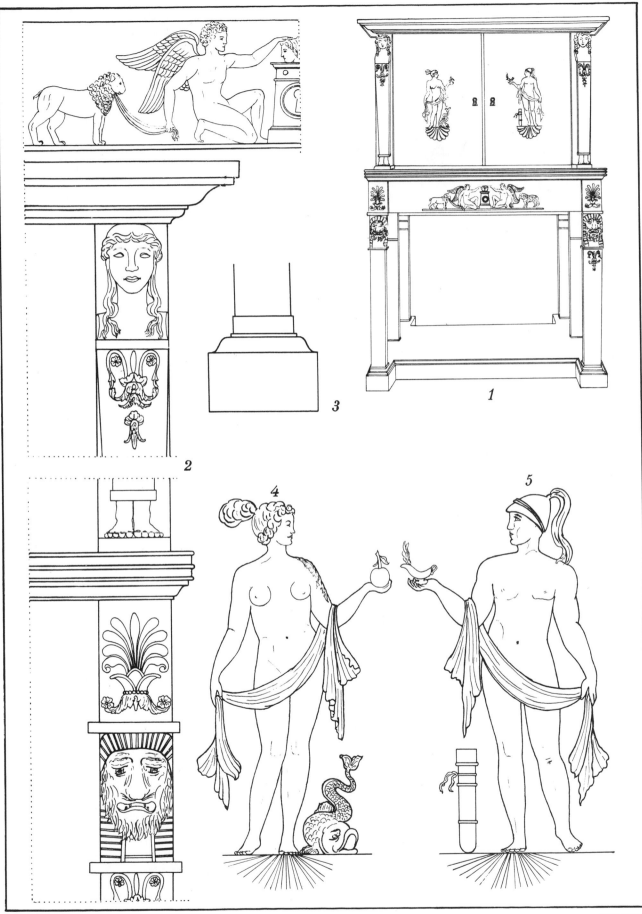

PLATE 399

1. Mahogany "bonheur-du-jour" paper cabinet, with gilt bronze decorations.    2. Detail of uprights.    3. Base.    4 and 5. Central figures.

*Private collection*

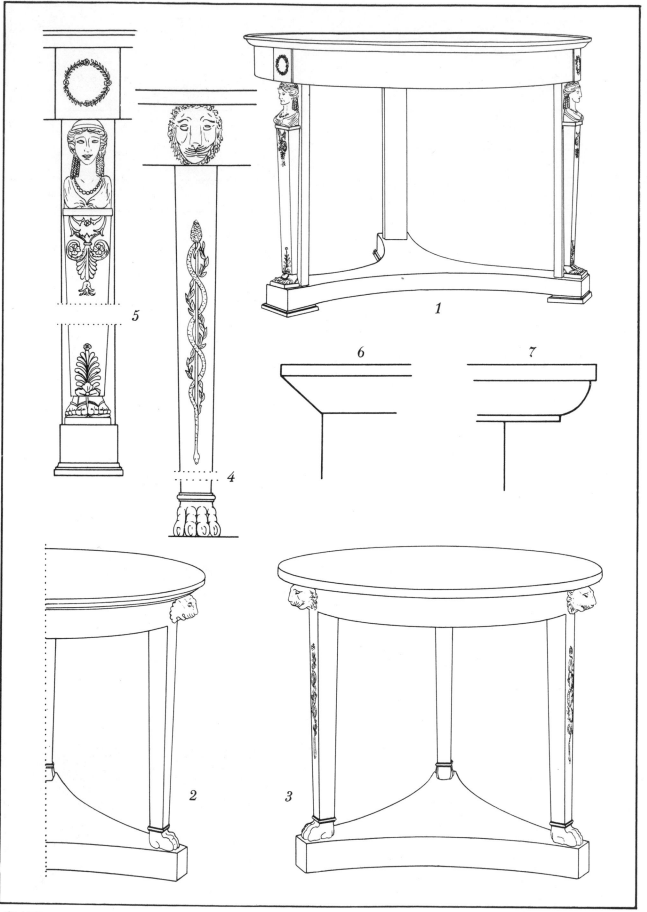

PLATE 400

EMPIRE

1, 2 and 3. Round mahogany pedestal tables with three legs, carved gilt bronzes, marble tops and decorated with sphinx's heads and lions' claws.   4 and 5. Details of legs.   6 and 7. Marble moulding.

*Museum of Decorative Arts, Paris and Compiègne and Fontainebleau Palaces*

PLATE 401                                                                            EMPIRE

1 and 2. Small round pedestal tables supported by four columns, with bronze decorations and white marble tops.   3
and 4. Details of columns.   5. Sketch of bronze decoration.

*Grand Trianon and Fontainebleau Palace*

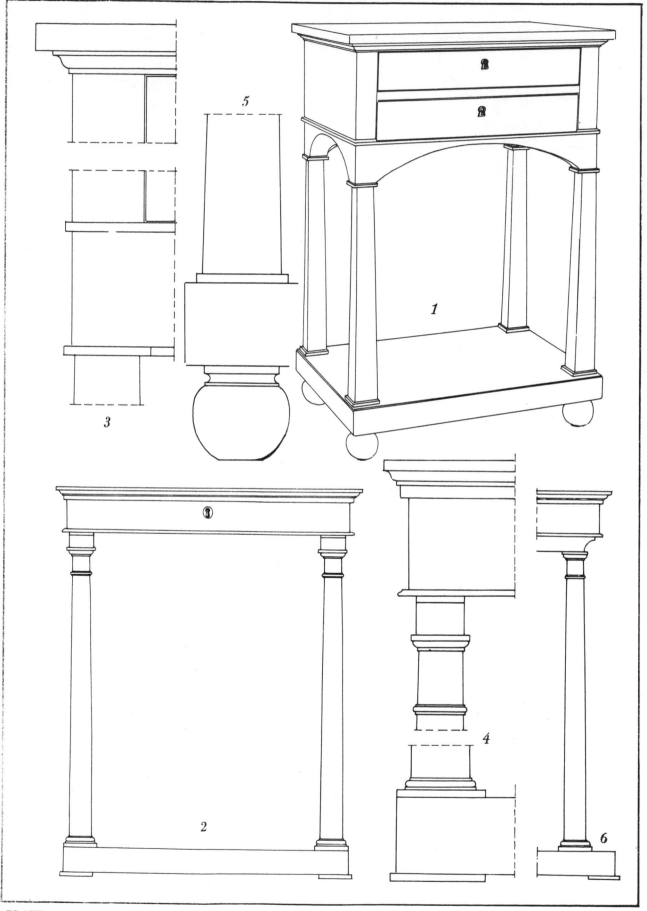

PLATE 402
1 and 2. Small worktables.   3 and 4. Details of uprights.   5. Foot.   6. Small column.

EMPIRE

*Private collections*

**PLATE** 403

1, 2 and 3. Small mirrors for dressing tables.   4, 5 and 6. Details of same.   7. Bronze decoration.

EMPIRE  (Restoration)

*Private collections*

**PLATE 404**

1 and 2. Elm-root and mahogany dressing tables with bronze decorations. 3 and 4. Uprights and legs. 5 and 6. Escutcheon plate decorations.

*Grand Trianon and Malmaison Castle*

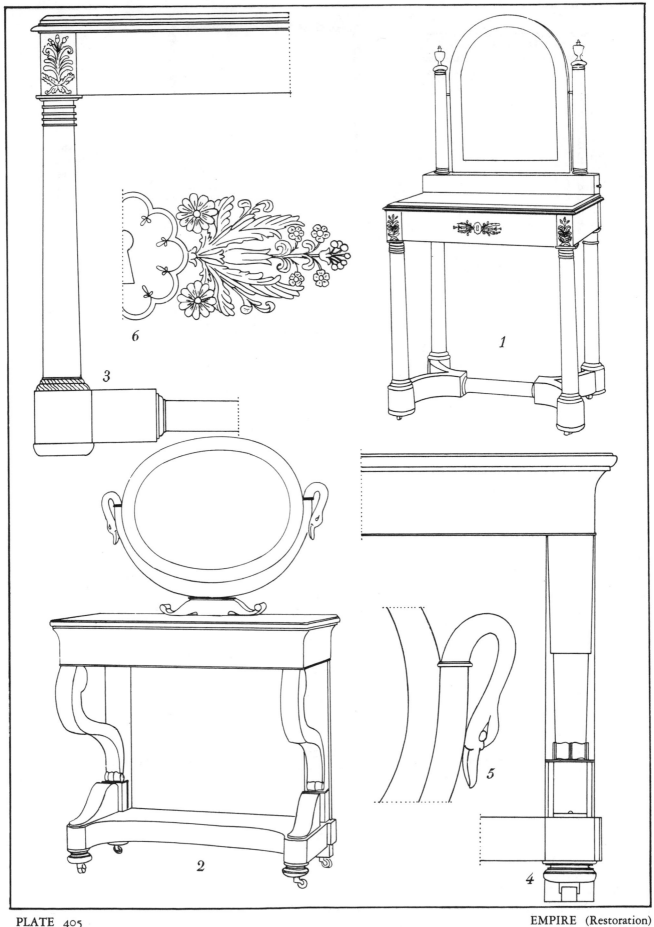

PLATE 405

EMPIRE (Restoration)

1 and 2. Mahogany dressing tables. The first one has bronze decorations; the second one has an oval mirror.   3 and 4. Uprights and legs.   5. Swan's head.   6. Detail of escutcheon plate.

*Ministry of Justice and Mobilier National de France*

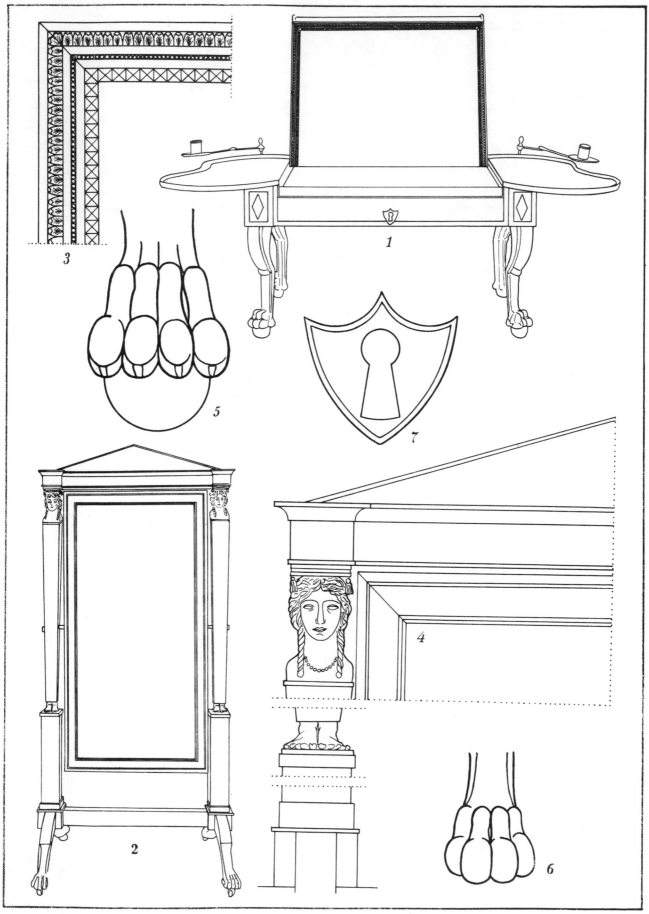

PLATE 406

EMPIRE (Restoration)

1. Small portable dressing table or bed tray of mahogany and maple with inlaid ebony and tin on the claws. 2. Portable mahogany mirror with gilt bronze decorations. 3 and 4. Details of frame. 5 and 6. Claws. 7. Escutcheon plate.

*Malmaison Castle and Fontainebleau Palace*

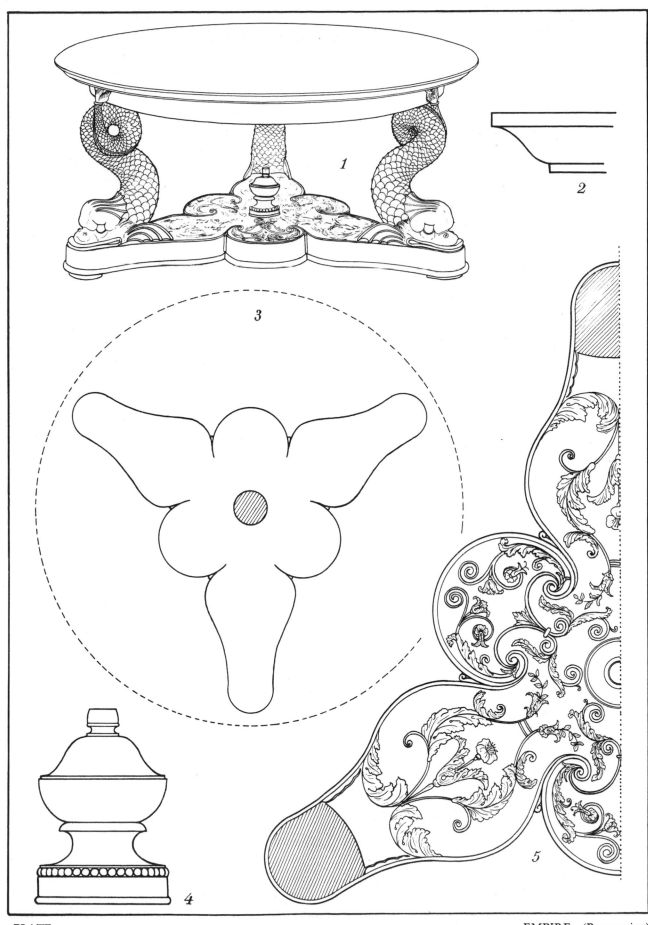

PLATE 407

EMPIRE (Restoration)

1. Round table with fine marquetry, supported by three dolphins.   2. Upper moulding.   3. Bottom.   4. Central finial.   5. Detail of marquetry.

*In a diplomatic building*

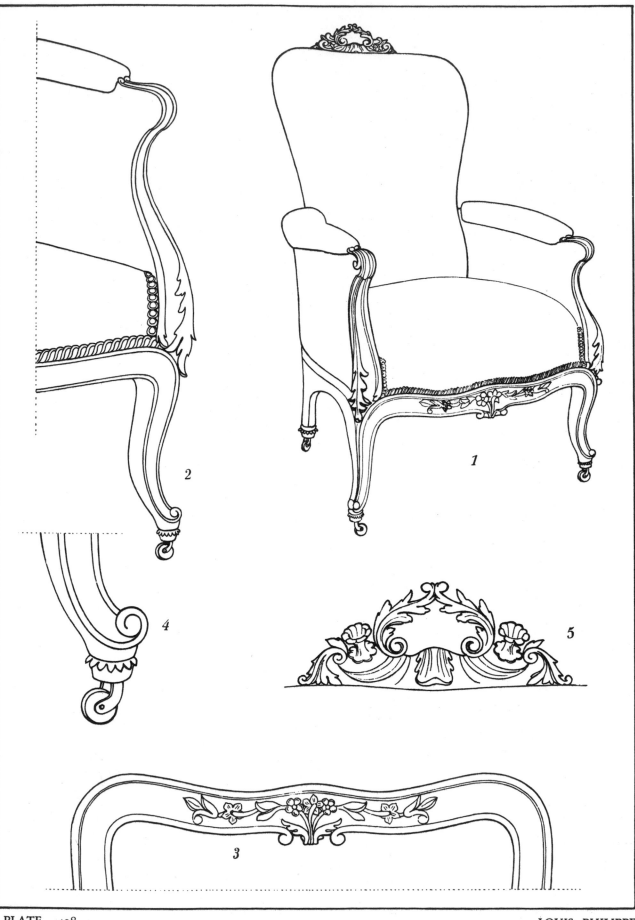

PLATE 408
1. Armchair.    2. Detail of arm and leg.    3. Sketch of middle lower carving.    4. Detail of foot.    5. Upper crest of back.

LOUIS PHILIPPE

*Fontainebleau Palace*

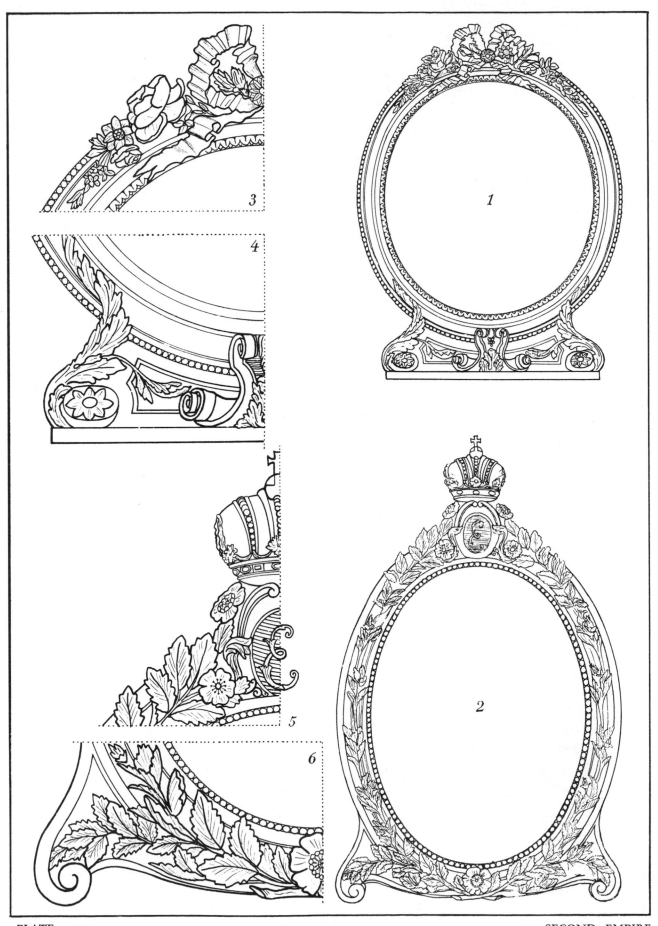

PLATE 409                                           SECOND EMPIRE

1. Medallion mirror of gilt carved wood.  2. Dressing-table mirror of gilt carved wood, belonging to Empress Eugénie.  3, 4, 5 and 6. Details.

*Mobilier National de France*

PLATE 410                                                                    SECOND EMPIRE

1. Portable mahogany mirror with bronzes, which belonged to Empress Eugénie.   2 and 3. Details of upright, frame
and support.   4. Candelabra.

*Mobilier National de France*

1. Small dressing-table mirror of carved gilt bronze which belonged to Empress Eugénie.    2 and 3. Details.

*Compiègne Palace*

# INDEX